MEN OF SPIRIT AND ENTERPRISE

MEN OF SPIRIT AND ENTERPRISE

Scots and Orkneymen

in the Hudson's Bay Company, 1780–1821

Suzanne Rigg

First published in Great Britain in 2011 by
John Donald, an imprint of Birlinn Ltd

West Newington House
10 Newington Road
Edinburgh
EH9 1QS

www.birlinn.co.uk

ISBN 978 1 906566 37 1

British Library Cataloguing-in-Publication Data
A catalogue record for this book is available on request
from the British Library

Typeset in Minion by
Koinonia, Manchester
Printed and bound in Britain by
Bell and Bain Ltd, Glasgow

Contents

Plates

1. Beaver and muskrat
   (Library and Archives Canada, R9266-2557, Peter Winkworth Collection of Canadiana)

2. Hudson's Bay Company banner
   (Stromness Museum)

3. Modifications of the beaver hat
   (Library and Archives Canada, C-017338)

4. Cannon used to signal the HBC's arrival in Stromness
   (Austin Ball)

5. Hudson's Bay Company and Northwest Company Forts at Île-à-la-Crosse, 1820
   (George Back, Library and Archives Canada, Acc. No. 1994-254-1.40R Acquired with the assistance of Hoechst and Celanese Canada and with a grant from the Department of Canadian Heritage under the Cultural Property Export and Import Act)

6. Portaging a canoe
   (Dennis Gale, Library and Archives Canada, Acc. No. 1970-188-1963 W.H. Coverdale Collection of Canadiana)

7. Indian hunters pursuing the buffalo in early spring
   (Peter Rindisbacher, 1806–1834, Library and Archives Canada, Acc. No. 1981-55-68 Bushnell Collection)

8. A hunter-family of Cree Indians at York Fort
   (Peter Rindisbacher, 1806–1834, Library and Archives Canada, Acc. No. 1988-250-16)

9. Beaded pocket-watch holder
   (Stromness Museum)

10. William Tomison's School, South Ronaldsay, Orkney
    (Charles Rigg)

Acknowledgements

This work is based on my thesis on Scots in the Hudson's Bay Company, which I completed at the School of Divinity, History and Philosophy at the University of Aberdeen. I have been fortunate to benefit from the expertise of three Scottish historians. Firstly, I am indebted to Marjory Harper who first sparked my interest in the Scottish Diaspora during my undergraduate studies at Aberdeen and went on to supervise my PhD. Her continuing support and advice has been invaluable. I would also like to thank my second supervisor, Andrew Mackillop, for injecting his infectious enthusiasm into this project as both a thesis and a book. Finally, I am very grateful to Professor Ted Cowan, an external examiner on my thesis, who kindly reviewed my work and has been instrumental in getting it published.

My postgraduate studies were wholly enabled by funding from the Arts and Humanities Research Council and I am extremely appreciative of the opportunity they provided. I would like to thank the staff at various institutions including the Hudson's Bay Company Archives in Winnipeg, Orkney Library and Archives, National Archives of Scotland, National Archives, Kew, Stromness Museum and the Manitoba Museum. I am also grateful to staff at the University of Winnipeg and Rupert's Land Research Centre for their assistance and permitting access to their library during my research in Winnipeg.

A number of people, including Jean Campbell, Mary and Forbes George, Katherine McLeod, Ron and Darlene Overby, and Doreen Pruden, provided a wonderful support network during my research period in Winnipeg and their hospitality was second to none. Across the Atlantic, special thanks must go to my brother Scott Rigg, Libby Daye, Austin Ball, Big Jack, Suzanne Hamilton, Sandra Hamilton, and Anne Daye, who all trawled the path alongside me, providing unwavering support and fellowship. Towards the end of the road, the contributions of David Tinto, Daniel Gravier, Gill Cloke, Mairi Sutherland and Tony Gemmell were much valued. Finally, my biggest debt goes to my parents. I would like to thank my dad, Charles, for engaging in endless discussions on Scots in the HBC, tirelessly reading drafts, and providing valuable feedback perhaps with the exception of his proposed title: 'Beavering away in a fur away country'! My mum, Dolina, endured the above with patience and good humour, and provided some much-needed light relief when discussions finally concluded. It is to my parents that this book is dedicated.

Abbreviations

CBMH/BCHM	*Canadian Bulletin of Medical History/ Bulletin canadien d'histoire de la médecine*
CHR	*Canadian Historical Review*
CMAJ	*Canadian Medical Association Journal*
HBC	Hudson's Bay Company
HBCA	Hudson's Bay Company Archives, Winnipeg
HJ	*The Historical Journal*
HoC	House of Commons
JEH	*The Journal of Economic History*
JPR	*Journal of Population Research*
NA	The National Archives, Kew, London
NAS	National Archives of Scotland, Edinburgh
NWC	North West Company
OA	Orkney Library & Archives, Kirkwall
OSA	*The Statistical Account of Scotland 1791-99*
SHR	*Scottish Historical Review*
SS	*Scottish Studies*
TRSC	*Transactions of the Royal Society of Canada*
WL	Western Isles Library, Stornoway

A Note on Terminology

Some of the eighteenth- and nineteenth-century terms used to describe the people and companies involved in the fur trade have been retained in this book, and require some explanation. 'Canadians' refers to people from the territory of Lower Canada, which is now in the present-day province of Quebec. The term 'Canadian' also applies to all employees of the North West Company, including its Scottish members, as the organisation's roots lay in the French-Canadian, Montreal-based fur trade; 'voyageur' refers to a French-Canadian canoeman who was employed to transport furs. References to the 'Nor'westers' and 'Canadian Company' also allude to the North West Company.

The terms 'native' and 'indian' refer to the indigenous people of Rupert's Land, now called the 'First Nations'. Other terms have been borrowed from present-day academic discourse: for instance, 'mixed-blood' is the accepted term for the mixed-race progeny of the fur traders and native women. However, 'Métis' refers exclusively to the mixed-blood descendents of the NWC.

I use the term 'sojourner' to indicate a temporary resident in a foreign country.

Names

The appearance of many very similar names is unavoidable in this area. Many Orcadians had the same name, and the HBC often differentiated by adding a number or a letter to the name. For instance, there was a George Flett 1st and a George Flett 2nd; a William Flett Jnr, William Flett Snr, William Flett 'A' and William Flett 'B'; a John Ballenden of Stromness, who served as writer, master and chief, and a John Ballenden 1st from Orphir, who was a canoebuilder.

Maps

Scotland

0   50   100 kilometres

Orkney
Stromness Kirkwall

Thurso
Caithness
Wick

Shetland Lerwick

Stornoway
Lewis
Sutherland

Harris

North Uist

Benbecula

Ross and Cromarty

Skye

South Uist

Inverness

Barra

Rum

Eigg

Inverness

Nairn Moray Banff

Aberdeen

Coll

Tiree

Mull

Argyll

Kincardine

Angus

Perth

Colonsay Jura

Clackmannan

Kinross

Fife

Stirling

Islay

Greenock
Renfrew Glasgow

Dunbarton

West Lothian

Edinburgh

East Lothian

Midlothian

Bute

Arran

Lanark

Peebles

Berwick

Ayr

Selkirk

Roxburgh

Dumfries

Kirkcudbright

Wigtown

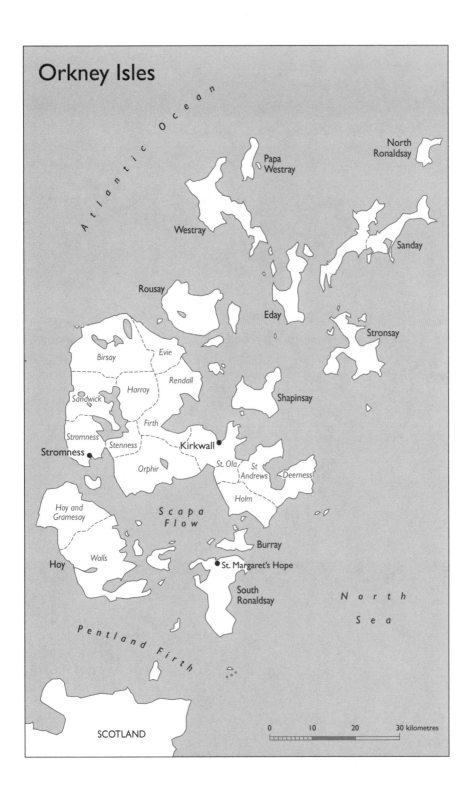

Orkney Isles

Atlantic Ocean

North Ronaldsay

Papa Westray

Westray

Sanday

Rousay

Eday

Stronsay

Birsay

Evie

Rendall

Harray

Sandwick

Shapinsay

Firth

Stromness

Stenness

Kirkwall

Stromness

Orphir

St. Ola

St Andrews

Deerness

Holm

Hoy and Gramesay

Scapa Flow

Walls

Burray

Hoy

St. Margaret's Hope

South Ronaldsay

North Sea

Pentland Firth

SCOTLAND

0   10   20   30 kilometres

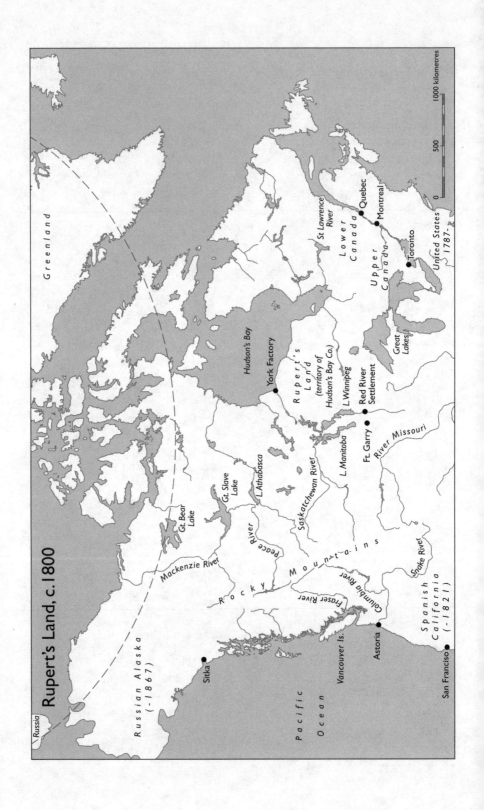

Rupert's Land, c.1800

Russia

Greenland

Russian Alaska
(-1867)

Sitka

Pacific
Ocean

Vancouver Is.

Astoria

San Franciso

Spanish
California
(-1821)

Snake River

Columbia River

Fraser River

Rocky Mountains

Mackenzie River

Peace River

Gt. Bear
Lake

Gt. Slave
Lake

L. Athabasca

Saskatchewan River

L. Manitoba

L. Winnipeg

Ft. Garry

Red River
Settlement

River Missouri

Rupert's
Land
(territory of
Hudson's Bay Co.)

Hudson's Bay

York Factory

Great
Lakes

Toronto

Upper
Canada

Lower
Canada

St Lawrence
River

Quebec

Montreal

United States
1787-

0   500   1000 kilometres

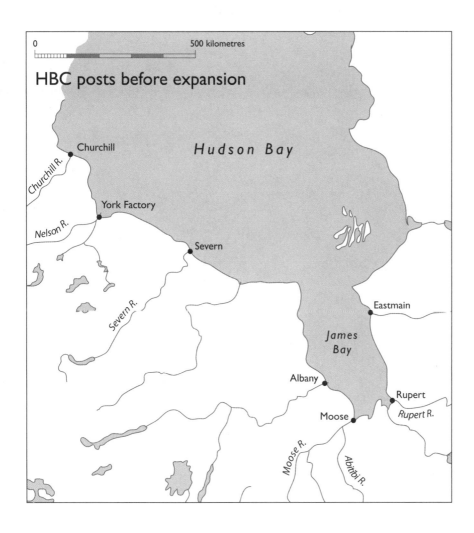

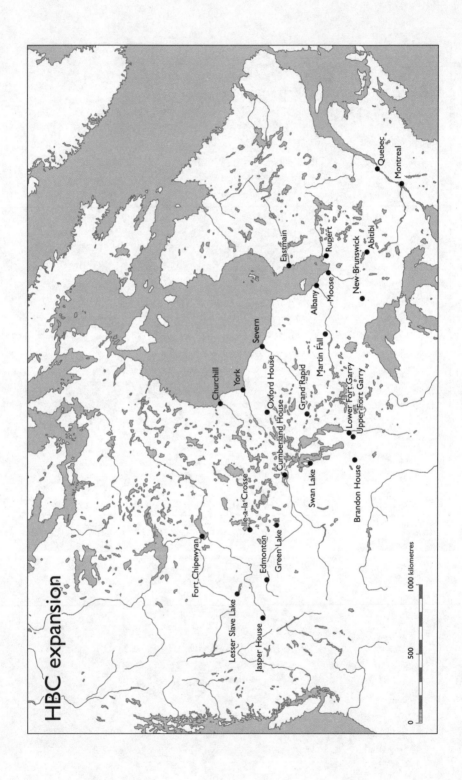

HBC expansion

Quebec
Montreal

Eastmain
Rupert
New Brunswick
Abitibi
Albany
Moose

Severn
Martin Fall

Churchill
York
Oxford House
Grand Rapid
Lower Fort Garry
Upper Fort Garry
Cumberland House
Swan Lake
Brandon House
Île-a-la-Crosse
Edmonton
Green Lake
Fort Chipewyan
Lesser Slave Lake
Jasper House

0   500   1000 kilometres

Chronology

NWC recruits in Orkney.

Canada Jurisdiction Act regulates that crimes committed in the fur-trading territories can be tried in Lower Canada.

1804   XY Company reunites with the North West Company.

1805   The HBC recruits from Sutherland, Caithness and Shetland.

1811   HBC's 'New System' of administration is established.

Lord Selkirk is permitted to create a settlement of Scottish colonists in Assiniboia.

HBC recruitment extends across Scotland.

1812   War of 1812.

1815   End of Napoleonic Wars.

The HBC attempts to consolidate its presence in the Athabasca.

1816   HBC recruiting agents are appointed in Inverness and the Western Isles.

Massacre at Seven Oaks. The Métis, many of whom are the sons of Scots, kill 21 Scottish settlers during a clash at the Red River settlement.

1821   The HBC and NWC unite under the name and charter of the HBC.

ONE

Introduction

In 1814, Edward Chappell boarded His Majesty's Ship Rosamund, destined for naval service in the Arctic. He divulged that 'Had we been ordered to the North Pole, there could not have been more long faces among us ... nothing remained, but the dismal prospect of a tedious voyage, amidst icy seas, and shores covered with eternal snows.'[1] The *Rosamund* voyaged from England in convoy with two vessels belonging to the Hudson's Bay Company (HBC) and routed via the Orkney Isles. Chappell found that in contrast to his own dejection, the Orcadian community eagerly awaited the reverberation of cannon which ushered in the ships of the HBC, as 'almost every person in the island is, in some way or other, interested in their coming'.[2] Orcadian anticipation was largely rooted in the knowledge that many local men would board the ships and temporarily migrate across the Atlantic as employees in the service of the HBC.

The HBC was a trading company that originated from the discovery of a rich supply of beaver to the south and west of Hudson's Bay in present-day Canada. Beaver pelts were in great demand in seventeenth-century Europe as the soft, warm, waterproof fur, underlying the pelt, was ideal for making into fashionable felt hats. Radisson and Groseilliers, the two French explorers who discovered this find in the 1660s, failed to secure the backing of their own country to launch a fur-trading venture in this territory and looked to England for cooperation. They were fortunate that King Charles II was keen to locate a northern trade route to China, and gained his support along with that of his cousin Prince Rupert and some wealthy merchants. Together they backed a speculative voyage to Hudson's Bay in 1668 to assess trading prospects and the viability of the route across the Atlantic Ocean, up the Hudson Strait, and into Hudson's Bay. Following the triumphant return of the *Nonsuch* bearing a cargo of beaver pelts, King Charles II granted a Royal Charter to its investors, and on 2 May 1670, Prince Rupert and the seventeen other members of this joint-stock enterprise became 'the Governor and Company of Adventurers of England traeding [sic] into Hudson's Bay'.[3]

Under the terms of the charter these men were considered 'the true and absolute Lordes and Proprietors of Rupert's Land'. The territory of Rupert's Land encompassed much of modern-day Canada, and was defined as the land drained by rivers flowing into Hudson's Bay. Within this huge domain the governing gentlemen were permitted to build castles, forts, plantations, colonies and towns, and were granted the right to establish laws and armies, as well as the 'sole right to trade and commerce': its true extent was unknown at the time, but this trading company had actually been awarded control of an empire fifty times the size of Scotland.[4]

Few members of the London Committee, as the governing body of the HBC became known, ever set foot in Rupert's Land, but directed and financed operations from the HBC's headquarters in London. Despite their large remit, the directors initially limited their sphere of activity to trade. They employed personnel to facilitate the fur-trading business around Hudson's Bay in return for wages, food and accommodation. Unlike British imperial ventures in the Montreal fur trade and in the Caribbean plantations, where local or enslaved workers occupied the lowest ranks of the labour force, the HBC developed a practice whereby British personnel were contracted, typically for three to five years, and sent thousands of miles across the Atlantic to the shores of Hudson's Bay.

The Company ships anchored at the southern end of this inland sea, at the mouths of the rivers draining into Hudson's Bay. Posts, also known as houses, forts and factories, were constructed on the nearby marshy landscape and soon came to include Moose, Churchill, York, Rupert, Albany, and Eastmain. Employees were stationed at these remote establishments, which were at least 100 miles apart, and had to adapt to working life in an extremely cold, sub-arctic climate.

At each of the posts, employees were organised by hierarchical rank and generally categorised into two distinct groupings: 'men', sometimes referred to as 'servants', and 'gentlemen' otherwise known as 'officers'. The former made up the bulk of the workforce, and their duties included hunting for provisions, felling trees for firewood and building or repairing wooden posts, for shelter and as a place to trade. Unskilled workers did much of the hard graft while skilled servants were generally occupied with making or repairing essential equipment to survive in the wilderness and execute the fur trade; this included producing tools, sleds, snowshoes, guns, traps, canoes, boats, and clothing. All of the aforementioned operations were supervised by officers of the HBC who served as intermediaries between the London Committee and the rest of the workforce. Each post was managed by a chief trader and a council of officers, and these gentlemen were entrusted with managing the business in Rupert's Land, maintaining accounts and journals, corresponding with other posts and carrying out the actual trade in furs with natives.[5]

In order to conduct the fur trade, the posts were stocked with British- and European-manufactured goods such as knives, axes, guns, powder, shot, kettles, tobacco, jewellery and blankets. Members of the Cree, Chipewyan and Assiniboia tribes canoed down to the posts on Hudson's Bay in late spring or summer to exchange furs for the imported goods. Although these native tribe members orchestrated the exchange of furs, they were often acting as middlemen on behalf of more distant tribes, such as the Blackfoot, who actually trapped the furs. They began the bartering process with the ceremonial ritual of smoking a pipe and an exchange of gifts, such as brandy and tobacco from HBC employees, and beaver pelts from the tribes.[6]

The standard of trade was then measured in 'Made Beaver', which was one good quality adult beaver pelt. All other furs including marten, otter, bear, deer, fox and wolf were measured against this standard and the imported trade goods were also priced in Made Beaver. When the seasonal trade was complete, the furs were then sorted and packed by HBC employees ready for shipment to London. A structured and long-standing routine developed whereby two or three HBC vessels made an annual trip to Hudson's Bay, arriving in summer with new employees, trade goods and supplies, and departing in early autumn before the winter crept in and Hudson's Bay froze over, carrying a cargo of furs and returning employees. The furs were taken to London to be auctioned at market and then made into fashionable apparel.[7]

For the first century of the Company's operations, which remained in Hudson's Bay, the personnel needs of the HBC were small. Initial recruitment practices drew heavily on Londoners in the first decade in which the Company operated, but much to the surprise of the directors, the urban recruits were found to be unsatisfactory employees. They possessed a poor work ethic and indulged in excessive alcohol consumption, both problems which hindered the Company's operations. A recruitment ethos was progressively established in which the London Committee prioritised the employment of Scots, largely due to their perceived qualities of subordination, sobriety, obedience and ability to endure deprivation; and English 'country lads' of whom it was believed that they were free of the debauched traits associated with city life, such as excessive drinking, which were visible in the earlier English recruits from London, and would thus work harder. In 1683 and 1684, Edinburgh tradesmen Thomas Bannatyne and John Fullartine, among others, pioneered the way for the numerous Scots who were to embark on the voyage to Hudson's Bay over the following two centuries.[8]

This early recruitment practice of hiring a few Scots in the 1680s was given impetus by shortages of English manpower during the French-British conflict in the 1690s, and the outbreak of the War of the Spanish Succession in 1702. The

HBC had no option but to look to other sources of labour, as few Englishmen were willing to join the Company and those who did were often press-ganged. Following futile attempts in London, labour was recruited in the Orkney Islands in 1702, when the Company ships made a final stop for supplies en route to Hudson's Bay. Ten to twelve young men were engaged and, as war conditions continued to disable the Company's ability to recruit in England, another seven Orcadians were sent to the Bay in 1712. These workers continued to enter the Company in the 1720s, and by the 1730s their employment had become firmly established.[9]

The recruitment of Orkneymen had several advantages, which became increasingly obvious to the Company management. The Orkney Isles are situated on the north-east periphery of Britain and are separated from Scotland by the Pentland Firth. It was convenient to hire men from that location as the Company vessels, like most destined for North America, paid a visit to Orkney before crossing the Atlantic. Aside from having good harbours, provisions that could be procured cheaply, and servicing for ships, Orkney was also remotely situated, so that in times of war routing via the islands helped avoid privateers. In addition, Orcadians could be supplied at short notice and any deficit in crew or complement could be instantly remedied. As the men were from a traditional society located in a peripheral region of Britain, they also fitted the Company's blueprint of the ideal servant: subservient, industrious, 'more sober and tractable than the Irish' and willing to work for low wages.[10]

Although the HBC had created a recruitment ideology to which it adhered for 200 years, and the Company had also succeeded in learning the business of the fur trade, the HBC still had to contend with the challenges of engaging in overseas trade in the Age of Empire. Its operations were rarely stable, often threatened by warfare and trading rivalries. Between 1686 and 1713, Britain's conflict with France encroached upon operations in Hudson's Bay as French interlopers attacked and seized HBC posts. The Royal Charter of 1670 had ignored the French presence near Rupert's Land, perhaps because they were allies at the time, but the Company's exclusive right to trade in Rupert's Land was certainly contested when French fur traders intercepted natives en route to exchange furs at Hudson's Bay. Hostilities ceased in 1713 with the signing of the Treaty of Utrecht and the French traders surrendered the posts and trade around Hudson's Bay. The HBC re-established its posts, but did not attempt to expand its activities further into its chartered territory.[11]

From a commercial standpoint, by the mid-eighteenth century, the Company had actually become inert: increased rivalry from Montreal traders, who intercepted the natives en route to the posts at the Bay, resulted in stagnation of trade. The HBC's inactivity contrasted poorly with the vigorous action shown by private French traders who crossed the continent towards the Rockies in the pursuit of quality furs. This led to a damning critique that accused the Company, which held chartered rights to a much vaster territory than that which it embraced, of 'sleeping by the frozen sea'. Negative attention fell upon the Company in Britain and this, followed by the British conquest of Canada in 1763 when British merchants began to move into the successful Montreal-based fur trade, provoked the directors to expand trading operations beyond the periphery of Hudson's Bay.[12] Aside from being able to compete more effectively against rival traders, this also meant that the HBC's reliance on middlemen declined, as its employees came into direct contact with the trappers.

When the HBC finally stirred in 1774, it constructed its first inland post, Cumberland House, which was 700 miles inland by canoe from Hudson's Bay. However, pressures mounted to continue expansion when some of the Montreal-based merchants, many of whom were Scottish Highlanders, formally coalesced as the North West Company (NWC) in 1779. Employing skilled and experienced French-Canadian *voyageurs* and injecting capital into the business, the new company immediately presented itself as a formidable rival. At the same time, in 1780, the ravages of smallpox wiped out some native trading populations and in several areas 'blasted' hopes of increasing trade; the expansion of commerce and settlements throughout Rupert's Land became a mandatory objective if an ample share of the fur trade was to be retained.[13]

The first century of the HBC's existence was long and difficult, but the era after 1779 was a particularly critical one. The HBC grappled with new challenges presented by the expansion of commerce and settlements throughout Rupert's Land. Its route of expansion followed the river networks leading from Hudson's Bay along the Churchill, Nelson, Severn, Albany and Moose rivers, and eventually west to the Rockies on the Saskatchewan River, north on the Athabasca, and south-west to the Red River and Assiniboine River, near present-day Winnipeg, Manitoba. The labour force already had to adapt to life in the freezing tundra, and now also had to contend with long expeditions through wilderness terrain, encountering thick forests, vast lakes, dangerous rivers, prairies, mountains, and wild animals, as they tried to establish new relationships with native tribes and set up trading posts.

'Country skills', such as a familiarity with native languages and the ability to operate a canoe, became increasingly important assets for employees engaged in inland work.[14] Birchbark canoes were the main form of inland transport, as they were fast, handled rapids well, and were light, making them easy to portage – carry overland – between bodies of water and around obstacles such as waterfalls. The main disadvantage of canoes was their fragility. A variety of boats, including those known as the Albany boats, Churchill boats, freight boats, and Red River boats, were also used on these inland expeditions as they had the advantage of pushing through ice and carrying more freight than canoes. However, they were difficult to portage and often had to be tracked, which involved towing the boat with a haul line. They did not come to replace the canoe as the main form of water transport until after 1821, when a uniform design was used, which later became known as the York boat.[15]

Aside from meeting the new demands of the developing inland fur trade, the HBC also faced an aggressive trading competition with the NWC. A feud developed between the two companies as they fought to win over new native trading partners, establishing posts side by side across the country, with the NWC approaching from the east, along the St Lawrence and Ottawa Rivers. Tensions were further heightened by the need to discover new sources of fur. The North American fur trade had been in operation for over 200 years prior to the onset of rivalry between the two companies, and the adherents of the trade had paid no attention to the ecological impact of the business during this time. They had disregarded the fur-bearing capacity of the territories where they trapped and traded.[16] The beaver was an immobile creature that could be hunted in forested areas of lakes and rivers throughout the year, and exhaustion of numbers had occurred as early as around 1635 in areas of the St Lawrence drainage basin.[17] The arrival of traders with ammunition meant that the beaver supplies soon diminished across the country generally, and the scarcity of the resource on which the fur trade depended only served to exacerbate competition between the trading companies, eventually pushing the trade into the beaver-rich north-west of the country. This rivalry only added to the HBC's problems as it increased the cost of furs at a time when the Company was already struggling financially, due to problems further afield in Europe.

Trouble brewed across the Atlantic with the outbreak of the French Revolutionary wars and later, the Napoleonic wars, both of which created complications for the HBC, including labour shortages and serious financial difficulties. The value of the Company's stock fell, the market for furs faltered, and the price of trade goods and provisions increased. With falling profits and mounting debt, the HBC reached a crisis point and, in 1810, finally addressed its problems through a reorganisation of the London Committee. One of the new shareholders, Andrew Wedderburn, was accepted onto the London Committee and gained extensive control over Company policy from 1810 onwards, introducing a plan of reform, which came to be known as the 'New System'.[18]

This new scheme, also known as the 'Retrenching System', was designed to increase efficiency in the HBC. One of the main aspects of the New System was the recruitment of more energetic and driven personnel to compete with the North West Company; and well-educated men to maintain methodical records and help manage the business in Rupert's Land more effectively, reducing reliance on the internal recruitment of servants. Economising strategies were also brought into play, which included the abolition of employees' bonuses and the delivery of fewer imported provisions from Britain. This plan of reform also affected the administration of Rupert's Land, splitting the fur-trading territory into two departments, north and south, each of which was managed by a super-intendent. One of the most radical facets of the New System was the institution of a colony at Red River in Assiniboia.

The establishment of a settlement at Red River emerged from the involve-ment of Thomas Douglas, fifth earl of Selkirk, as a shareholder in the Company from 1808. In 1811 he was given a tract of land covering 116,000 square miles, on which he could settle Scottish Highlanders in return for providing labourers and provisions from the colony, as well as lots of land for retired HBC employees to settle on. However, the NWC, believing that the colony was a conspiracy to ravage their fur trade, became determined to oppose it to the full, and supported attacks on the settlement by the mixed-blood population of Assiniboia (later known as the Métis), which culminated in bloodshed in 1816 when at least twenty-two people were shot dead. This turbulent phase in HBC history drew to a close in 1821 when the two trading companies, suffering substantial human, material, and financial losses, were compelled to merge, resulting in a complete reorganisation of the trade.

This book is a history of the HBC fur trade from a Scottish perspective during the era of trading competition between the HBC and the NWC, and as a result the main body will concentrate on the era 1780 to 1821. Numerous scholars have remarked on the prominence of Scots in the HBC, but it was only recently that Scottish participation in the fur trade was touched upon from a Scottish perspective, in the broad context of diaspora and empire.[19] In an attempt to delve into the issues pertinent to Scots, a thematic structure and empirical approach have been chosen.

Chapter 2 examines the rationale behind, and the evolution of, the HBC's recruitment drive from the 1780s until 1821 when it merged with the NWC. The chronological examination of recruitment is largely carried out from the official perspective of the directors, who ruled the enterprise from London. Scottish participation was truly phenomenal in this period, escalating to over 80 per cent of all HBC employees at the turn of the century and comprising over 60 per cent at any other time. Regional contributions within Scotland shifted throughout the period as the Company management re-evaluated and tailored its recruitment practices to overcome problems caused by commercial expansionism, inter-fur trade rivalry and imperial conflict.[20] The gradual intro-duction of Scots from other areas including Shetland, the Western Isles, and the Highlands was quite remarkable, and coupled with the modest presence of Lowland Scots, meant that by 1821, few areas of Scotland had been untouched by the HBC.[21] This chapter demonstrates the ways in which Scots, and Orcadians in particular, became disproportionately numerous and increasingly visible in the HBC, setting the framework for the rest of the book, which largely, but not exclusively, focuses on the experience of Orcadian employees.

In contrast to the London Committee, which explicitly recorded the grounds for its recruitment policies and practices, Orcadian employees left few records explaining why their personal engagement with the fur trade was so appealing and enduring. Chapter 3 probes the underpinning of Orcadian persistence in the fur trade. In 1801, the population of the islands was enumerated as 24,445, but 'great emigrations' were emanating from Orkney and the islands encountered a 'constant drain of men'.[22] Economic outlets in Orkney were insubstantial and often unfruitful at this time, providing a motivation to depart the islands. Yet, there are some indications that opportunity, rather than despondency and destitution, provided the main spur for sojourning and relocation from Orkney. The islands' economic shortcomings were surmounted by their location, offering disillusioned inhabitants easy access to alternative employment in the mainland and overseas, thereby constructing a versatile temporary migratory tradition.

Prospective sojourners found an array of avenues through which they could seek to better their fortunes and many were lured into the service of the HBC. The accessibility and durability of employment in the HBC, coupled with the promise of financial success, attracted many Orkneymen to service. Individual impetus to enter the Company was also influenced by the receipt of encouraging feedback from friends and relatives who were already serving in Rupert's Land. One further appeal lay in the considerable scope for advancement within the HBC.

Yet employment in the fur trade was not by any means wholly attractive: Chapter 4 examines the perils that accompanied work in the geographically isolated environment of Rupert's Land. HBC employees engaged in physically demanding work and the strains of such drudgery were heightened by severe climatic conditions. The Hudson's Bay area experienced a six-month long sub-arctic winter in which the temperature could plummet as low as minus 50°F. Historians frequently note that Orcadians were accustomed to such a harsh climate and were particularly well-equipped for, and suited to, the rigours of the fur trade. Some of these environmentally deterministic views may have arisen from the recommendations of HBC Governor, John Nixon who suggested that in 1682 the Company should recruit Scots 'for that countrie is a hard country to live in' and Scots were 'a hardy people ... to endure hunger'.[23]

Yet there are no indications that Scots were any more habituated to the extreme climes than any other ethnicity. Orkney experienced 'tempestuous winds', rain, and snow once a year for 'perhaps a fortnight at a time', which were not tantamount to the 'long gloomy, and most severe winter' experienced by fur traders in Rupert's Land.[24] There is a need to put pre-conceptions of hardiness and suitability aside and examine exactly how Orkneymen did fare against the hazards of the fur trade. This chapter also discusses the ways in which the paternalistic directors endeavoured to mitigate such suffering and tended to the welfare of employees and their dependants in Scotland.

The hardships of the fur trade were particularly oppressive in the years prior to the union of the HBC and the NWC due to the pressures imposed by their trading competition. Chapter 5 offers a re-interpretation of the trading conflict and documents a rising antagonism between the concerns in the eighteenth century, which intensified in the first decade of the nineteenth century with increasingly frequent encounters of intimidation, robbery and violence. Until 1811 it appears that provocation and aggression emanated largely from the NWC, but following administrative reorganisation in the HBC, a policy change from passive to active opposition, and the creation of the Red River colony, the course of the conflict thereafter changed. Pressures resulting from the incompatibility of commerce and settlement exacerbated enmity and the struggle, largely centred on Red River, became more organised, militarised and violent.[25] This chapter argues that the open hostilities, which emerged after the Red River settlement was instituted, were merely a continuation of the escalating discord evident in the earlier period.

The brutal feud is of even greater importance when examined from a Scottish perspective. During the heat of the struggles, Scots from all over the Highlands, Hebrides and Lowlands worked in the HBC, alongside the Orcadian faction. Likewise, there was a substantial Scottish element to the NWC. There was a significant contingent of Highlanders, and many other participants hailed from Aberdeenshire, Glasgow and Ayrshire. Also, the Red River settlers were largely from Sutherland, many of the Métis were progeny of the Scottish members of the NWC and native women, and Lord Selkirk was from Kirkcudbrightshire. Some of the early skirmishes involved Scot attacking Scot, and when the conflict expanded, Scots or half-Scots were involved in every aspect of the fur trade contest.[26]

The Scots' engagement with the fur trade constituted far more than contractual participation in a commercial enterprise. It was also characterised by a complex set of social and cultural circumstances, which is explored in Chapter 6. HBC employees were sojourners who temporarily left their homelands and families to become transient members of a unique social, cultural, and economic sphere. Although their status as temporary migrants suggests that their cultural baggage would be negligible, particularly in comparison with Scottish immigrants, traces of Scottishness were clearly manifested in the territory of Rupert's Land.

Despite the transience of service, Scots were also confronted with the process of acculturation in Rupert's Land. They were in an isolated environment, and partook in work that encouraged immersion in a new way of life, which often included embracing the custom of acquiring an indigenous partner as a 'country wife'. Entrenchment in the fur trade social field clearly had the potential to alter servants' objectives and to modify their identity. It has been suggested that they subsequently severed ties with their home societies, and became so immersed in Rupert's Land that all of their significant relationships, friendships and ties were derived from their sojourn.[27] Although it is possible that their encounter with the fur trade fractured their relationship with 'home', the HBC's paternalistic administrators helped to mitigate the effects of acculturation.

It is clear that the fur trade social sphere did not exist in isolation and although endeavours have been made to uncover the implications of the fur trade for indigenous societies, the impact on British societies has been awarded considerably less attention.[28] It would be expected that the temporary absence and eventual re-influx of HBC employees had a potentially huge impact on the donor society, particularly on a small locus such as Orkney. Chapter 7 looks at the ways in which employees repatriated the profits of the fur trade.

Members of employees' home societies were a crucial factor in the decision to undertake a sojourn as most servants had the explicit intention of making money to support their families during their absence, to fulfil their own personal aspirations upon their return, and to safeguard the future of their relatives after their decease. Since the location in which they plied their trade and earned that money was so far from home, mechanisms had to be set in place to ensure that wages and savings were successfully, safely and expeditiously sent back to Scotland. To this end, a regulated, although not flawless, system of remittance was instituted in the HBC in the 1780s. This chapter looks at the ways in which employees' modest gains from the fur trade benefited themselves, families on both sides of the Atlantic, and the local community in Orkney.

TWO

Recruitment Policies and Practices

Inland exertions: 1780–1791

Scots became an integral part of the HBC in the first 100 years of its existence, although they did not truly monopolise the fur trade until the 1780s when a significant change took place in the HBC's trading operations. Business had largely been confined to the shores of Hudson's Bay, forcing natives to travel a long distance to barter their furs at the HBC posts. They increasingly found it preferable to conduct trade with men encountered along the way, regardless of whether these people had an allegiance to the HBC or operated out of Montreal. When the HBC's rival traders formed the NWC in 1779 and constructed temporary trading posts in the interior, there was even less reason to journey down to the Bay. To counteract this development, the HBC decided that expansion and moving inland beyond the periphery of Hudson's Bay ought to become its 'first consideration'. With this came a need to expand the workforce with 'most able and enterprizen Labourers' and Orkney, both for its location and abundant supply of cheap labour, became the obvious source.[1]

However, the Company directors had neglected to lay the foundations that would fully realise their inland plans. The crucial flaw in the plan of expansion was the absence of an organised recruitment scheme, customised to meet the new demands of the fur trade. Recruitment to the HBC remained a casual affair as the Company directors embarked upon their inland programme; ships' captains selected workers at Stromness en route to Hudson's Bay.[2] Several obstacles to expansion arose from the management's naïve oversight, including labour shortages and the employment of men who were unsuitable, being either unfit or unwilling to undertake inland expansion.

In the early 1780s, the labour force totalled around 250 employees and the complement had barely increased in size by 1786, with 258 men spread throughout numerous posts, including newly established Brunswick House on the Moose River. The workforce began to increase more substantially thereafter as labour was needed to press ahead with the development of the inland trade: approximately fifty new recruits were engaged annually, and by 1789 the complement totalled 308 servants. Orkneymen soon took a firm hold of all key sectors in the servant class, constituting the majority of labourers, carpenters, blacksmiths, coopers, tailors, and bricklayers in the Company.[3]

Even with this addition, the workforce remained insufficient, and deficiencies in the complement at Moose restricted expansion to Abitibi, near the present day Ontario–Quebec border. At the same time, Manchester House, situated on the Battle River to the east of the Rockies, was in need of at least twenty more men. The employees who operated in the interior were inadequate to carry out the necessary duties and by 1790 it was stated that overall 100 more men were required. Yet, reports from York Factory cautioned that although double the number of men and canoes could be employed with success in the inland trade, this could not be done until more competent servants were engaged.[4]

This stemmed from a failure of the Committee members to consider whether the servants who had previously been suitable for the fur trade – obedient, hard-working and content with low wages – would remain so in the new environment in which the Company operated. Inland work was entirely different from employment in the confines of Hudson's Bay. It required long wilderness journeys along the network of rivers leading out of Hudson's Bay and men prepared to acquire experience in canoemanship. The waterways were often rapid and dangerous, and the canoes and their cargo had to be portaged. The workforce was not trained in such pursuits and although Orkneymen were accustomed to seafaring, none of them came equipped to build or handle a canoe.

In addition, many of the rivers froze over in winter and expeditions had to be carried out on foot. Those on inland duty could spend as long as two months travelling in winter, covering up to thirty miles a day, hauling loaded sleds and wearing snowshoes, which were a hindrance, frequently resulting in sprained ankles from stumbling in the snow. These men were expected to exert themselves, often while suffering from hunger and fatigue; although previously strenuous, fur-trade occupations had become exceedingly demanding.[5]

The directors prevailed upon the ships' captains to recruit young men, aged eighteen to thirty years old and fit for such physical challenges, but the captains do not appear to have been very efficient recruiting agents. Many Orkneymen were found to be unfit for inland service, being either too old or too decrepit. Officers revealed that 'aged infirm, and cripples unfit for labouring duties constitute the whole at this place' with the exception of tradesmen.[6] They were referring to York factory, where in 1788 the officers had been able to send only seven young recruits inland, as the rest of the hands were ill-equipped to embark on the journey. Two years later, Joseph Colen, chief officer at York Factory expressed concerns that the Company settlements would soon be full of debilitated men as 50 per cent of the fifty-seven men at York were 'objects fit for hospitals & are a burden to the factory'.[7] One of the captains admitted to willingly engaging invalids and some without limbs, so it is not surprising that employees unfitted for laborious duties and inland expeditions continued to occupy the posts. With no penalties for shoddy recruiting, it was probable that the captains simply wanted to fulfil their quota of men and set sail across the Atlantic without delay.

Yet, even those men who were fit enough to undertake the new rigours of the fur trade were not always willing. Out of the total complement in the 1780s, between 20 and 25 per cent were intended to construct or reside at inland trading posts and conduct business. Although some employees had ventured into the interior during the previous decade and received an allowance of forty shillings for the exertions involved, along with forty shillings for any canoe built and ten shillings per journey undertaken, many were simply unwilling. Orkneymen were content to work for low wages, but arduous and potentially life-threatening employment was less appealing for the same meagre salary, regardless of any gratuities offered. Some collectively refused to work inland, and one man who loathed inland travel endeavoured to spread this aversion among his companions. Another reluctant Orcadian servant, William Laughton, refused to work beyond Henley House, which was over 150 miles upstream from Albany post on James Bay, and a fellow servant would only go inland if bestowed with 'various presents'. In fact, in order to build the quantity of settlements necessary to compete effectively against the NWC, an officer warned the managers they would have to resort to bribery.[8]

Offering financial encouragement to undertake inland work was proving to be a double-edged sword; some men were successfully enticed to work but a precedent had been set, at least in the employees' psyche, and they would refuse particular duties if they were not paid for it. One officer complained that employees used to be compliant but had become increasingly refractory and whereas the older servants knew better, the rest were no longer afraid to refuse duty and in fact now 'deny with a face of brass'. They would not return inland unless certain terms were met and when the payment of forty shillings for building canoes was stopped, the men became markedly less industrious.[9]

Bargaining and negotiating was already customary within the workforce, but by being bribed to work, servants had become more aware of their significance to the Company's ability to fulfil plans and, consequently, their value as commodities. They exploited their awareness of labour deficits and took the opportunity to assert themselves for better conditions and terms that would prove financially beneficial. According to officers at York, the Orkneymen were aware of understaffing in 1788 and took advantage of the situation by forming a combination, also known as a strike, to bargain for better terms. In another instance that year, some of the Orkneymen refused to return to their inland stations until their officers demanded that the London Committee permit the homeward-bound vessels to stop at Orkney to allow passenger disembarkation. This stipulation was in order to return home without having used up a huge portion of their wages in travelling from Gravesend, where the ships docked, to Orkney. They appear to have succeeded in this endeavour, as the Company altered the routes of the *King George III* and recorded the ship's detour via the Orkney Islands in 1795.[10]

Successful bargaining such as this proved to the servants that radical measures worked. To this end, employees also refused to sign contracts or would only sign if certain conditions were met. Those whose agreements expired in Rupert's Land attempted to increase their wages on the next contract by railroading their superiors into their terms of employment. Negotiations were carried out when the return ship was anchored in Hudson's Bay, so that if a salary increase or bonus was not permitted, the servants threatened to step on board the ship back home. Officers were warned that this was 'mere Tricking' and to disregard such manipulative behaviour. If any servant was singled out as a ringleader, then he was to be sent home with the knowledge that he would not be engaged in the service again.[11] It is ironic that the Orcadians, whose tractability had been prized over the insubordination of English recruits, became intransigent, partly as a result of the HBC's policy of selective financial inducements.

Another area to which the Company failed to give enough attention in the light of the new demands of the fur trade, was its conditions of service. Each first-time recruit was committed to a five-year contract and could subsequently opt for a one- or three-year agreement after the original expired, or alternatively, return home to Britain. Colin Robertson, a fur trader from Perth, later commented that Orcadian men in particular were inclined to return home once they were capable of carrying out their duties. The Committee's disapproval of this behaviour arose from the cost and length of time it had taken men to acquire experience and skills such as canoeing, and the expense in shipping men across the Atlantic. Some employees had completed their contracts and decided to terminate temporary migratory work in the fur trade, but many others, such as Adam Mowat from Stromness, sailed back to Orkney simply to re-engage with the Company on better terms. These employees wanted to renegotiate the agreement on which they were originally hired, hoping to offer their own terms of higher wages and a shorter contract.[12]

The London Committee chose to implement some strategies in order to regain control over its workforce and re-engagement procedures. The first was designed to ensure that the Company would only re-hire efficient workers. Instructions were issued in 1787, that all men leaving the service must be awarded a reference, signed by a chief officer. The future engagement of all servants in Orkney would be wholly dependent on the production of this certificate reflecting their good character. In a second stratagem, which was intended to create a distinction between those who stayed in Rupert's Land and those who chose to return home, the Company decided that more support would be given to employees who renewed their contract in Rupert's Land and thus remained in continuous service. But men who re-entered the Company after returning to Orkney, however briefly, would do so at their old wages, not at increased remuneration, and if they stayed for another three years rather than five, then they would be shown less favourable regard. They also took the unpopular decision of prohibiting re-engagement on short one-year contracts, insisting that there was a three-year minimum. Therefore, a servant such as Magnus Twatt found that his options had been reduced to continuing in the service for three years at £20, or returning home to Orkney and not being allowed out again.[13]

Unfortunately these resolutions were ineffective and men continued to resist authority, wrangle over the particulars of service and return home to re-engage. This conduct exasperated the directors, to the extent that they claimed they were 'totally indifferent whether such old servants, as they style themselves, are ever employed again or not'.[14] As in the early years of the Company's existence, when Londoners failed to meet expectations, the management sought new employees free of such problems. Introducing recruits from a new arena was a remedy to which the Company directors were to resort repeatedly whenever they perceived problems with a group of existing servants. In the 1780s, they turned to French-Canadians in the hope of alleviating their tribulations.

The Committee's justification was that Canadians were well-equipped for inland work. They had invaluable experience, being familiar with the territory and adept at canoeing. Although Canadian voyageurs traditionally served the Montreal trading companies and the Committee was concerned about the extent of their loyalty to the HBC, it was felt that fidelity to the HBC could be secured by mixing them among the Scottish and English servants.[15] Canadians were not, however, particularly well regarded within the service. Officer William Walker described them as a 'parcel of Shifting Fellows', and although he had categorically criticised Orkneymen for 'worse and worse behaving', as soon as Canadian servants became the alternative option, he backtracked and claimed that the Company already had fine servants.[16] In addition, Canadian employment came at an expense, for, although not incurring the costs of a voyage across the Atlantic, they engaged at double the wages of a new Orcadian recruit. Few Canadian engagements materialised anyway, primarily because the Company did not adopt a purposeful recruitment strategy towards them.[17]

By the end of the 1780s, the Company management seemed more aware that expansion and recruitment were complementary processes and that the unsophisticated, century-old method of recruitment was no longer suitable. By relinquishing the responsibility of recruitment to the captains, the directors realised that they had little control over the composition and size of the lower-ranking labour force. Perhaps Orcadian William Tomison's assertion in 1790, that there was a great quantity of Orkneymen willing to enter the service and fifty more could have been procured if wanted, prompted them to react.[18] Although Orkneymen were proving problematic, the fact that they remained cheap and plentiful kept them attractive. The Committee realised that in order to capitalise on this rich labour supply, change was imperative. They took a significant step towards formalising the recruitment process in 1791 by hiring an agent to be permanently stationed in Stromness.

The utility of a Scottish-based intermediary had emerged in the 1780s when the Company hired Andrew Graham, an ex-officer, to organise the payment of servants' accounts from Edinburgh. The need to recruit more men and the forthcoming additions to the payroll meant that managing the employment of Scots had become a permanent occupation. An administrative figure situated in the Orkney Isles meant that all aspects of Orcadian employment could be handled locally. It was hoped that David Geddes, a merchant in Stromness who had connections with one of the Company captains, would establish an agency in Orkney.[19] His responsibilities would include recruiting servants for the trading posts, the advance of recruits' wages, administering contracts and the payment of wages and support money to servants' families. Overall, this measure testified to the increased Orcadian presence in the Company – at least 70 per cent of all employees in total in 1789 – and reasserted the Company's determination to continue staffing its settlements with Orkneymen.

Recruitment, war and rivalries: 1791–1810

The benefit of the agent, 'a man well qualified for business, and attentive to the interests of the Company', was that he could distribute printed advertisements in advance of the HBC vessels' arrival in Stromness.[20] Geddes was asked to procure 100 or more Orcadian servants in 1791 and likewise over the following two years, receiving a commission of ten shillings for each recruit engaged. Although Geddes only engaged sixty-six Orkneymen in 1791, the annual entry rate was higher than previously and Orcadians became more prominent in the Company, prompting the London Committee to comment that there are 'so many Cromarties Isbisters Spences … in the Company's Service'.[21] The benefits of organised recruitment had become apparent, but competition for Orkney-based manpower, coupled with negative public opinion, served to hinder

Geddes' recruitment efforts almost from the outset.

During the Mercantilist Age in which the HBC burgeoned, Britain's foreign relations were rarely stable. In the 1790s, imperial conflict had once again broken out between Britain and France and since the Company's ideal labour force consisted of males in their prime, the competitive demands of war inevitably had an effect upon its attempts to increase and sustain a sufficient workforce. Military recruitment during both the Revolutionary and Napoleonic wars, from 1792 until 1815, was considerable; the Navy alone grew from 16,000 men in 1789 to 140,000 in 1812.[22] Seafaring was an attractive option for many Orkneymen, but the army was generally reviled; nobody had enlisted as a soldier from the parishes of Birsay and Harray in the eighteenth century. Rev. James Watson confirmed that in the southern islands of South Ronaldsay and Burray, the inhabitants' affection for a nautical career was only matched by their 'aversion to a military one'.[23] However, during the French wars, bounties were offered to entice men to enlist, and press-gangs operated assiduously to secure those recruits who were less inclined to volunteer.

Throughout the Revolutionary wars and much of the Napoleonic conflict, complaints of war-induced labour shortage proliferated in the HBC. The Committee members frequently reflected on how the war in Europe was resulting in a scarcity of hands and prohibiting them from meeting the needs of the business. Competitive outlets for manpower had a significant effect upon recruitment and as early as 1793, impressments of seamen in England had caused the ships to depart later than usual. In that same year there were complaints in Rupert's Land of a shortage of men to carry out essential plans of expansion.[24]

In order to overcome the labour deficiency, two approaches were informally commissioned by the Company directors: incentives and coercion. Although the Company Secretary had stated, in response to a communication concerning a meagre labour supply in Orkney, that 'there is no forcing Men to go against their will', there were other ways in which the Company could attempt to secure recruits.[25] The first approach was to offer potential employees financial inducements, a tactic that had proven effective with Orcadian employees in the past. In 1794, David Geddes was authorised to offer recruits a bounty of one or two guineas, and the ensuing year it was again hoped that diligent men could be recruited through the offer of advances and bounties, in addition to the usual gratuities for inland service.[26]

The management had to sustain a diplomatic balance between attracting fresh hands and mollifying existing servants, who might resent new recruits engaging on more favourable terms. Geddes had the task of procuring at least 100 men in 1795 and suggested that his recruitment quest might be more

successful if the initial wages were raised to £8 on account of the war, as opposed
to the usual £6. He also advocated a reduction in the length of contract from the
standard five years to a three-year agreement. However, the directors rebuffed
this proposition, concerned that men already on full-term contracts at a lower
wage, might feel aggrieved. They were torn between the need to augment their
complement and to retain the workers already in service. They made one
concession by permitting 'old' servants who had returned home at the expiration of their contract to re-engage at their existing wages for one year, followed
by a rise, instead of serving the full term on their previous salary as usual. Yet,
only a couple of years later, as the wars continued to rage, the Company was
desperate, and further acquiesced by permitting Geddes' former suggestion of
'War Wages': new recruits were offered £8 per annum for three-year contracts.[27]

Attracting new recruits was difficult, but preserving the level of personnel
in the service had long been a significant challenge to the directors. Equilib-
rium needed to be maintained between the number of men departing the fur
trade and those being recruited. Officers in Rupert's Land complained that the
balance was slipping, which was detrimental to the trade, and attributed this to
a want of tighter regulations on the renewal of contracts. Some servants such
as Andrew Johnson refused to sign three-year contracts, professing that they
would stay only one year. In fact, annual agreements made in Rupert's Land
became a frequent occurrence, which came at a heavy cost to the business.
Aside from forking out higher wages for each new contract, such short-term
service damaged continuity. It created uncertainty over the next year's quota of
men and, on occasion, resulted in posts being abandoned as employees had to
travel from their inland posts to Hudson's Bay to renegotiate their contracts.[28]
In order to sustain a sufficiently sizeable workforce, the Committee members
had to resort to extortion.

The astute directors were able to identify and then exploit their servants'
fears. By reminding servants of the military need of the state, the management
hoped that Orkneymen would choose to renew their contracts as opposed to
returning home to the press-gangs. It is ironic that in a time of war-induced
labour shortage, the *Statistical Accounts* for Orkney suggest that for some,
employment in the Company was preferable to serving in the war. The minister
in Orphir, Rev. Francis Liddell, complained that 'for the moment war is
proclaimed, for fear of being pressed, they skulk away to this distant settlement'.
Similar reports came from the parishes of Firth and Stenness where Rev. John
Malcolm confirmed that many local men sought to join the HBC when news of
war arrived. Apparently, Orkneymen preferred the 'rigour of the severe climate
of Hudson's Bay, to the idleness and showy appearance of a soldier'.[29] To this
end, the Committee suggested to officers in 1793 that 'It may not be improper to

intimate to those useful Hands who are desirous of returning to England that it is more than probable on the ships arrival they will be press'd into his majesty's service'.[30] They also forewarned their servants that men returning home would meet with an unpleasant welcome on arrival as soldiers and sailors were in such desperate need, and on top of that, the men would find no other employment.

The Company's officers were also dragooned into retaining servants in the fur trade. They were instructed to convince men who wished to return to continue in service for another year. Despite their efforts, the shortage of hands became so acute in 1797 that the Company feared it would not be able to maintain the existing number of employees, never mind increase the workforce. Aside from those voluntarily returning home, others were sent back by officers as punishment for misbehaviour. The management had earlier dictated that the servants who transgressed ought to be discharged, unless they possessed valuable canoe skills, but it would appear that during the war the Company was suffering as a result of its own stringent rules. Officers were chastised that 'it will be to very little purpose that our agent in the Orknies procure Men annually for the company at a very considerable expence if they are thus injuriously to Our Interest sent Home'.[31] They were instructed to fine employees for misdemeanours rather than send them home and to dismiss only those who had committed an absolute breach of the regulations. In order to enforce this order, the directors ruled that the charge of five guineas for the servants' voyage home, would be placed on the officer's personal account. A couple of years later, they became even more authoritarian and threatened the servants who wished to return that they would have to pay their own passage home. The captains were targeted too, and directed not to take on board any returning servants unless an equivalent number of men had been recruited from Orkney.[32]

By the turn of the century, the directors had prevailed; economic incentives, coupled with coercive measures, had resulted in a substantial increase in the workforce. Orcadian participation had risen almost two-fold since 1789 and their level of involvement in the Company was at its peak. Rev. William Clouston had speculated in 1794 that of the workforce, 'three-fourths are Orknese'.[33] Indeed, by 1800, the Orcadian faction had risen to at least 79 per cent of the total number of servants, amounting to 418 men out of the entire 524 employees. Examination of recruitment levels and Orcadian participation in the decade thereafter, however, indicates that such levels were not, and possibly could not be, sustained. The Orcadian contribution had decreased by a colossal 30 per cent between 1800 and 1812. It is feasible that the labour supply in Orkney had actually been exhausted and that the management, with expansion at the forefront of its collective mind, held unrealistic expectations about the abundance of its principal source of manpower. Furthermore, the coercive measures taken by the Company directors in the late 1790s to secure a workforce may have backfired. It is unlikely that those servants who were detained in Hudson's Bay against their will would have brought favourable reports of service when they finally did return home.[34]

Public opinion was something to which the directors paid little heed but their virtual disregard of looming unrest in the 1790s was to prove detrimental to the recruitment efforts in the early 1800s. It was paradoxical that while the Company had been successfully increasing the size of the Orcadian percentage of the workforce, public opinion had actually been turning against the enterprise in Orkney. William Tomison, a native of the islands, had informed the Company management that he 'heard no Gentlemen in Orkney say anything against this country' aside from one person.[35] He had, however, made this statement before the outbreak of the Revolutionary wars, when public opinion on migration and its proponents became far more antagonistic. War induced a strong negative response towards emigration, primarily because it was believed in the eighteenth century that a large population equalled a powerful nation: military strength and industrial and agricultural viability were dependent upon an adequate supply of men. Therefore, the removal of the industrious as opposed to surplus population, and of essential manpower for the British navy, army and industries, was bound to cause disquiet. Mercantilists such as Samuel Johnson, James Boswell and various anonymous authors wrote extensively on the subject between the 1760s and early 1800s. The consensus agreed with Dr Johnson that emigration was 'hurtful to human happiness' as it 'weakened the defence of a nation'.[36] Although Orkneymen in the HBC were typically sojourners, contemporary opinion did not differentiate between temporary and permanent emigration.

In 1794, William Clouston inferred that the Company's recruitment demands had elicited some grievances in Orkney. Although the fisheries, army and navy also tapped into the Orcadian labour supply, Clouston noted that complaints were generally targeted at the HBC as their recruitment was more visible, with a substantial annual intake of fresh hands. This had not been a problem in the past, but the want of men to serve in other fields made it harder for Orkney to spare those for the HBC.[37] One vocal adversary of the HBC, Rev. Francis Liddell of Orphir, echoed other opponents of emigration when he criticised the Orcadian servants in 1797, who

> instead of offering an honourable service to their King and country, or
> staying at home to cultivate their lands, and protect their wives, their
> children, and their parents, for the sum of L.6 *per annum*, hire themselves
> out for slaves in a savage land, where, in the language of Scripture, they

are literally employed as hewers of wood and drawers of water; or, what is a still more distinguishing badge of slavery, in dragging along large loads of timber, yoked in the team, like beasts of burden. My God! Shall man, formed in the image of his creator, desert the human species; and, for the paltry sum of L.6 a-year, assume the manners and the habits of the brutes that perish. Fy be on the man, who would rather be the slave of a Company of private merchants, than enter into the fleets and armies of Great Britain, and bravely fight for his King and country, our religion, our liberties, and our laws.[38]

The effect of such influential parties publicly denouncing the Company in a small society was potentially ruinous. Engagement in the service was often a community affair that involved recommendations from school-teachers and ministers, who petitioned on behalf of servants who appeared hard-done-by, or families of servants requiring financial support. It is unclear whether the opponents of migration did wield any effect on recruitment from Orkney during the wars, but Rev. William Clouston noted that those who objected to sojourning in the HBC enlightened recruits on the harshness of wilderness employment; emphasising the severe climate, hazards of frostbite, and danger of being killed by natives.[39] Clouston believed that such opinions did not deter the men from signing up, but there is evidence to suggest that uncomplimentary representations did hamper the recruitment effort.

Negative rumours among returning servants spread like any intelligence in Orkney, 'with the rapidity of wild fire'.[40] These reports centred on aspects of life working in the HBC. For instance, the dangerous nature of service was highlighted when the Esquimaux murdered some employees at Eastmain in 1794. It seemed 'to operate very powerfully at the Orknies against Men engaging' and it was believed that it would take some time to expunge. Another rumour was based on differing strands of treatment between the posts. In this respect, Orcadians returning from Churchill in 1794 were critical of the harsh treatment they had received, serving on poorer terms than their colleagues at York.[41]

In both sets of circumstances, however, the Committee members noted that the abhorrence was to a particular post and not the general service. The servants at Churchill were not discouraged from continuing in the fur trade, but simply left the service in order to re-engage with the hope that they would be allocated to a different locale in Rupert's Land, where the bounties on offer were higher. When the Company recognised this discrepancy, it endeavoured to allow bounties for Churchill servants, consisting of forty shillings for canoe-building and the same for trip money; voyages that were exceptionally long would be rewarded with a double payment of the bonus. Yet, if anyone was caught leaving the post to re-engage at York, they were to be banned from service, since Churchill had been made equally advantageous.[42]

While the disadvantages of consistently drawing upon a localised pool of labour had not fully materialised in the 1790s, the drawbacks were clearly evident in the next decade. The Peace of Amiens in 1802 had provoked optimism within the Company and a respite from labour shortages was eagerly anticipated. However, it proved to be a vain prospect as the fisheries required a huge number of men, making available HBC workers few and far between. More troubling, and in contrary to Clouston's belief that negative representations did not dissuade recruits, unfavourable reports circulating in Orkney caused men previously set to engage to change their minds. William Tomison, an officer from South Ronaldsay, wrote from Cumberland House to John Ballenden, a fellow Orcadian at York Factory, that 'Mr Geddes informs me there was more Men to come out, but as soon as the Ships arrived in Orkney it was rumoured all over the Country there was no provisions on board the ships'.[43] It is likely that the recruits who changed their minds received a warm reception at the northern fisheries that year.

Circumstances deteriorated further when eighty-four men returned home; the directors were so alarmed by the numerous servants on three-year contracts disengaging from service that they 'determined to put a stop to it'.[44] In order to compensate for those who had returned and to carry forward some much-needed expansion, the agent was required to engage double the number of recruits in 1803, amounting to 150 men. The management cautioned the Orkney agent that 'it might be good Policy not to let it be known that so great a Number of Men is requested this year'.[45] In tradesmen alone, they required thirteen men, along with nine sailors, seven tailors and a large consignment of labourers. However, on account of peace, the directorate had opted for a restoration of traditional terms and again insisted upon the full five-year contract. This immediately counteracted the recruitment drive, and hopes of attaining the optimum number of recruits required soon dissolved when Geddes struggled to obtain any hands at all.[46] He petitioned the Company to shorten the contract for fear it was repelling men, which it probably had, but it later transpired that the usual annual increment obtained in Orkney had been poached by the NWC.

For those experiencing discontent and disillusionment with the HBC there were alternative employers ready to highlight the attractions of their services and primed to accept the disgruntled. Conspicuous rivals for manpower in war-time were the army and navy, while other less discernible contenders had also emerged; engaging in the fur trade had actually opened up new avenues of employment for Orkneymen, namely, service with rival traders, the NWC. For servants with a serious grudge to bear, this constituted the ultimate revenge.

The Montreal-based company was not immune to the strains caused by expansion and competition and it too struggled to obtain sufficient quantities of men to stimulate trade. Despite the HBC administrators' almost blinkered view of the French-Canadian voyageurs as ideal workers, the NWC experienced similar problems with its labour force as the HBC did; at times workers could only be attained and retained through the bait of money and advance of wages.[47] There is some evidence to suggest that either due to labour shortages, or as a tactic to gain advantage in the commercial competition, the NWC directors encroached upon the Orcadian labour supply.

The HBC management informed the Orkney agent in 1793 that they had received a tip-off concerning former servants re-engaging in the fur trade with the rival company. To make matters worse, these ex-servants had then tried to engage Orkneymen for the NWC's service. Despite this intelligence, and knowledge presented by their own officers in 1789 that a handful of Orcadian servants had threatened to sign up with the Canadian traders immediately on arrival in Britain as they were intent on injuring the HBC, the directors disregarded the possibility that their rivals would tap into their established labour supply.[48] It was an unlikely supposition, they felt, because the rival company was located, and undertook recruitment, in Montreal.

Yet, the recruitment of Orkneymen was a serious concern of the rival company in 1798. One of the Scottish NWC members, Aeneas Cameron, was home on leave and ordered to correspond with a NWC acquaintance in the Orkney Islands. He was requested to recruit seamen for a period of three to five years, advance them money and assist them to the port of Greenock.[49] It is uncertain whether he succeeded and if so, the number of men he engaged. It is also unclear to what extent the executives of the HBC were aware of their rival's plans, but rumours certainly proliferated in Rupert's Land in 1798. Whether or not the plan was leaked, the managers confidently avowed that the Company's able servants would not be swayed to leave their employ by the opposition, and experience had proved this to be the case.[50]

It therefore must have been a revelation to the London Committee when in 1803, Captain Richards, formerly of the HBC, entered the 'Employ of certain Canada Merchants of this Metropolis' and commanded a ship to Quebec and thereafter Hudson's Bay, carrying former HBC servants. The vessel stopped at Stromness on the outward voyage and the captain circulated adverts around the islands encouraging Orkneymen to enrol with him. Between forty and fifty servants were engaged, most of whom were previous HBC employees, and their arrival at Charlton Island in Hudson's Bay did 'excite some Degree of surprise'.[51] The captain seemingly boasted about having several ex-servants and, bizarrely, of the fact that they had been engaged at high wages; the minimum salary on offer was £18 for young hands.

Although the Company management advised officers that its opponents might endeavour to entice more employees away, this warning may have arrived too late, as the officers at Hudson's Bay feared that their rivals had already signed up some existing servants for the subsequent year. Thomas Isbister, a trader, was reportedly offered £80 and a free passage if he would join the NWC, at a time when the HBC was trying to secure him for £30. The directors ordered a tight rein to be kept on current employees and to limit interactions between them and any defectors. The managers were confident that their former servants would be submitted to harsh treatment and eventually regret their decision to side with the Canadians, but they were adamant that no favours should be granted to the traitors and under no circumstances would these renegades be permitted back in the HBC's service.[52]

This encroachment upon the HBC's traditional labour supply served as a significant hindrance to the HBC's recruitment, particularly as the NWC's intake of fifty servants matched typical levels of HBC recruitment at this time. Although the rival company had offered excessively high wages, its success in hiring so many servants also indicates that the unfavourable reports disseminated about the HBC may indeed have impinged on the recruitment effort. Only one year later, an ex-servant, William Tilloch, threatened to slander the Company with unsavoury reports affixed to church doors in Orkney. This was followed the subsequent year by a combination between existing servants, former employees and their friends and relatives in Orkney with the purpose of inhibiting the Company from attaining the necessary intake of hands for service. The latter recalcitrance did not appear to arise from genuine grievance but, according to the directors, was formed with the objective of forcing over-inflated wages.[53]

Faced with the devastating effects of negative opinion coupled with a fierce competition for manpower, the HBC directors were compelled to broaden their recruitment sphere and establish new sources of Scottish labour. The extension of the catchment area to other regions of Scotland was not a new strategy for the management; such a step had been considered in the 1790s. They had been advised in 1792 that the Highlands could supply them with a significant number of hands, and two years later, on fur trader George Sutherland's advice, they asked Geddes to investigate the eligibility and expense of engaging Shetlanders. It was perhaps hoped that both Highlanders and Shetlanders would display the same qualities as Orkneymen; but although Geddes was to visit Shetland in the summer of 1794, the prospect of procuring workers was apparently poor.[54] Nothing materialised out of either impulse; the Scottish contribution, excluding

Orcadian participation, constituted only 1 per cent in 1800, and all but one recruit came from Caithness and Sutherland, which is understandable given the close proximity of these counties to the Orkney Isles.

Yet, in 1804 the directors could not determine how many recruits Geddes would procure and feared that military pressures had bled the country of suitable men, making Geddes' Orcadian recruitment drive futile. In addition, a demand for servants who were specifically able and willing to prosecute the inland trade, and protect it from neighbouring rivals, was growing vociferous in Rupert's Land. This urgent need prompted the Committee members to sanction active recruitment in the Highlands and Shetland Isles; Francis Heddle was subsequently directed to recruit from Shetland in 1805, while Donald McKay and William Auld, Scottish officers who were on leave, recruited in Sutherland and Caithness.[55]

Geddes had exerted himself in his recruitment campaign during the war, but the new agents appear to have pursued recruitment more vigorously, under the auspices of the Committee. A two-guinea bounty was offered to encourage new hands, but the recruiting agents were warned that a 'great deal, indeed, in order to procure Men in the first Instance must depend entirely on yourself'.[56] William Auld was instructed to inform potential recruits of the benefits of service and to flaunt the material successes of former employees in order to entice them to engage. The directors reassured him that these representations were not embellished and they were confident that such success stories would motivate men to enter service.

In contrast to claims that the plans came to nothing, Donald McKay was successful in procuring men from Caithness, and while Francis Heddle declared it unlikely that he would engage any men in Shetland, the vessel *King George III* was ordered to stop in Lerwick and collect new hands before proceeding to Orkney. This is the first time that there is any record of a Company vessel voyaging to Hudson's Bay via the Shetland Isles, and attests to the desperation of the Committee.[57] Therefore, as with the introduction of Orcadians to the fur trade in the early eighteenth century, imperial conflict and the associated shortage of men fuelled a new recruitment practice in which they turned to other Scots such as Shetlanders and Highlanders. The involvement of mainland Scots during this period should not, however, be overstated. Although non-Orcadian Scottish participation had increased with the recruiting efforts of the first decade of the nineteenth century, they still comprised less than 3 per cent of servants in 1812; Orkneymen continued to make up the bulk of the workforce.

Overlooking the Orcadians' turbulent behaviour in the early years of the decade, the management had continued to lure Orkneymen with financial awards, despite their own economic sufferings as a result of both the lengthy war and commercial competition within the fur trade. In 1806, the Committee announced that sizeable bounties had been offered to encourage new servants to sign up and old employees looking to re-engage. A sliding scale was employed to differentiate between fresh recruits and experienced hands. New personnel were offered a four-to-eight guinea gratuity, depending on their qualifications, while former servants were offered as much as twelve guineas extra, per three-year contract. The bounties were not fixed and were largely dependent on the agent's discretion as well as the servant's skill and experience. The other incentive offered that year was orientated towards the recruiting agent; he was granted increased commission of one guinea per hand for each person he engaged. Financial inducements seemingly produced the desired results, as Geddes informed the Committee in March that he had obtained a sufficient number of new recruits.[58] This success, together with the continuing manpower exigencies of war, pushed the HBC to consent to a bounty again in 1807.

However, the administrators hoped that they would not have to resort to such an expensive method of recruitment in future, and terminated such gratuities the following year. This decision was taken partially out of fear that current hands would return home, only to re-engage and obtain the bounty. As an alternative, they decided to offer a re-engagement bonus to existing servants in Rupert's Land. Twelve guineas were offered to any man earning less than £25 who renewed a five-year contract. If that was not persuasion enough to remain in the service, the example of two fellow servants being pressed in 1806 on their way to Stromness, coupled with the passing of the Local Militia Bill, which obliged all able men to act as soldiers, served to secure the workforce.[59]

The financial and coercive measures taken by the Company, coupled with attempts to extend recruitment to other parts of Scotland, only just ensured the survival of the enterprise. But such approaches could not be continued indefinitely. Commercially, the business was really struggling, particularly after 1806, when a continental blockade obstructed access to the European markets, and the usual exports to northern Europe were stopped. Unsold furs piled up in the London warehouses and the HBC had to suspend the payment of dividends on Company stock. On top of this, war conditions meant that trade goods had become increasingly expensive, and war taxes still had to be paid. Additionally, increased competition between the fur-trading entities in Rupert's Land was draining the availability of quality furs. As the HBC debated how to continue its business, recruitment reached a virtual standstill.[60]

Scots in the New System

Fortunately, the Company soon developed the New System, which aimed to breathe new life into the business with the recruitment of more active, dynamic and industrious Scottish servants. Although the Napoleonic wars continued to rage, trading rivalries within the fur trade became a more pressing matter and dictated recruitment patterns until the two competitors merged in 1821. Whereas earlier concerns during the war had centred on the problem of an inadequate supply of labour, the main objective under the New System was now to tackle the long-standing inefficiency of its workforce, which was impeding effective operations in the era of trading competition. Colin Robertson, a Scotsman who had previously been in the employ of the rival Company, offered his advice on the adverse circumstances of the HBC. He opined that the main advantage held by the NWC was energetic, obedient men and conversely, the London Committee's chief impediment was a supply of men 'very ill calculated for the country'.[61]

The management reassessed its recruitment policies and regretted that unsuitable men had been sent from Orkney over the years who had been found to be completely unfit for their duties. At least two of the men in the service were described as lunatics, and they received a host of criticism regarding the engagement of boys, as these youngsters served little use for the first three years of their contract. Of equal hindrance was the prevalence of aged men and the fact that one servant commissioned a personal copy of 'a guide to old age' would suggest that they were right to be concerned. Geddes had been instructed not to send infirm, disabled or aged men but, as the Company acknowledged, it had been difficult to compete with the military needs of the country. Infirmity had been a long-standing complaint in the HBC but the war had contributed to a dearth of suitable recruits, removing the majority of men in their prime and leaving only 'dwarfs' available to enter the fur trade.[62]

The mentality of the workforce was perhaps even more detrimental to inland commerce. Compliability, subordination and a positive work ethic continued to be displaced by complacency and insubordination among the Orcadian employees. Four Orkneymen were fined for the refusal of duty at York Factory in 1801, while one non-Orcadian was applauded for resisting their pressure to join the rebellion.[63] In another instance, Nicholas Tate, a boat-builder at Severn, gave an outright refusal when ordered to commence inland duty in 1807. His superior, James Swain stated that 'he did not consider me as having any Business to order him to any thing of the kind'.[64] Even though Tate was aware that he faced a fine for his poor conduct, he retorted that he could still not be forced to go. Swain appealed to the directors not to let such disrespectful behaviour go unpunished, as subordination was crucial to the effective administration of Rupert's Land.

Efforts were made to amend this type of misbehaviour by sending home the worst culprits and the ringleaders of collective action. The instigators of unrest were singled out and fined, before being banned from future service. Accordingly, Orkneyman John Robertson was denied re-engagement after inciting others to act disobediently, and in 1807, Magnus Loutitt was informed that he was not allowed back as a result of involvement in a combination injurious to the HBC.[65]

These measures proved ineffective and in 1810, Colin Robertson confirmed the growing obstinacy among the Orcadian sector. He noted that when 'Orkneymen were either discontented with the post or their Master, you can never get them to do their duty but by halves' and 'if the place they are ordered to has only the name of being hard, or the voyage difficult to perform, they will throw a hundred obstacles in the way'.[66] The Committee members were aware that servants now had the tendency to deliberate over whether they should obey the Company's rules or not. However, the directors did not consider this intractability to 'arise from any intrinsic defect in the character of the Orkney men'.[67] They believed that the officers were at fault as they had not upheld firm boundaries of authority and had essentially pandered to the servants, which would have made any group of men difficult. This attribution of refractory behaviour to poor administration, rather than disposition, partially explains why Orcadians continued to be the mainstay of recruitment despite similar evidence of insubordination twenty years earlier.

The environment of the fur trade was changing however, and, in the new climate of hostile rivalry, the Orcadian tendency to negotiate and bargain over duties, wages and orders became of paramount concern to the Committee. In the face of increasingly aggressive NWC opposition, unruliness had the potential to utterly disable the Company. Obedience was vital as an officer needed men who were prepared to back him, defend Company property and carry out commands without questioning whether those orders constituted a part of their obligations or not. Orcadian lack of deference was already proving problematical in the competition, and William Auld acknowledged that their lack of fervour and cooperation were cited as reasons for not effectively withstanding their opponents' hostile behaviour.[68] The Committee informed its managers at the Bay that it did not 'despair of your succeeding in curing these bad habits among the old hands by… enforcing the obedience that is due. But where habits of insubordination have been continued by a long system of mismanagement, they are not to be cured at once, nor without a great effort; & there was reason to expect that the object might be more readily attained by the introduction of a new set of men, from other parts of the Kingdom.'[69] Conforming to earlier practices, the Company pursued a facile solution to its problems. Instead of countering Orcadian misbehaviour, the management strove to introduce new employees devoid of such waywardness.

Between 1810 and 1815, the Company revolutionised its recruitment agenda, and the overhaul happened swiftly. The directorate had taken a decision in 1810 to substantially increase the enlistment of men in Rupert's Land. Seventy-two men returned home and it was predicted that another fifty would go back the following year, which, in conjunction with the death of six employees, meant that substitutes were urgently needed; 200 men were envisaged as an adequate augmentation.[70] The Committee adhered to its old recruitment ethos and selected men from peripheral regions of Britain in the hope of attaining the quintessential hard-working, tractable and affordable servant.

Agents were appointed to hire 'stout active young people' from the Hebrides, Glasgow, and Ireland. The directors appealed for the engagement of men used 'to the management of Boats in rapid & intricate Places'; probably reflecting the HBC's growing use of a variety of boats for inland transport.[71] One of the Scottish agents, Charles McLean, was solicited to secure 100 men from the Western Isles alone. Blacksmiths, carpenters, and coopers were also sought, along with fifteen seamen to navigate schooners, all positions that had previously been the domain of Orkneymen.

Again, the recruitment efforts of these agents appear to have been more far-reaching than those of Geddes; perhaps in areas where the Company did not have a reputation and history of recruitment, such lengths were necessary. An advertisement seeking new hands was placed in the *Inverness Journal* and this was complemented by an active recruitment drive in the Western Isles. McLean engaged one young clerk and asked him to accompany him on a tour of Lewis, recruiting additional men. He was instructed to inform budding recruits of a new Company policy that any employees who honoured the terms of their contract and finished with a good reference would receive 100 acres of land in Assiniboia if they wished to settle there. For every further three-year contract they would be awarded an additional grant of 100 acres.[72]

Enticement in the form of land grants was perhaps requisite to compensate for the recent abolition of bounties, trip money, and all allowances under the New System. These measures had been taken as part of the new rigorous approach towards the business and although short-term, three-year and longer-term five-year contracts were still permitted, employees were to be engaged at fixed wages. These were, however, at considerably higher rates than previously, due to the competitive demands of war: £18 a year for the short labouring contract, £20 for a five-year commitment, and £25 for tradespersons.[73]

A diverse group of Glaswegians, Irishmen, Western Islanders and men from Ayrshire and Galloway was secured to descend upon Hudson's Bay. They were followed the next year by fifteen men from Caithness, engaged by Donald Sinclair, and a group from Islay hired by Charles McLean. The Committee believed that the recruitment methods had been more fruitful than in previous years and optimistically assumed that within a few years there would be an abundant supply of men and 'of a much superior class to any that have been hitherto sent out to the Bay'.[74]

Ironically, while one facet of the New System was directed towards revitalising the service with feisty men to combat the increasingly aggressive trading competition with the NWC, the Company managers inadvertently fuelled that hostility, through their sanctioning of the Red River colony. The land grants offered to the new recruits were in Lord Selkirk's new settlement in Assiniboia. Aside from providing lots of land for HBC employees, Selkirk was also committed to recruiting on behalf of the Company. He had been advised to overlook Irish recruits in 1813 as a result of some strife created by those sent to Hudson's Bay in 1811, but in the following year, as the incensed NWC became increasingly riled, the presence of such Irishmen appealed as it was believed that they were capable of withstanding the NWC's mounting hostility.[75] The directors did not state explicitly that they needed men willing to fight, but their plan to succeed in the commercial competition was to counter force with equal strength. In fact, one Orcadian trader, James Sutherland, thought that the HBC was actually 'adopting such wild plans that they will get very few to remain in their service'.[76] This apprehension may have contributed to the Committee's belief that Irishmen, rather than Orkneymen, were most appropriate to challenge the Canadians.[77]

It was clear that the management's stereotypical views of ethnic character traits remained intact, for while they believed Orkneymen to possess a 'docile spirit', Irishmen, Scottish Highlanders and Western Islanders were alleged to be capable of withstanding belligerence. George Simpson, Scottish administrator and future governor of the HBC, later commented that 'in time of danger two highlanders are worth half a Doz. Canadian Bullies'.[78] To this end, the Company also boosted its quotas of these men; an agent, John McDonald, was instituted in Inverness, and Donald Mackenzie was appointed agent in Stornoway on the recommendation of Andrew Colvile in 1816.

The influx of new recruits considerably altered the ethnic make-up of the HBC workforce. Men from counties across Scotland became part of the labour force.[79] Recruits from Caithness and Sutherland continued to enter the Company in increasing numbers and, for the first time in the HBC's history, men from Inverness-shire and Ross-shire also peppered the list of personnel. At Edmonton alone there were over forty men listed from Lewis and Inverness, although 'Inverness' servants actually encompassed recruits from all over the

Highlands, as far south as Blair Atholl in Perthshire and as far north as Reay in Sutherland.[80] In total, these new Scottish recruits constituted 12 per cent of the workforce in 1816, while the overall Scottish contribution amounted to more than 60 per cent.

The position of Orkneymen in this New System had at first been unclear and in many ways it appeared that they had become marginalised. Contravening years of tradition, the Company vessels had not stopped in Stromness in 1810 to pick up recruits. In addition, officers in Rupert's Land were instructed to retain only those Orcadian servants who were necessary, useful and worth their salaries; those who were regarded as undeserving were to be let go.[81] The directors also stressed to officers to treat the new servants of non-Orcadian origin particularly well, 'without abusive language or unnecessary harshness' as 'the report which these men may make of the Country & their treatment in it, our future success in recruiting will in a great measure depend'.[82] It appeared as though their intention was to supplant Orkneymen, but the management hoped that the arrival and integration of new servants from different locations would actually have an advantageous effect upon their old servants. It might demonstrate to the latter that they were not indispensable and consequently make them accept the new agreement. The overhaul of the recruitment scheme could have been the death knell for Orcadian employment, but this was not to be the case.

Although hiring Orkneymen in 1811 was merely to substitute those who had been influenced by NWC rumour-mongering in Stornoway and had abandoned their engagements, there were clear signs that the Company was unwilling to discard its traditional labour supply. Having been subjected to the repercussions of negative opinion in the previous decade, the Company directors had wisely made a pointed effort in 1811 to address 'ill reports propagated in the Orkneys' concerning an officer at the Bay, in the fear that it would dissuade men from engaging.[83] They insisted that if unfavourable impressions had resulted from the rumours then Geddes was to reassure potential employees that nobody was under that particular officer's control. This does not suggest that the HBC was prepared to abandon the Orcadian contingent.

There were in fact clear signs that the directors still viewed Orkneymen as their core workforce: a prospective recruit from Yorkshire petitioned the Company for employment in 1815 but was advised that its labour force came from the Orkney Islands.[84] Orcadians represented two-thirds of the Company payroll in 1812 and although this was not early enough to see any effects of the New System, between 1812 and 1816 Orcadian participation had decreased by less than 9 per cent to 266 servants out of 528. Despite a profession to the contrary, upon inauguration, the New System appears to have been of little

consequence to the recruitment of Orkneymen. Their participation as a proportion of all employees had fallen to 50 per cent of the growing fur trade population by 1816; but although they had fallen quite considerably as a proportion of
the Company, they had barely dropped in quantity.

It is quite remarkable that Orkneymen managed to sustain such a considerable presence in the Company, given the negative reputation that they had
acquired with the London Committee. An important factor in this was that
although the Committee members complained about the quality of Orcadian
hands, they never doubted that suitable men could be obtained in Orkney.
Stipulations attending Orcadian recruitment had been far more stringent since
1811, and the directors had insisted that recruits were to be of better quality
than previously so that more competent men were procured. An age limit of
thirty years was imposed, although as usual the Company had offered some
latitude, including that experienced men could be up to forty years old. The
Committee had also stressed that it would not consider itself bound by any
agreement Geddes made unless the Orkneymen met the given description. The
latter directive had perhaps two purposes: to act as a financial safeguard for the
Company in case unsuitable men were advanced money, and to ensure Geddes
sincerely sought appropriate recruits.[85] A final resolve had been attended to in
1812, to ensure that adequate men were sent to Rupert's Land. A surgeon was
appointed to examine recruits in Stromness before sailing to the Bay. Every man
boarding a vessel was to be inspected and if any were 'found to be labouring
under any disease, debility, or contagious distemper' their services were to be
declined.[86]

However, like the measures formerly taken to guard against the engagement
of inappropriate servants, these provisos proved ineffective. Aged men still
entered the Company, some of whom lied about their age in order to be accepted
and, unable to cope with the extreme climate, were subsequently shipped back
to Orkney the following year at high cost to the business. Orcadian John Inkster
returned home as he was declared to be in poor condition for the fur trade by
the surgeon, and another three men were sent back in 1816. Officers at both
Albany and Moose posts objected to their particularly hopeless recruits that
year. The directors did query the judgement of some officers who discharged
men from service, particularly if the reject was still young. The management
countered that, with 'health & youth on their side', the men could not possibly
be unfit, and if they were defective in some way, the officers should have stated
the flaw so that the agent could be made answerable.[87]

The recruiting agents were held accountable but the only retribution they
received was repeated complaints and instructions about the qualities to look
for in hands. The inattention of both the Orcadian agents, David Geddes and

latterly his son, George Geddes, was frequently complained about. One man, Robert Garson, was described as being one of 'Mr Geddes' bad bargains, almost useless'.[88] The directors criticised the damage that had been suffered by the Company owing to the employment of infirm and elderly men. When John Rae, father of the future explorer Dr John Rae, succeeded Geddes as the recruiting agent for Orkney, he was forewarned that a surgeon would painstakingly examine them to prevent people unsuited for the service going to the Bay. It is not clear whether it ever occurred to the London Committee that problems could arise from employing some recruiting agents who had no direct personal experience of the fur trade, or that the Company might actually benefit from accepting the offer of some of its ex-servants to procure men for the service on their return to Scotland.[89]

In any case, it was fortunate for the Orkneymen that recruits from other parts of Scotland showed similar shortcomings. William Sinclair from Pulteney, near Wick, had contracted to the Company for three years in 1812 but returned home the year he went out. Likewise, John McPhail from Inverness possessed a fragile constitution and was sent home after one year as he could not perform his duties.[90] Perhaps even more advantageous for the Orkneymen was the unruly behaviour of other recruits. In the 1780s, Orkneymen had gained a bad reputation for united action and obstinate behaviour and in 1814 the Committee had reversed its earlier decision to integrate men and recommended that the new recruits be 'employed apart by themselves so as not to be contaminated with the faults of the old hands'.[91] Regardless of whether or not they had been corrupted, the Glaswegians and Irishmen had fully surpassed Orkneymen with their mutinous behaviour.[92]

In addition, the long-coveted Canadians had proven to be overrated. In 1816, the Company had proceeded with the mass engagement of voyageurs whom they had often considered but only tentatively recruited. Colin Robertson had impressed upon the Company the advantages of hiring energetic Canadian men who were apparently more resolute than Orkneymen and adhered to their superiors even when suffering from the hardships of service.[93] In fact, the expense of their employment remained the only visible drawback. In 1807, officers had been granted the freedom to engage a few Canadians in Rupert's Land and, five years later, the Committee had given in to temptation and hired an agent in Montreal. Maitland, Auldjo and Co. were asked to recruit twenty canoemen and ten middlemen at £20 to 30 a year, but none of these men was interested in serving the HBC.[94] However, three years later when the directors endeavoured to venture into the Athabasca, a more serious attempt was made to engage the voyageurs, with the offer of higher wages. They wanted 100 men, including a set of clerks accustomed to the French language and manners who could command them. Drawn in by decent pay, they rapidly engaged and soon formed a predominant group within the HBC; by 1820 there were 350 Canadians and 420 Europeans in the service.[95]

However, the Canadians failed to impress the directors and in 1818, perhaps realising that such bulk recruitment had been too hasty, the management discussed gradually replacing them with Europeans, one district at a time.[96] By the end of the decade, recruitment patterns appeared less erratic than earlier in the century, and regular sources of labour came from Inverness, Lewis, Orkney and Canada. In the servants' list for the year 1818–19 the total Scottish contribution was slightly under 70 per cent and most of those were still Orcadian. Eighteen per cent were other Scots, largely from Ross-shire, Inverness-shire, Sutherland and Caithness, but the complements also included recruits from Lowland Scotland, and the urban centres of Glasgow, Lanark, Edinburgh and Dumfries were all represented.[97]

The end of the Napoleonic wars had enhanced recruitment opportunities for the Company. International peace could not have come at a better time, as the trading competition with the NWC was at a climax and leading to financial straits. Recruitment pressures eased as there were plenty of men available to engage due to the general depression that hit Britain when peace arrived, bringing unemployment and low wages. The Company asserted that it could have sent any number of men in 1816 and, in fact, could easily have sent as many as double the number required but wanted to give preference to its long-standing servants.[98]

The Company did however take some advantage of the situation and altered its wage policy. The difficulties in obtaining work at home after the war and the poor wages on offer meant that the HBC was able to secure an ample supply of men at a salary of £15 a year. The Committee members, therefore, stipulated that wages should not be higher than £20 for an experienced labourer and £24 for a steersman. Tradesmen were also affected; all new hands from Orkney were to enter the service in the capacity of labourer, regardless of ability, and receive a salary of £15. If they were capable as mechanics, coopers, carpenters and boat-builders then they would obtain a wage increase once their aptitude had been determined.[99]

Additionally, despite the Company's profession that it wished to retain its old hands, those servants were increasingly informed that their services were not required. This was not a calculated shift away from the recruitment of Orcadians, but simply a recognition that the Company was finally in a position to be more selective about the men engaged and only wanted first-rate recruits.[100] Fitting men, however, were still a rare find in Orkney, and hands wishing to re-engage were frequently refused, while those who made it to Rupert's Land continued to meet with dissatisfaction. Yet, the realisation that other workers also had their flaws, coupled with the Orcadian experience of the fur trade, may have reinforced the Company's belief that Orkneymen were an asset, and upheld the desire to continue engaging them despite the increasingly aggressive nature of the fur trade and alternative recruitment options available. The Company management had experimented with hands from a variety of locales since the institution of the New System, including Scandinavians, but Orkneymen remained the soundest option, being orderly and accustomed to inland work. The courage of some Orcadian servants, the aptitude and experience of canoeing and boat-building of others, along with a familiarity with trading practices, native tribes and their language, and continued low cost compared to Canadians, made them irreplaceable.[101]

The Orcadians' principal redeeming factor was probably their perceived loyalty to the Company. The Committee had queried Orcadian fidelity during the early years of the French wars, but from the commencement of the New System, Orkneymen had served well in meeting quotas and acting as a fallback when recruitment fell short elsewhere. A slight decline of interest in the Company was noted in 1819, arising from the lure of work with herring curers and, perhaps, news of the violent trading conflict with the NWC, which may have deterred Orkneymen from signing up as they found military pursuits so deplorable.[102] However, the dependability of Orkneymen had generally continued in the post-war period and stood them in good stead. For instance, when agent John McDonald was unable to meet his small quota from Inverness in 1820, the Orkney agent was asked, and able, to provide a surplus. McDonald and the Inverness servants were overlooked the following year, and when Donald McKay suggested that the Company take on some willing young men from Sutherland, he was informed that they were not employing any Highlanders that year. Rather, the HBC looked to the Lewis and Orkney agents who were able to provide the required quantity of recruits. Donald McKenzie procured forty in Stornoway, while between fifteen and twenty men were expected from Derbyshire, and another fifty from Orkney.[103] John Rae had also been requested to obtain coopers and was asked not 'to look further than the Orkneys, as the hands from the neighbourhood of Glasgow will by no means answer for the Service of the Company'.[104] It was expected that in Orkney the entire quota would be reached and this actually amounted to sixty servants in the end, as the English recruits failed to arrive at the ships.[105] Rae's ability to supplement the numbers at short notice once again raised the esteem of Orkneymen and the Committee resolved not to send any more Canadians.

When the fur trade rivalry ended in 1821, Orkneymen were again the mainstay of recruitment, with the assistance of men from Lewis. The Company vessels routed first via Stromness, and then by Stornoway, before proceeding to Hudson's Bay. It is clear that Scottish sojourners truly underpinned the HBC throughout the entire period under examination, and that Orkneymen in particular were of fundamental and persistent significance. Yet, the endurance of the HBC's recruitment practice was only facilitated by the Orcadians' regard for temporary migratory employment in the Arctic. It is thus necessary to explore the appeal of sojourning, and service in the HBC, from the Orcadian perspective.

THREE

Orcadian Poverty and Arctic Opportunity: Constructing a Career in the HBC

The Orcadian economy and traditions of migration

The location of Orkney dictated the islands' economic prospects: both maritime and agricultural opportunities were available to the population. However, the economic condition of Orkney in the late eighteenth century was by many accounts unpromising, as the islands' potential remained undeveloped. The Orcadian economy was largely agricultural, with five-sixths of the working population engaged in that employment, but farming was considered by many of its inhabitants to be backward.[1] George Low, minister in Birsay and Harray, contended that husbandry was in desperate need of improvement, and his depiction correlates with the general portrayal offered in the *Statistical Accounts*. Although the northern islands such as Sanday experienced more favourable conditions than the rest of Orkney and had some of the finest and largest farms, agriculture was generally condemned throughout as inefficient, rude and neglected.[2] These ills were believed to be the result of short leases and inadequate farming methods. Land was 'in such a bad state of cultivation, from idleness and want of manure', that one observer, Edward Chappell, commented 'that at least five weeds are produced to one blade of corn'.[3]

The poor condition of agriculture was exacerbated by periodic crop failures. Famine afflicted the Orkneys in 1782 and 1783, when the crops completely failed due to the poor seasons and damaged feed. Following one death from starvation and others looming, the government was forced to intervene and provide meal to avert further mortality. Orkney endured almost constant crop failures until 1788, and even the indifferent yields of later years were to leave families in straitened circumstances. At the turn of the nineteenth century, Patrick Neill who toured the island confirmed that many Orcadian farmers continued to be run down by poverty.[4]

The Orcadian economy was not exceptional, as many farming counties in Scotland endured agricultural adversity and devastating crop failure at this time. Farm workers in Orkney and neighbouring counties alike failed to sustain the local economy through crop cultivation alone. Many were forced to supplement their annual income with seasonal employment. Participation for a few months of the year in occupations such as fishing and kelp manufacture became the norm, and in some Orcadian parishes, it was reported that virtually all farmers were also fishermen and kelp manufacturers.[5] There was little else in the way of economic pursuit in Orkney so the access to, and profitability of, these supplementary industries largely determined the extent to which the population could be sustained.

Seas abounding with fish, including cod, haddock, ling, dogfish and lobster, surrounded the Orkney Isles. Herring was also readily available by 1804, but commercial fishing appears to have been as undeveloped as agriculture. Low verified that there was once a substantial fishery in Orkney, but by the late 1700s, this industry had faltered. There were no professional fishermen in the parishes of Kirkwall and Holm, and few fish were dispatched from Birsay and Harray, except dogfish, and even that failed on occasion. There were few herring nets in the islands and despite the profitability of lobster fishing, this activity was only pursued in a few areas such as the southern isles, and apparently would have been more lucrative were it not tempered by insufficient demand. To this end, fishing was generally only embarked upon to meet the immediate needs for family sustenance.[6]

The want of fisheries on the islands was deplored, as the country faced the wretched paradox of 'the poor inhabitants starving for want, while the sea, at their doors, was thus teeming with neglected food'.[7] The reasons for such a stunted fishing industry are not clear but one possible bar to the execution of a fruitful fishing economy was insufficient wealth among the farmers and cottagers in Orkney. Estate policies in Shetland meant that landlords provided the capital for tenants' fishing equipment, and thereafter sold the produce from the estate. Orcadians, on the other hand, had to establish themselves independently. It is plausible that the inhabitants of Orkney did not possess the capital that was required for the initial investment in fishing equipment. A large boat, long lines and a train of nets amounted to an estimated £30, and most Orcadians could not afford such a cumbersome outlay. Additionally, unlike their neighbours in the Caithness herring industry, who were virtually guaranteed a plentiful catch and a market in which the fish would sell, Orkneymen did not experience the same security as there was no fish market in which to get rid of their haul.[8] Therefore even those who could afford to fund their own fishing wares were possibly not willing to take the gamble of being unable to market their catch.

Patrick Neill suggests that the neglect of both agriculture and fishing emerged, at least partially, from proprietors' preference for the production of kelp, which entailed fewer risks and less capital.[9] The manufacture of kelp – used in the manufacture of glass, soap and alum – was initiated in Orkney in the early eighteenth century and soon became a prosperous branch of trade, truly flourishing from the 1770s onwards. Although the topography of Orkney confined kelp manufacture to the sandy eastern parishes, as the western side of the mainland was characterised by a rocky coast, many of the isles benefited from the annual extraction of that profitable commodity. The manufacture involved gathering seaweed, laying it out to dry and burning it in a kiln to produce alkali, which was then sent away to be used in the manufacture of kelp. This process involved the employment of numerous hands, and in Kirkwall as many as 3,000 people were employed in summer. Participants could earn an estimated £2 for their efforts and it meant that many islanders had remained financially solvent.[10] However, it was not as remunerative as other seasonal employment like herring fishing, and one visitor to the islands, David Thompson, 'could not help comparing this hard, wet labour for tenpence a day where not even a whistle was heard, with the merry songs of the ploughboys in England'.[11]

The Orcadian economy was clearly limited, but by many accounts, the labour market was not saturated. Parish ministers complained of a dearth of farm hands to work the land throughout the islands. One observer pronounced that 'None leave the parish for want of employment; indeed we want hands, because our young fellows go off in hopes of greater wages, as the farmers well feel'.[12] Although many inhabitants would have preferred to earn their bread amongst their kin at home, in consequence of limited or unprofitable opportunities in agriculture, trade and manufacturing, there was simply no means of retaining the young population in Orkney. With little hope of prospering at home, Orkneymen adopted the habit of relocating across the world to seek a livelihood.[13] Despite the impoverished state of some of these migrants, temporary migration does not appear to have been a last resort for these men: it was the preferred option.

Fortunately, the geographic location of the islands meant that there were multiple alternative employments readily available to those who intended to better their prospects elsewhere. Orcadian mobility within Britain was fostered by the proximity of the islands to Caithness, coupled with extensive export and import shipping links between Orkney and the coastal urban centres of Aberdeen, Glasgow, Newcastle, Whitby, London and Leith.[14] These links were either developed or reinforced during the kelp boom in the 1770s, which increased the frequency of ships travelling south. Accessibility to shipping had a far-reaching impact upon the local population, as it also provided a convenient gateway to overseas opportunity. The islands were well-located on the waterway between the North Sea and Atlantic Ocean and served many foreign trade and fishing routes. At the same time, the British-French conflicts had forced maritime traffic northwards in order to avoid the English Channel, so whaling

vessels also frequently routed via Orkney. Sailors frequently called into the port
of Stromness as it was a fine, easily accessible harbour, where vessels could be
serviced and supplies procured for their outward-bound voyage.[15] Prospective
migrants therefore built up knowledge of, and had easy access to, a variety of
locales, which meant that local inhabitants were as likely to seek melioration
abroad, as they were to migrate to the urban centres of Britain.

Distinct gender-specific traditions emerged within this broad sphere of
migratory opportunity. Orcadian women frequently ventured across to the
British mainland and acquired employment as domestic servants in urban
households. Rev. George Barry observed their preference for Newcastle,
London, and Edinburgh in particular. For most, this relocation was intended
only as a transitory undertaking, for the purpose of short-term or seasonal
employment. However, Barry noted that these female servants rarely went back
to Orkney due to the formation of marital and familial commitments during
their sojourn. Although industrial development also attracted male artisans to
these locales, it was more common for tradesmen and unskilled workers to ship
abroad temporarily in their quest for employment.[16]

The migratory opportunities favoured by Orkneymen embraced their
natural predilection for seafaring. This leaning towards the sea, rather than the
land, was evident among the youths from an early age and many indulged their
enthusiasm for seafaring through naval service. Rev. George Barry observed
that 'in the last war, as well as in some of the preceding, when the navy books
were from curiosity looked into, there were found in them upwards of 2,000
Orkney men'.[17]

Ambitious and adventurous Orcadians found another forum for overseas
employment in the northern fisheries. Young men joined the whaling vessels
from Newcastle, Whitby and Hull, when they stopped at Stromness on their
outward voyage to the fisheries in Greenland and Iceland. These three- to four-
month sojourns became a migratory tradition for Orkneymen, to the extent
that the fishermen became reliant on Orkney to supply a crew.[18] These long-
established links with seafaring predisposed Orcadians to seek a living overseas,
and service in the HBC was congruous with this established temporary migratory employment pattern.

The lure of Hudson's Bay

Despite the seclusion and inhospitability of the Arctic, employment in the HBC
held multifarious attractions for the restless, impoverished and ambitious inhabitants of Orkney. Inducements were largely economic, but unlike their Scottish
counterparts in the Caribbean plantations and East India Company, who
sought to make vast fortunes, Orkneymen signed up with the modest ambition

of 'gathering a few Pounds'.[19] For most recruits, the anticipation of alleviating household poverty and securing a more prosperous future for themselves and their families underpinned their decision to enter the service. The extent to which they succeeded in fulfilling this objective is discussed in Chapter 7.

Young, impecunious Orcadians were prime fodder for the HBC's recruiting representatives, who highlighted the advantages that could be reaped through a sojourn in Rupert's Land. Printed handbills were posted on church doors and other noticeable venues in Orkney, detailing the salaries on offer. Wages varied according to the position and skill of each man and compared favourably to those available in local occupations at home. In the 1780s, unskilled workers received £6 a year, skilled employees, including blacksmiths, boat-builders, coopers and shipwrights, earned between £15 and £36 per annum, depending on their ability and experience, and the minority of well-educated Orcadians who entered the service as writers or clerks were offered salaries of £15 each year.[20] Of course, the HBC's wage policy altered in relation to changing economic circumstances in Britain and, following the onset of the New System in 1811, labourers started on wages of at least £15.

Irrespective of the amount, regular wages and a fixed income appealed to most Orkneymen, and this attraction was heightened by the fact that they were guaranteed for a longer duration in the HBC than most other migratory employment. Each new recruit could commit himself to a five-year contract and employees thereafter negotiated the length of subsequent engagements.[21] There was longevity to employment if recruits wished, and this meant that men with financial commitments could enjoy a degree of economic security.

The Company also provided basic utilities such as accommodation and provisions in Hudson's Bay, stimulating further encouragement for economically motivated recruits. The directors recognised that this might encourage men to serve in the HBC, particularly as it was impossible to subsist at home without spending their wages. There was little prospect of spending or frittering away money in the wilds of Rupert's Land and the management emphasised that all employees could save money if they were willing. They stirred up additional anticipation with their claims that 'in Hudson's Bay you may nearly save the Whole of your Wages yearly'.[22] This prospect of improving future economic circumstances was matched by the hope of easing the immediate grinding poverty facing their families at home. Recruiting agents promoted this inducement to potential recruits and informed them that a portion of their wages could be remitted to their friends at home during their sojourn. The prospect of securing their future and warding off penury was probably sweetened further by the offer of money upfront, as servants were given an advance on their wages when they engaged.[23]

The recruitment propaganda probably incited some men who were looking for either long-term, subsistence-based migratory employment or lucrative opportunity to enter the service of the HBC. This beckoning of financial betterment was bolstered by the knowledge that family and friends would be working alongside them in the remoteness of Rupert's Land. In fact, the Company drew so many of its employees from one small society that members of the local community already in the fur trade may have exerted as much influence on recruitment as the official agent. Recruitment propaganda and advertising could be persuasive, but kinsmen offered first-hand experience of Company employment, details of which were transmitted in correspondence, during leave from service, or upon return to Orkney. Negative reports acted as a deterrent to recruitment, but equally, positive encouragement could entice men into the fur trade and help uncertain recruits reach a decision.

Familial guidance seems to have encouraged many Orkneymen to enter the service, and there was a high quantity of siblings in the HBC. In the parish of Orphir, as many as two or three immediate family members followed an original participant into service and in some instances up to four brothers joined the Company.[24] This trend was replicated elsewhere, and brothers William and James Wass from South Ronaldsay both served in the Company in the 1780s. In some cases, such as that of the Birston brothers from South Ronaldsay, the eldest, Magnus, joined first in 1790 and presumably gave favourable feedback as his brother Alexander entered the service three years later.[25]

Insight into the composition of such feedback is offered through correspondence from Orcadian James Sutherland 3rd to his brother John, in St Margaret's Hope. In 1817, twenty years after leaving his homeland of South Ronaldsay, James Sutherland offered guidance to his younger sibling who expressed a desire to move abroad in his quest for betterment. He advised against rushing into a decision to migrate temporarily and recommended that his brother weighed up all the possibilities open to him as, for instance, it would be a 'wild plan' to move to America without capital, because he would be reduced to a life of drudgery. These words of caution in choosing the means through which to seek advancement confirm that there was a variety of overseas outlets accessible to Orkneymen and that optimism, rather than domestic discouragement, was often the driving force behind such migration.

Sutherland went on to offer his young brother some qualified encouragement to follow him into the fur trade. He reassured him that his anticipation of improvement would be realised during service with the HBC: 'You know my sentiments regarding your coming to the country … You may think that it is from an attachment to the country that induces me to remain in it <u>no</u> it is from the attachment I have for my family as I am completely tired of the country.

Yet for young ones of spirit and enterprise money may be gained here probably easier than in any other country. I therefore leave it to yourself whether you come out or not, and would much rather see you here than hear that you have done worse.'[26] Sutherland concluded his counsel by discussing the various occupations available within the Company, and resolved that if his sibling was unable to settle himself at home, then he ought to join the service as a clerk.

Indeed, for those with a restless disposition and an adventurous nature, work in the HBC seemed ideal as it offered recruits diverse career opportunities that were unavailable in their homelands. The HBC built 242 new settlements throughout Rupert's Land between 1774 and 1821, and this expansion of the fur trade broadened the career opportunities of employees.[27] A wide range of unskilled, semi-skilled, skilled and managerial stations meant that men looking to alleviate poverty, squirrel away savings, or simply looking for a change in circumstances, were likely to find a suitable position in the HBC.

Mechanisms of advancement

The Company provided a basic career structure, at least in the lower ranks, and various promotional opportunities, which meant that upward mobility was a realistic ambition for the majority of the workforce. All employees had a favourable prospect of forging a successful career, and a variety of factors served to increase the likelihood of their advancement within the Company. Means of promotion included the development of country skills, such as canoeing and a familiarity with native languages or tribes, as well as education and patronage.

In the HBC, personnel were organised by hierarchical rank, but the occupational structure was more complex. Unskilled workers, namely labourers and canoemen or middlemen – who were effectively labourers in the middle of a canoe – formed the lowest ranks of the Company. Tradesmen, such as coopers, blacksmiths, armourers, boat-builders, cooks, and carpenters, were higher up the occupational ladder and formed another coherent group. Officers comprised a group of writers and clerks, masters, traders, surgeons, chiefs and any other employees in positions of authority. The masters were sometimes differentiated into occasional masters (a servant who filled in as 'master' on a temporary basis when the permanent master was away from the post), post masters, and district masters, but many of the terms such as trader and master appear to have been used interchangeably, as men were often described as holding slightly different stations in the various HBC administration files. Besides, the salaries of the different stations did not really differ, and Orkneymen in any of the trader or master positions could earn from £25 to £50 a year, and very occasionally more.[28]

There were many other occupations in the Company which did not fit specifically into these categories. The boundaries of rank were often blurred between and among these other stations. Labourers with additional country skills, such as bowsmen who were positioned as guides at the front of a canoe, and steersmen who were positioned at the rear of a canoe to steer, were higher-ranking than labourers and may be referred to as semi-skilled. Interpreters and linguists probably fit into this category as well, although they occasion-ally overlapped into the officer class and were often more akin to officers than labourers in terms of salary. Another enigmatic set was the assistant traders, who were not clearly identified as a group of officers, but some of whom were referred to as 'officer' individually. They often took charge of posts, and after the merger in 1821 were frequently ranked as clerks.[29]

The route of advancement through the lower ranks of the Company was clearly structured. When the fur trade spread to terrain that was only accessible via waterways, employees had the opportunity to advance through the develop-ment of canoe skills. Numerous recruits entered the service in the capacity of an unskilled labourer and although some were reluctant to go inland, others were willing to master the manoeuvres and navigation of canoes upon the often-turbulent rivers. In consequence, many labourers progressed to the station of canoeman by the end of their first contract and although these positions were synonymous in rank and salary, canoemen had better career prospects. Once employees had grasped the rudiments of canoeing, they were promoted to the second tier of proficiency, as bowsmen, and thereafter, to the station of steersman. Progression through the ranks was accompanied by increased wages depending on qualification and merit, and as the latter position involved responsibility for both the canoe and the transportation of trade goods, it was particularly well recompensed at between £16 and £30 per annum. The manage-ment stressed that no-one would be awarded the status of steersman unless officers in Rupert's Land had confirmed their qualification.[30]

The rate of mobility through the different levels of canoeing varied according to natural ability and determination. Young Orcadians, John Allan, Peter Brown, and William Groundwater rapidly progressed through the ranks. They were among many who entered the Company as labourers in 1785 at a rate of £6 a year but re-contracted in 1790 as bowsmen or steersmen, commanding salaries of between £12 and £15, bonuses aside. Likewise, Magnus Annal, a lively eighteen-year-old from South Ronaldsay, entered the service as a labourer in 1778. This young man had progressed to a canoeman by 1785 and moved up the ladder to the station of steersman in 1788. Even long-established labourers such as James Spence Senior, who had served thirteen years in the HBC, demonstrated a willingness to advance and learn new skills, resulting in his promotion to the capacity of steersman in 1786.[31]

Developing an aptitude for canoeing also benefited semi-skilled and skilled employees, as they too were financially rewarded. John Harper, an Orcadian tailor, also became a bowsman, and John Ballenden 1st, a carpenter from Orphir, diversified his abilities, becoming a steersman and canoe-builder. Others, such as John Davey, actually experienced upward mobility in two stations simultaneously; he engaged as a labourer and carpenter's assistant in 1790, and three years later had qualified as a canoeman and carpenter.[32]

A natural progression for many employees with canoe skills was to learn the art of canoe-building. This emerged as another essential occupation when the Company expanded its trade across Rupert's Land, and it was one in which Orkneymen developed a particular aptitude. John Irvine Senior from Sandwick served as a labourer in 1783 and by 1788 had progressed through the ranks to steersman and canoe-builder. He may have possessed knowledge of boats prior to entering the Company, or was simply stimulated to learn by the good remuneration that occurred with the job. This salary increase was significant: for example canoeman James Davey earned £14 a year in the 1780s and this was to be augmented to £20 if he could build canoes.[33]

Ambitious employees who wished to improve their prospects beyond the confines of hard physical labour really needed to acquire trading skills, such as thorough knowledge of a native tribe or their language. Fluent communication between the indigenous tribes of Rupert's Land and employees of the HBC was essential to the development of a good trading relationship. The traders encountered a variety of language families during their sojourn in Rupert's Land, including Algonkian, Siouan, Salish, Athabascan and Eskimo-Aleut.[34] Alexander Mackenzie contended that some Orkneymen had learned to communicate with the Eskimo, but Algonkian was most familiar to the HBC traders.[35] Numerous tribes, such as the Cree, resided within the vast territory in which Algonkian prevailed and many had their own language as well as peculiar customs and humours. For this reason, the directors considered their young recruits to be of limited use to the Company until they acquired some knowledge of a native language and hence the servants engaged for a term of five years.[36]

In order to form successful trading relationships, and to assist employees gain essential knowledge of local languages and customs, the HBC sent its servants to live with native tribes. During these residencies, employees endeavoured to build a good rapport with native traders, master indigenous skills such as hunting and trapping, and learn the tribe's language. This method proved effective and James Norn from Stromness had gained a good understanding of the natives through his winter residency with them in 1818. Likewise, Robert Cumming was commended for his competency in native interactions in 1819.

He was apparently so familiar with the indigenous tongue that he communicated fluently, while Orcadian Donald Gunn, who was considered active and intelligent, also spoke a native language well.[37]

Despite a common distaste for the tribal lifestyle, Scots demonstrated a flair for learning native languages.[38] Their endeavours were often rewarded with a promotion to the station of linguist or interpreter. For instance, Orcadian Magnus Spence entered the Company as a labourer in 1783 and soon became adept in country skills, occasioning his promotion to steersman and linguist in the 1790s. James Whitway also discovered that his linguistic faculties were advantageous and he served one contract as an unskilled labourer before upgrading to an interpreter in 1803.[39] The success of uneducated men in such semi-skilled positions actually prompted a remark from officer Joseph Colen in 1794, who observed that 'the men who are active and expert, at the same time ignorant of Letters are the most ready in learning the Indian Tongue – here are several clever men in this service who scarcely know a Letter in the Alphabet are good Linguists'.[40]

Employees who aspired to make inroads into the higher ranks of trading and management undoubtedly benefited from honing their communication skills. On many occasions when a lower-ranking employee was selected to take charge of an inland trading post, the chosen individual was particularly well-acquainted with a native tribe or language. James Gaddy Snr, from Evie in Orkney, entered the service as a labourer in 1781, and spent two years of his service with the Peeagan Indians learning their language. He seems to have been more at ease with the native way of life than many other servants as he was the only one willing to winter with the Muddy Indians at Stony Mountain in 1789 when the rest of the men at Manchester House 'was in one mind not to go'.[41] His readiness to reside with the natives meant that he became the only person familiar with the Blackfoot and Blood language. Consequently, Gaddy was appointed the summer master of Manchester House in 1792 and held the same position at South Branch House in 1794. Likewise, Orcadian Mitch Oman entered the service in 1771 and advanced from the position of labourer to canoeman in 1783. During his subsequent employment as a canoeman at South Branch House he was awarded charge of the post. Oman was deemed the most suitable person for this position in 1789 because he was well-acquainted with the local natives, having become skilled in their language and earned their respect. Following a brief return to Stromness in 1791, he re-entered the Company in 1793 in the official capacity of inland trader and master.[42]

A familiarity with native language and culture did not guarantee promotion, but it was an attribute favoured when advancement was considered, particularly within the upper ranks of the Company. George Sutherland, a long-term linguist and trader from Wick, had good knowledge of the language and method of treating natives in the 1780s. For this reason, he was considered qualified to assist the chief, Joseph Colen at York in 1787 and to become chief trader inland in 1794. Likewise, Orcadian trader, Adam Snodie, had a fine grasp of the Chipewyan language at a time when there were few officers who shared that competency. Although the directors did not elect to promote him in 1814, they decided to bear him in mind as an officer of great potential and he was later promoted to the station of district master.[43]

Some employees successfully infiltrated the upper ranks of the HBC through their skills and experience in the field, whereas others already possessed the virtues sought in officers when they initially entered the service. The structure of the HBC meant that literacy and education were particularly valuable assets. The directors were situated in London, and as the actual business was practised on the other side of the Atlantic, the Committee required officers to provide written details on every occurrence, in order to manage the Company effectively. They requested daily chronicling at individual posts and on inland journeys, copies of written correspondence between the personnel at separate posts in Rupert's Land, servants' accounts and post accounts, as well as annual communication with themselves in London. Therefore educated men had remarkably good prospects for advancement.

Well-educated recruits often entered the HBC as writers or clerks and were automatically primed for promotion. They were awarded the honour of dining at the chief's table during meal times and it was hoped that this would stimulate their ambition. The upward mobility of these young writers tended to be rapid, and James Russell, from Shapinsay, rose to the position of district master only seven years after his entry as a writer in 1807. In fact, four of the most renowned Orkneymen in the service, William Sinclair 1st, Alexander Kennedy, James Sutherland 3rd and John Ballenden of Stromness, served as writers in the late eighteenth century, before rising to prominence as chief factors in the early nineteenth century.[44]

Yet the Company even appreciated a basic literacy in its employees as the ongoing establishment of new inland houses generated an urgent need for additional masters. Inland posts were often small and required minimal administration. Therefore the Company endorsed the appointment of less well-educated, but literate, men to these stations.[45] This offered low-ranking employees who could maintain simple records an exciting opportunity to scale the ranks to promotion. Literacy seems to have assisted in promoting the successful career of Orcadian James Tait. He entered the service as a labourer in 1778 and demonstrated his literacy when he maintained journals at Manchester House. He was left in charge of Manchester House in 1790, being the most appropriate man for the job, and subsequently served as master and trader until his return to Orkney in 1812.[46] James Kirkness' ascension of the career ladder was also furthered by his literacy. Leaving his homeland of Harray in 1797, Kirkness entered the Company and served as a labourer until 1802 when he was promoted to assistant writer: by 1812 he had upgraded to the station of writer and trader.[47]

Country skills and literacy undoubtedly facilitated the upward mobility of men in the HBC, but perceived loyalty to the Company also won considerable favour with the London Committee. The directors stated in 1789 that 'merit and that alone shall be the Road to our favour', but some promotions, generally to the most senior positions within the Company, were granted by the directors to reward the long service of employees.[48] James Sutherland was chosen over Englishman Matthew Truthwaite to fill a vacancy of second-in-command at Gloucester House in 1780 because his 'services are of so much Older date We could not pass over him when other considerations give no preference'.[49] Likewise, when officer John McNab was asked to resign his post as chief factor at Churchill in 1802, and take over the same position at York, William Auld, who had 'long as well as local experience', was invited to take his place at Churchill.[50] Another officer, John Sutherland, also benefited from his long and faithful service as he was promoted within the upper ranks at Osnaburgh in 1806.[51]

Yet it seems that high-ranking employees had the potential to be as influential on a fellow servant's career as the directors, and many appointments and promotions were aided and encouraged by the support of a senior colleague. Officers were entrusted with managing the business in Rupert's Land and served as intermediaries between the London Committee and the workforce. They delivered instructions to employees and also passed on commendation or reprimands on behalf of the directors. Their role as brokers was far-reaching because, although they were also the subordinate servants of the directors, their opinions were valued and the management often deferred to their judgement on personnel matters. The Committee asked the officers to provide a just character reference for all employees and welcomed recommendations regarding any servants worthy of their notice.[52]

The HBC's officers also came to possess some discretionary powers within Rupert's Land. The communication system between inland posts, Hudson's Bay and the Company's headquarters in London was so long and delayed that the directors' orders were often invalid by the time they reached their destination. In addition, the Committee's inexperience of the practicalities of the fur trade meant that some of their directives were ill-informed. This was detrimental to the business and, for instance, James Sutherland complained that if he followed orders and moved to Portage de l'Isle in 1795, he would lose the spring trade.

The management then decided that such experienced officers should be allowed some discretionary authority to make 'on the spot' decisions.[53]

Officers were given the latitude to meet the needs of the business in Rupert's Land, and this included appointing traders and post masters as the Company moved inland. The existing officers were insufficient to manage all the new establishments in the interior as well as further expand commerce, so high-ranking employees were permitted to assign men to new management positions until they received further orders from the directors.[54] These discretionary powers, teamed with the Company's reliance on its officers' insights and recommendations, meant that existing members of the HBC actually had the ability to influence the careers of other men. Officers had a bearing on appointments, promotions and salary increases, which facilitated the employment of ethnic-based patronage within Rupert's Land.

New recruits had no difficulty in obtaining labouring work in the HBC, but the acquisition of skilled and managerial positions, which were prestigious and therefore highly sought-after, was often problematical. The London Committee did not outrightly discriminate against Scots, but they had a marked tendency to favour Englishmen for high-status occupations.[55] In order to facilitate access to desirable stations, existing employees endeavoured to influence the London Committee on behalf of their relatives in Orkney. For instance, John Moncrieff petitioned the directors in 1797, in support of his youngest brother. His sibling was currently employed as a schoolmaster, but wished to enter the service as a writer. Moncrieff appealed to the directors' empathetic nature and informed them that two of his brothers had lost legs in His Majesty's Service and another had lost part of his jawbone. Although the HBC secretary believed that all the administrative positions had been filled in Hudson's Bay, he did request, on behalf of the Committee, that agent Geddes make enquiries. Likewise, in 1817, John McNab requested that his grandson should be considered if a surgeon needed appointing.[56]

James Sutherland also did his utmost to assist his Orcadian relatives and, in his letter of advice to his brother in 1817, added that he had already personally written to the Orkney recruiting agent 'to apply to the Company to get you as a Clerk'.[57] Over the ensuing years, he also determined to promote the preferment of his mixed-blood son, William. By 1825, he had trained William for a clerkship by getting him voluntary work in the counting house and writing at the Red River settlement. Although he did not receive any wages, Sutherland hoped that he would 'reap a benefit by it – next year I hope to get him in the service as a Clerk or as a kind of Midsipman [sic] on board a Ship of the Companys that trades in the Columbia North West Coast of America'.[58]

The operation of such family networks conflicts with the view that employees had few former connections to assist with their advancement.[59] Furthermore, useful career ties were not confined to kin; local fellowship in Orkney also shaped recruitment. Alexander Kennedy's career-break emerged out of the patronage of a senior Orcadian officer in the HBC. Kennedy was selected as writer in 1798, under the auspices of John Ballenden of Stromness and it was hoped that 'he may do credit' to the recommendation.[60] His subsequent rise through the ranks to the station of chief factor suggests that he was indeed a source of satisfaction to both his patron and the London Committee.

A glowing reference from a current employee occasionally secured a coveted position in the workforce, but it was more common for a recommendation or introduction to be followed up with a local enquiry into the advocated individual. In this sense, it appears that the principal recruiting agents also held an integral role in the advancement of Orkneymen. The successive Orkney agents, David Geddes, George Geddes, and eventually John Rae, pursued these investigations, often with the assistance of local school-teachers and clergy. Typical research included determining an applicant's qualification, age, previous employment, and manner of education, sometimes supplemented by a sample of handwriting.[61] Although such enquiries may have been undertaken from a strictly professional perspective, it is clear that on some occasions, the agents' personal connections with individuals did influence the selection procedure. For instance, David Geddes was permitted to engage the carpenter and boat-builder that he had 'so strongly recommended' in 1793.[62] Additionally, in 1808, it appears that David Geddes' own son George entered the Company as a school-teacher, prior to taking over as the official Orkney agent in 1814. George, in turn, was permitted to engage some of his friends from the Orkney Islands. One of the Geddes' successors, John Rae, also appears to have taken advantage of his connection to the Company, as the directors were pleased to inform him in 1821 that his 'young friend Mr Hamilton' had been appointed surgeon of the *Eddystone*.[63]

Local connections continued to be of use to Orkneymen who wished to advance within the HBC. It was mentioned earlier that James Kirkness had risen into the senior ranks of the Company, aided by his literacy. Thereafter, his advancement continued within the upper levels of the HBC and seems to have been fostered by the patronage of chief factor, William Sinclair. Both men originated from the parish of Harray in Orkney, and in 1812, Kirkness worked under Sinclair's command in the Winnipeg district. These men would have shared social and working lives as well as a connection based on common local origin, and perhaps even a prior friendship. Kirkness clearly benefited from these circumstances as Sinclair recommended him to the Company directors and increased his wages from £25 to £40 a year. The bond between the men was cemented when Kirkness married Sinclair's mixed-blood daughter, Jane, in Rupert's Land. It is probable that the support of a chief factor assisted in Kirkness' ongoing advancement, which culminated in a promotion to the station of district master in 1818.[64]

William Tomison, another prominent Orcadian, and the senior officer in charge of the York inland district, also appears to have been instrumental in the advancement of various Orkneymen in the HBC. Although Tomison's scope to offer positions of responsibility was limited, he had some successes, such as appointing fellow Orcadian Magnus Twatt in charge of Cumberland House in the summer of 1792.[65] The aforementioned progress of James Gaddy and Mitch Oman was also made in the York inland district in which Tomison wielded considerable influence. Gaddy was one of Tomison's 'trusted subordinates' and after serving one contract at the rate of £6 per annum, renewed his contract in 1786 on better terms, which at £20 a year was a much higher sum than usual, 'on account of Mr Tomison's recommendation'.[66] John Ballenden 1st, a canoe-builder from Orphir, also benefited from Tomison's support as he gave him an excellent reference in 1800, believing that Ballenden really merited the Committee's attention. Although Ballenden was not promoted, he did receive a wage increase from £25 per annum to £30 for a three-year contract.[67]

In fact, the patronage of William Tomison appears to have been sought out by some Orkneymen. James Sandison, a canoeman and steersman from Orkney, was keen to retain his acquaintance with Tomison who was one of his local associates from South Ronaldsay. They were situated at different posts and Sandison had to contend with the sheer size of the territory in which the HBC operated, in what seemed to be an attempt to secure support from Tomison. In 1791, Sandison requested an acknowledgement in correspondence from the English master of his post to Mr Tomison at York. The letter duly stated that Sandison 'is desirous to be remembered to you'.[68] During the remaining years of the decade, Sandison was promoted from the low ranks to the station of trader in the York district under Tomison's jurisdiction.[69]

Pre-existing ties assisted Orcadian advancement, but new helpful bonds were also forged among Scots within the fur trade. The successful career of Orcadian John Ballenden of Stromness seems to have been assisted by the ethnic-based patronage of senior member and fellow Scot, Andrew Graham. Ballenden entered the HBC in 1770 as a servant to Andrew Graham and although it is not clear whether they had a prior friendship, a strong relationship certainly developed between the men. Graham was obviously impressed with his young assistant as it was noted in 1772 that the 'young men Umfreville, Walker & Ballenden will most probably turn out well, if properly managed'.[70] This was to be the case as six years after his entry Ballenden was promoted to the station of writer.

Although Graham subsequently departed from Rupert's Land, the two men retained their connection across the Atlantic and Graham assisted Ballenden with the management of his Company finances from Edinburgh. Their mutual regard was evident when Ballenden named his son after his friend and, in turn, Graham made a provision of £60 for Ballenden in his will.[71] It is probable that Graham continued to exert an influence over Ballenden's career following his departure from the Company, as he remained an important advisor to the London Committee. It would therefore not be surprising if Graham's support assisted in Ballenden's phenomenal advancement to master and then chief at York in 1800.[72] In fact, the benefit that Ballenden gained from patronage may have been what prompted him to offer similar support to fellow Orcadian, Alexander Kennedy, as mentioned earlier.

The role, and perhaps limitations, of patronage as a mechanism for advancement in the HBC are also exemplified by the experience of Orcadian William Yorston. He entered the Company in 1796 and departed the service in 1812, following what he deemed to be unfair retribution as a result of his involvement in a mutiny at Brandon House the preceding year.[73] Upon his return to Orkney, Yorston instigated a petition to the Committee concerning his unjust treatment and included a chronicle of his career in the Company, which illuminates some of the forms of support available to servants in the HBC.

Five years after entering the service, William Yorston acquired the benefaction of his post master at Brandon House, John McKay, an officer from Clyne who considered the young Orcadian to be the 'most usefull Hand he had'. When Yorston's contract was due to expire in 1802, he decided that he would re-engage with the Company, but on more favourable terms. His previous salary was £8 per annum and he wanted an increase to £15 for the first year of a three-year contract and £18 for the remaining two years. McKay's backing was patently evident in Yorston's endeavour as this Highland officer formally guaranteed the payment of £18 for the latter two years. If the Committee decided that Yorston's proposed wages were too extravagant, then McKay, who had £867 of earnings in his Company account, promised to pay the difference, as he firmly believed that the Orcadian servant was 'a Man fit for this Country'.[74]

William Yorston then went on to secure the patronage of another officer, Thomas Vincent, who had briefly taken over McKay's command of Brandon House in 1806. He promoted Yorston to second-in-command and trader, possibly on McKay's recommendation, as he had a continued attachment to the young hand. In this station, Yorston held increased responsibility and was entrusted with sole charge of the post when Vincent was absent. He must have conducted himself well, as a strong bond also developed between these men and Vincent took 'a warm Interest in his Welfare', sending a small gift for Yorston's wife in 1808 and a pair of trousers for himself.[75] He offered paternal advice to his young friend, encouraging him to behave well so as to stay in favour with his superiors, which would lead to the continuation of his position as summer master at Brandon House. Yorston seemingly followed this advice as, although he officially continued as second and trader, he received temporary command of the post in 1808.

When John McKay resumed his position of master at Brandon House, he again adopted the role of patron and did his utmost to further Yorston's career. In 1810, he wrote to the Company secretary recommending Yorston as the most qualified for the position of master at Brandon House or any other, due to his long services and good acquaintance with the local natives and their manner of trading. McKay also mentioned that Yorston had £417 due to him in wages and, maintaining his promise to Yorston, wanted to clarify whether he or the Company should pay it. The HBC responded in 1811 – unaware that McKay had since died in July 1810 – and informed him that 'in respect to your engagement with W. Yorston... no one has been authorised to engage any person for the Company's Service but the Chief Factor'.[76] This suggests that McKay had actually attempted to appoint, rather than simply recommend Yorston for the permanent position of master.

It is clear that Scots endeavoured to exercise patronage within the HBC, but their overall success in this is less impressive when compared to the utility of Scottish connections in other imperial enterprises. Planters in the British West Indies assisted their Scottish relatives by providing career openings as attorneys, overseers, book-keepers, doctors, and executors. This resulted in huge networks of family members, such as the Campbells from Argyll, who became particularly prominent in Jamaica. Many others drew upon their local connections and regional affiliations and this resulted in concentrations of migrants from specific regions in Scotland in the Caribbean, including a network of Scots from Banff, Elgin and Huntly, which operated in Tobago.[77] Nonetheless, it is clear that Orkneymen also carried family and local parish connections into the fur trade, and formed new connections on the basis of shared ethnicity. Their ability to influence the HBC management and introduce relatives and acquaintances into sought-after positions was certainly greater than has previously been assumed.

However, it seems that patrons had more success in obtaining initial appointments and raising wages, than securing promotions. For instance, James Sutherland was able to influence the preliminary opportunities available to his brother in the HBC, but warned him in 1817 that despite his own prominent position as a chief factor, there were limits to his leverage. He declared, 'never be so mad as come out as a foremast hand, for however much I be able to befriend you, it would be impossible to raise you either to rank or respectability from so menial a situation'.[78] In fact, there is an absence of evidence clearly demonstrating the successful operation of kin-based patronage in the HBC. John Nicks observed that the three brothers of Orcadian officer Adam Snodie, and the siblings of officer James Tait, failed to forge successful careers in the Company.[79]

This contrasts with the success of the Scottish shareholders in the NWC, which was attributed to the exploitation of kin networks. They were notorious for the recruitment of relatives from Scotland, and nepotism towards kin members was so prevalent that young men holding direct ties to the proprietors were almost guaranteed entry to a good position, future promotion and a successful career.[80] Considering that such kin networks were among the most reliable sources of support for Scots in the empire, this suggests that patronage as a mechanism for advancement was circumscribed in Rupert's Land.[81]

The efficacy of Scottish support networks was perhaps impaired by the vastness of the territory in which the HBC operated, and the English monopoly on senior positions in the Company. Despite the increasing number of Scots in the senior ranks, Englishmen retained a firm hold over this domain. For instance, at long-established posts in Hudson's Bay such as Severn, the three most superior employees in 1797 – out of a complement of twenty-one – were English. Senior and influential Scottish officers such as Tomison, Sinclair and Ballenden remained a minute proportion of the aggregate Scottish contribution to the Company, and competition for their support would have been high. Junior Orcadian officers were frequently found in the management positions of inland posts, which tended to be smaller and manned by a handful of men, but a lack of evidence means that the extent of their clout is opaque. There was a high turnover of officers at these inland houses and the master was often only temporarily in charge, so even if he wished to support the advancement of an employee, it is possible that he was not in a senior enough position, or in command for long enough, to wield much influence over his subordinate's career.[82] Therefore there was absolutely no guarantee that Scottish employees, who were dispersed at posts across Rupert's Land, would have a master who was influential, well known to them, or even Scottish.

In addition, the structure of the posts encouraged the formation of strong relationships within the patriarchal 'household', and Scottish employees were probably as prone to form patron-client relationships with whoever their master was, regardless of ethnicity. The English monopoly on high-ranking positions, and high turnover of masters, may explain why some Scottish employees such as William Yorston had multiple unconnected patrons, one of whom, Thomas Vincent, was English. Although some men such as James Sandison, who had an English master, endeavoured to overcome the problems of dispersion, and cultivate pre-existing ethnic bonds, it is unlikely that many would have had such success, or even made such an attempt.

Not only did the structure of the posts encourage strong relationships within each house, but rivalries between the HBC's posts may have worked against the establishment, or fostering, of ethnic-based patron-client relationships across Rupert's Land. In the 1790s, the directors had noted an 'unaccountable jealousy subsisting between each other of our Inland Masters who seem to lose sight of the General Interest for their own partial purposes'.[83] Discord was still evident between individual posts in 1805 and this rivalry may have served to reinforce the bonds within each post.[84] It is therefore possible that unless a master or supervisor was Scottish or known to them, ethnic bonds would have had a nominal influence on Orcadian careers in Rupert's Land.

Yet the fundamental framework of the HBC probably had the most significant bridling influence on the extensive and effective operation of patronage in Rupert's Land. Unlike the business associations that formed the NWC, and many of the sugar plantations in the Caribbean, which were largely owned and managed by Scots, giving them direct influence over the hiring and promotional procedures, the HBC was not Scottish; an authoritative Committee of Englishmen directed it from London. The directors were reluctant to devolve much power to their employees and ultimately retained full control over the recruitment and promotional process.[85]

Until 1810, employees could exert their influence on the Committee, but the apparent constraints on the implementation of patronage became even more debilitating after the institution of the New System. The Committee declared that only the chief factor and superintendent were at liberty to represent to the Committee the abilities and qualifications of employees who maybe warranted an increase in salary or advance in station. For instance, Jacob Corrigal had been informed in 1811 that when a vacancy opened internally his long service would be taken into consideration.[86] However, he was then notified in 1814 that promotion depended on the recommendation of the governor of the district.[87] Patronage became more paramount to career advancement, but the availability of patrons was seriously curtailed. This was even more the case for Scots seeking direct assistance, as by 1818, only one of the uppermost high-ranking men, James Sutherland, was Scottish. Therefore between 1810 and 1821, fewer officers had any direct leverage over their compatriots' careers, although officers could probably still influence their superiors, both chief factors and superintendents.

In view of these checks to the employment of patronage, it is even more remarkable that Scots succeeded in assisting one another to the degree that they did. Also, because webs of patronage did not operate to anywhere near the same extent as they did in other imperial enterprises, employees in the HBC did not hold such high expectations of support and thus avoided the disappointment often felt by hopeful Scots seeking patronage in the British West Indies.[88] The other avenues to advancement in the HBC were equally as valid as patronage, and overall, the opportunities for upward mobility in the HBC were prodigious. A variety of mechanisms assisted Orkneymen in their endeavours to scale the career ladder and many were conspicuously successful. In fact, the extent of advancement among the Orkneymen was such that some non-Orcadian employees seem to have resented their good fortune. In 1790, English officer William Walker informed the Committee that 'if any person from the Orkney Isles should be placed over me' he wanted them to 'recall me next season'.[89]

Circumventing obstacles to advancement

There were many opportunities for employees to advance within the HBC, but some Orkneymen encountered significant obstacles in their quest for improvement. Unlike Scots in the British West Indies and the NWC, who were generally wealthy and literate men, Orcadian servants in the HBC were often poor and uneducated.[90] Illiteracy, inadequate education, low social status, and the HBC's wage policy hindered the ambitions of some employees who sought to forge fruitful careers. Some of these were actually self-imposed constraints, while other impediments arose out of the Company's policies, which appeared to favour well-educated men with good social connections. However, employees who endeavoured to rise to positions of responsibility, as well as those who simply sought high wages, found that these obstacles to betterment were often illusory, easily circumvented, or could be endured in the short term for the sake of long-term benefits.

One significant hurdle to advancement was a lack of basic literacy amongst Orcadians. Levels of illiteracy appear far greater than is often assumed, given the vast quantity of contracts signed with 'x' as opposed to a signature.[91] In view of the fact that high-ranking positions in the Company required written work and numeracy, illiteracy had the potential to be a real impediment to betterment. The duties of an officer were considerable and even the temporary masters in charge of subordinate posts had to comply with these written mandates. Men who could not read or write would obviously struggle with the regular tasks required of them as officers.

However, some Orcadian employees successfully overcame the barrier to upward mobility that illiteracy had imposed upon them. Mitch Oman, master of South Branch House, was, according to David Thompson, 'without education, yet of a superior mind to most men, curious and inquisitive, with a very retentive memory'.[92] He could not write and signed documents with a cross, but in order to surmount this obstacle when managing a post in 1789, Oman's superior, William Walker, sent a literate employee to South Branch House to act as writer to Mitch Oman.[93] The practical help that was offered by colleagues in both reading and writing meant that illiteracy did not have to be a significant hurdle to ambitious employees, but some servants were uncomfortable about resorting to the assistance of literate men. For instance, Edward Wishart from Orphir had worked as a labourer since 1778, toiled his way up through the ranks, developed both canoe-building and navigating skills, and was eventually rewarded for his efforts with the offer of the position as summer master at an outpost of Nelson River in 1794. He declined the promotion as a result of his poor literacy; as Joseph Colen explained: 'he cannot write his own name and being obliged to apply to the men to read his Letters of Instruction exposes him to their ridicule and contempt'. Indeed, Colen noted that many employees that were right for the position of master did not accept the station because they were 'fearful to undertake it knowing that they would expose themselves to the Ridicule of their fellow Servants'.[94] Thus the social ramifications of illiteracy were perhaps greater then the practical obstacle.

Social problems did emerge from the promotion of uneducated men who had originated in the labouring class. The HBC believed in social stratification and wanted its officers to uphold social divisions between the ranks and assert authority over subordinate employees. High-ranking Orkneymen lay in a social limbo as they were expected to disassociate from their former friends and colleagues in the low ranks, but struggled to assimilate into the upper ranks. A cultural gulf separated them – the illiterate or poorly educated – from the externally appointed officers, many of whom were well-read. A scholarly ethos was certainly evident among high-ranking Scottish officers: James Sutherland, John McNab, John McKay, John Sutherland and William Auld read dictionaries, encyclopaedias, and philosophy, political economy, and history books sent from Britain.[95] Orcadians may have felt more comfortable among their comrades in the low ranks but their relationship had also altered. Officers were expected to dine separately from the servants to keep an appropriate distinction and they were also warned against undertaking the labour of low-ranking servants unless necessary, as aside from being undignified, it reduced their authority over the lower ranks.[96]

There are certainly indications that Orkneymen found adjustment to their newly acquired status as officers quite challenging. Many were faced with disapproval for having next to no subordination among their men. For instance, George Budge, who advanced to the position of clerk and master after twenty years' service, was criticised for being uneducated and unable to maintain appropriate order among the men under his control. According to a senior officer, the combination made him unsuitable for a higher rank and it was recommended that he take responsibility of only a small outpost under a district master.[97]

Low social status and want of a good education became considerable stumbling blocks for Orkneymen, particularly after 1810 when the management introduced the New System. Boundaries between the ranks were to sharpen as the directors attempted to unify the officer class. They wanted officers who were already well-educated, possessed good connections, and reflected their own attitudes and aims.[98] As part of the New System, which was initiated between 1810 and 1821, the directors made changes to their recruitment and promotional policies that were consistent with these aspirations and the upper sector of the Company was gradually overhauled.

The first step was to introduce well-educated men from England and Scotland and to assign them to the position of junior officer or clerk. At least three men of 'respectable connexions' were engaged from Inverness in 1818, along with two or three clerks from Stornoway.[99] The advantage of hiring men who already possessed a good education was that they would be able to cope with the numerous demands of administration, which included increasingly vast amounts of record keeping, accounting and chronicling. It was thought that externally appointed officers such as William Nourse from Edinburgh, and William Christie from Inverness, showed good potential and would become very valuable officers in a short amount of time. The directors assumed that these new men would simply require a term of residence with the natives in order to learn their languages, habits and customs, and master the rudiments of the fur trade. Senior officer James Bird was of the same mind and believed that within a few years, the HBC would have a string of experienced traders.[100]

Another facet of the New System was to inhibit the advancement of unsuitable employees. The Company took the opportunity to expeditiously demote or dismiss some of its personnel and, to this end some officers were relegated or stood down, because they did not meet the 'true spirit of our new regulations'.[101] The internal recruitment of officers was to become a rarity and opportunities immediately diminished for Orkneymen to ascend to such careers. Few low-ranking Orkneymen were newly appointed into the high ranks under the New System, and it seems that the influx of educated Scots into managerial positions had to some extent lessened their opportunities for promotion. Employees' advancement would depend on the governor's report reflecting their education, sobriety, activity, obedience and willingness to fight against the North West Company, and only properly qualified men would be appointed to the station of trader.[102] Therefore uneducated servants who had risen from the low ranks discovered new limitations to their aspirations and, for instance, John Robertson, who climbed the occupational ladder from a labourer to an outpost master at Nelson River, was now regarded in 1814 as unqualified for a higher post.[103]

However, some of the senior officers in the Company did not approve of the HBC's new policies, which was evident in their treatment towards the newly-appointed clerks. Long-serving officers had not shared their luxuries with the new clerks, which pushed these men to mix with the lower-ranking servants instead. The poor conduct shown towards the new officers was actually such that it had put them off the service altogether. It turned out that the workforce's unwelcoming spirit partially arose from the belief that the freshly appointed officers were spies. The Committee stressed in 1816, that it 'was not our intention (& we cannot too strongly impress this upon your mind) that the clerks should be considered as spies on the conduct of the Trader'.[104]

Aside from harbouring suspicions about the motives of new officers, some of the long-established personnel simply opposed the Company's new recruitment and promotional strategy, as it conflicted with the needs of the trade in Rupert's Land. William Auld observed in 1811 that 'the very considerable time which is requisite to form Steersman Guides and Interpreters is equally requisite to qualify as an officer to perform with success the duties of his station'. He complained about externally appointed officers who were 'utterly incompetent to a charge among Indians of whose language and customs they are alike strangers to'.[105] The new clerks may have been perfect for the Company in theory, but in reality they lacked the essential skills of the trade. Nicol Finlayson, a clerk from Fodderty, did not impress his superiors, as they had to offer repeated instructions on how to manage his posts, which was hampered by his frivolous and careless nature.[106]

High-ranking personnel in Rupert's Land recognised the superior benefit of skill and experience over education and social background, and accordingly supported internal recruitment practices. The continuation of their role as middlemen between subordinate employees and the London Committee meant that they still had some influence over the careers of personnel under the New System. In the servants' character references, they acknowledged the apparent faults of employees, particularly those that conflicted with the aims of retrenchment. However, they also highlighted the ways in which enterprising employees, who did not fit the directors' description of the ideal officer, compensated for their supposed shortcomings by exhibiting other desirable qualities such as country skills, experience, and good character.[107] Therefore poorly educated, socially inept and illiterate men found that the impositions evoked by retrenchment could actually be overcome.

According to Company policy, James Slater was ill-equipped for his position as outpost master at Osnaburgh as he was illiterate and had insufficient authority over his subordinates. Yet he offset this apparent deficiency by his proficiency as a trader, and his aggregate trade return was such that senior officers believed it counteracted his lack of education. His trade skills earned him the respect of his colleagues in the officer rank and by 1818 he had been promoted to a district master and was officially noted as 'an Officer of much merit'.[108] Likewise, Peter Spence had a poor education but his superiors in Hudson's Bay thought his common sense and enterprising spirit made him well-equipped as an officer, and he was promoted from cooper to clerk in 1816, and thereafter to district master. Another successful but illiterate trader, Donald Sutherland from Clyne, also progressed through the ranks from the position of tailor, to district master in 1818.[109]

Through their natural merit and the support of senior colleagues, many Orcadians held their place in the high ranks and continued to advance within the HBC. In 1819, Scots held seventeen out of the thirty-two highest-ranking positions of governor, chief factor and district master, and nine of these officers were Orkneymen. Another twenty-seven Orkneymen, while not obtaining the most senior positions, continued to serve as clerks, outpost masters and assistant traders.[110] Therefore despite the designs of retrenchment, poorly educated men had retained a remarkable hold on superior stations, as their skill and experience in the field rendered them essential to the business. In fact, it appears that even some illiterate employees continued in the senior ranks of the Company, as one officer relied on a literate labourer, Donald Mathison from Lewis, to act as writer for him in 1818. This was confirmed in 1821 when George Simpson condemned the poor abilities of the HBC's officers and especially the junior ones, as many 'of these fellows can hardly sign their own Names'.[111]

Some employees used practical measures or compensated for their perceived deficiencies and overcame obstacles to promotion, but between 58 per cent and 65 per cent of Orcadian employees remained in the lowest ranks of the Company between 1789 and 1819.[112] Although these figures suggest that vertical mobility was restricted in the HBC, caution ought to be employed in assessing Orcadian advancement, as it is to some extent a subjective issue. It is not clear in what terms employees viewed their careers and defined their own success. Some men may have viewed advancement as simple vocational progress, others may have defined it by their social standing and whether they were ranked as officers or servants, while others, and perhaps the majority, considered it in terms of financial remuneration.

The basic labouring wages offered in the HBC were marginally better than those on offer in Orkney, but labouring was generally considered to be an unremunerative and unfulfilling vocation. One potential recruit, John Sutherland, was warned by his brother that as a labourer he would have 'the chance of being a slave … and earn little or nothing'.[113] The wages had not advanced in the century since Scots first entered the Company, and as the position involved heavy drudgery, the 'paltry sum' of £6 a year for a five-year contract in the 1780s and 1790s was deemed an inadequate reward for toiling in a dangerous and distant wilderness. The wages increased to £8 a year during the early years of conflict with France and £15 to £20 in the latter years of the Napoleonic wars, but still met with criticism in Orkney.[114] Even the Company management admitted that the preliminary labouring wage was dismal, and although they were aware that the wage might raise complaints, they justified their policy on the grounds that new recruits were virtually ineffectual owing to their inexperience in the business.[115]

Menial work was initially unattractive to financially motivated recruits, but in practice, it was not the unrewarding occupation that many assumed it to be, and the vast number of recruits that signed up each year testifies to this. The meagre salary was actually misleading, as without accommodation costs most of the income remained intact. Furthermore, it was only the minimum income that labourers could expect to earn, as there were actually ways, whilst in the Company, in which that sum could be augmented. Opportunities were available to all servants to increase their income through inland work, and it is possible that the bounties accompanying such work compensated for the unfavourable terms of the initial contract. Although inland residence was generally not appealing because it incurred physical hardship, it did become financially rewarding. In the 1780s and 1790s when the annual salary was £6, each servant earning less than £10 who resided at an inland settlement received an extra £2, raising his annual income to £8, the maximum he could expect to earn through farm labouring and kelp manufacture in Orkney. In addition, any trip taken in the interior of Rupert's Land merited the reward of £1 and if the journey was particularly long or difficult, £2. The trip money had the potential to enhance annual wages considerably, as Robert Flett experienced; he earned £8 per annum but gained an extra £3 to £4 each year for his inland travels. Likewise, William Thompson from Ronaldsay received war wages of £8 a year and gained another £5 in bounties, taking his wages to £13 per annum.[116] Therefore one labouring contract was potentially lucrative: the advantages were simply obscured.

In addition, labourers may have accepted low wages on the understanding that it was merely a temporary situation that would improve in the second and third contracts with better remuneration. Officially, men were awarded wage increases upon the expiration of a contract and according to their merit and station. The Committee requested that the servants send their resolves from the posts to the Company headquarters, detailing their intentions to return home or continue in the service, and if so, the length of contract and wage they would favour. In order for the executives to ascertain an appropriate wage increase, officers sent certificates of employees' abilities and a description of their station such as 'labourer' or 'steersman'. A basic salary and career structure existed for the lower-ranking servants, and in 1788 the Company submitted the terms upon which men would advance. The first contract as a labourer was of five years' duration at £6 per annum, accompanied by a 40-shilling bounty; the second contract was for three years at £12 per annum as a canoeman; and the third contract was for three years at £16 per annum as a steersman.[117]

Yet some low-ranking employees did not climb this occupational ladder. Many of the servants were reported to be very indolent unless 'an immediate Prospect of gain presents itself'.[118] The development of country skills and other attributes favoured in advancement took time and effort, which some men were not willing to tolerate. However, even these men who remained in the lowest ranks of the Company stood to profit from service, as salaries were not only increased in relation to their abilities, but they were also advanced in proportion to the time that servants remained in service. Accordingly, labourers such as John Cromartie, who entered the Company in 1780 and received the standard wage of £6 a year, did not learn any canoe skills, but still earned double the amount in his second contract as a labourer. Likewise, George Taylor served a five-year contract at £6 a year in 1792 and then re-engaged for a second contract of labouring in 1797, at £12 a year.[119]

In fact, although an occupational hierarchy existed within the Company, this was not always reflected in salary. It seems that in financial matters, longevity of service was actually held in higher regard than station. Indeed, the Company openly declared that fidelity to the Company through long service earned their regard. This was evident when old labouring hands, such as James Short from Orphir, who had a history of fourteen years' service, received salaries as high as £28 in 1806. Likewise, in 1800, unskilled labourer Thomas Miller earned £25 to £30, when £25 was the equivalent salary of Orcadian officer Andrew Moar, master of Neoskweskau.[120]

In addition, employees often received wage increases that were far greater than the Company had intended. Officers frequently deviated from the customary wage policy and amended salaries on the ground, in response to practical needs. Orkneymen frequently bartered over their duties and contracts in Rupert's Land to ensure that they received the highest pay possible and that their absence from their homelands was ultimately worthwhile. At the same time, the Committee had stressed to officers during the war to retain servants at the Bay, due to the shortage of hands. Often the only means of retaining employees was to grant exorbitant wages and, for this reason, a custom emerged in which officers promised wage increases to servants without the directors' permission.

For instance, labourer Magnus Flett served one five-year contract at £8 a year and submitted his resolves towards the end of his first contract, notifying the Committee of his intention to return home in 1802. This may have been an example of the Orcadians' 'great share of art and Cunning' in financial matters, whereby they threatened to depart the service only in order to receive better earnings.[121] His superiors in Hudson's Bay persuaded him to continue in the service for a second contract, at the elevated rate of £25 per annum. Likewise, Nicholas Folster desired to engage in 1801 for three years at £15 a year and the Committee agreed to his request, but before the officers in Hudson's Bay had received these instructions from the incoming ship, they had used their discretionary powers and increased his salary to £18 for one year.[122] Some employees really manipulated the system and after being guaranteed a wage increase from their officers, subsequently demanded a higher salary in their resolves, which were sent to the London Committee. For example, William Ballenden received £12 per annum in 1801 and after the officers agreed to raise his salary to £18 for one year, he then requested £22 a year from the Committee.[123]

The digressions from the conventional method of increasing wages led the directors to complain that the lack of heed given to their regulations was disappointing. The exasperated Committee pointed out that increasing wages so extravagantly was a drain upon the Company and stressed that the aggregate cost of servants' wages and provisions were far heavier than the officers could ever imagine.[124] The directors had explicitly decreed in 1797 that any unapproved increases, guaranteed by officers, would be charged to the account of the officer who took the authority to make the promise. It appeared to vex the management further when officers then took this on board and willingly offered to pay the difference. Officer John McNab increased Magnus Birsay's wages in 1797, and the perplexed Committee exclaimed that it did 'not understand what Mr McNab's intention is in offering now and then to pay the additional advance wages which he makes to various servants'.[125]

It did not occur to the directors that the officers were simply obeying orders and retaining essential hands, and that those who were responsible for trade in Rupert's Land needed quality hands in order to achieve sufficient returns. Officers did not increase salaries needlessly and ensured that employees received wages equal to their value. For example, John Johnston was unwilling to remain in the service for less than £12 a year, but his superior, Mr Hutchins, held the opinion that £8 matched his abilities. Likewise, the council at Moose Fort was forthcoming about John Cromartie's resolves in 1790, stressing that in its view he demanded higher wages than he deserved.[126] Therefore it was only if a servant was sincerely useful to the business that officers ensured that he would remain in the service by raising his wages.

Overall, both official and unofficial wage practices meant that unskilled men, who like most others entered the service to make money, were often not any financially worse off by remaining in the lower ranks. It is thus possible that some servants who did not ascend, or only partially ascended the occupational hierarchy, refrained from doing so as a calculated choice. Additionally, because experience and perceived loyalty were valued as much as merit, other employees who may have failed to ascend the occupational ladder as far as they had hoped, still found profit in service due to the financial remuneration. Yet temporary migratory employment in the HBC was still a gamble; embarking on labour-intensive work in Arctic conditions meant that permanent disability, or even death, were real possibilities, either of which could render the original economic objective futile.

FOUR

Occupational Hazards, Medical Care and Welfare

Accumulated miseries: hunger, fatigue and cold

The entrance to Hudson's Bay is nestled between the Foxe Basin, leading to the Arctic Ocean, and the Hudson Strait, connecting to the Atlantic Ocean. The southern inland coasts experience a sub-artic climate and, as one of the first Scottish HBC employees, Thomas Bannatyne, observed in 1684, 'in the wintertime it is very cowld and all the rivers and a great part of the sea is frosen fast'.[1] Although polar bears, walrus and wolves thrived in this territory, it offered a remote and relentless environment for humans. One Company officer claimed that servants were not 'kept out at labour so as to hurt by freezing', but the very nature of the work meant that employees had to endure long periods of time outside.[2]

Building trading posts, cutting wood, hunting and other outdoor expeditions such as transporting letters between posts, exploring Rupert's Land, and visiting native encampments to foster friendship and trade, were part and parcel of the fur-trade experience. It is therefore not surprising that many suffered from exposure to the elements and departed the HBC service with severe disabilities, the consequence of frozen limbs. John McDonald, the Inverness recruiting agent, confirmed the dangers of freezing when he reported in 1819 that a number of young hands returned home after a sojourn of only one year, disabled by frost.[3] In minor cases the servants experienced frostnip that rendered the 'face, point of our nose, under the chin, points of our fingers, and the laps of our ears' to freeze 'a little, which only exchanges the old skin for a new one, and in some complexions ... leave a mark for ever'.[4] The more widely reported condition was frostbite, in which the actual tissue beneath the skin froze; this often prevented a servant from being fit to work, as in the case of Orcadian Andrew Kirkness, who was immobilized after his hands froze all over. Occasionally, however, the damage was so extreme that the only solution was amputation of the affected part. It was feared that a young lad who had served the Company for only one year would be crippled for life after he froze in 1789, and an extremely frozen servant at Eastmain was fated to suffer the loss of part of his nose in 1816.[5]

Winter expeditions were particularly conducive to the onset of frostbite as, according to fur trader David Thompson, 'the falling snow with the movable snow on the ground, causes a drift and darkness in which the traveller is bewildered'.[6] Such was the case of John Malcolm from Walls in Orkney who became disorientated and subsequently froze at Gloucester Lake in 1817. He had to be sent for surgical assistance and suffered the misfortune of having both his feet amputated. Another servant John McDonald also froze on a journey in 1810 and lost all the toes from one foot.[7]

The above men were actually fortunate not to perish, as prolonged exposure to the elements was a common cause of death. In 1817, James Clouston, a labourer from Stenness, embarked upon a team-hunting expedition near Capusco in the Albany district, which ultimately resulted in his demise. Originally a grouping of nine men, they separated into two parties. The trailing contingent consisted of three men, one of whom had identified his comrades' tracks to follow in the snow. Clouston, however, believing he could actually see the party ahead in another direction, parted from their company. Although his companions attempted to communicate with him, they received no response. Alone, in the cold of the winter night, Clouston was with 'neither Hatchet flint or Stick, to make a fire'. His tracks were visible the following morning but the rest of the men did not look for him, feeling powerless in the knowledge that he must have been in a helpless condition. Exactly when he perished is unknown but the 'inhumanity of his Country men for not looking after him' was later criticised. A fellow Orcadian, Jacob Corrigall, argued that had the men found Clouston in the morning they might have saved his life, and that seeing his footprints in the snow was the same as seeing the pitiable lad in person and not offering him any aid.[8]

However, even when comrades did search for one another, it was often too late to be of any assistance. In January 1801, some Eastmain servants were ordered to haul fish from the tents twenty miles away. One of the party, George Harvey, a young servant with only a year's experience, was unable to keep up and advised the others to go ahead. When he failed to reach the tents, the remainder of the crew set out to look for him and eventually found his body three miles away, 'entirely covered with blood and a great quantity all round him; it is supposed (as no wound was found about him) that from too much fatigue, he had burst a blood-vessel inwards and after much trying to reach the Tent had fallen down & expired, blood was in his track half a mile from where he was laying'.[9] Again, a servant collapsed in 1816 and his companions were unable to provide him with any comfort at all, as they too had endured five days without any nourishment, and so the man froze to death.[10]

The cold weather exacerbated the strains of fatigue and hunger and the servants often had no choice but to relinquish their comrades in order to preserve their own lives. In January 1815, two servants arrived at Albany Fort in a weak state, having abandoned Henley House, which was depleted of provisions. They had commenced as a group of four but two were forsaken along the river. The following year a similar fate befell employees, Robert Gill and James Gaddy, who struggled on a journey with a native woman and child. Having consumed all of their provisions, they battled on for another six days until Gaddy was unable to continue any further. His companions constructed a shelter for the night and after making a fire, left him lying there to die. They proceeded for another five days until Robert Gill also 'sank under the accumulated miseries of Hunger fatigue & Cold'.[11]

Scarcity and scurvy

Inadequate sustenance was the root cause of ill-health, widespread misery, and unrest in the fur trade. This was particularly true for those who worked inland and who, through lack of provisions, were increasingly reduced to an appalling state of starvation. Provisions were imported from Britain and included pork, beef, pease, bacon, flour, cheese, oatmeal, barley and butter, while country supplies such as fish, geese, partridges, plover, duck, rabbits, buffalo, venison, and moose were obtained in Rupert's Land.[12] The growth of vegetables and maintenance of livestock were also encouraged at the Company settlements. Theoretically, the posts would have sufficient resources to provide effectively for the workforce, but the system of supply was precarious. European provisions were sent only once a year, and much of the workforce was reliant on locally obtained provisions, which were never guaranteed due to the unreliability of the natural environment.

Employees' levels of vulnerability depended on their degree of isolation, and their ease of communication with the outside world. Bayside posts were usually well-provided with European goods, but even they had to rely upon natural resources to some degree, and it was feared at Eastmain in 1809 that their supplies of imported meat would dwindle before they could obtain country provisions from the geese hunt in spring. On the other hand, inland servants rarely had much recourse to European provisions, and at York inland they each had fifty pounds of flour, four gallons of oatmeal and two gallons of brandy, although barley was sometimes taken too.[13]

The regular European provisions bestowed upon inland employees in the HBC compare unfavourably with those awarded to the NWC. The Nor'westers were based in Montreal, and as they had supply lines running across the country, inland employees had access to fresher and more varied food. One HBC officer visited an NWC house near Red Lake in 1790 and, 'to my great surprise found entertainment suitable for any gentlemen, boiled Beef, Pork, Beaver, Portugal split peas made into fine soup, fat Cake, Chocolate, and very good wine'. He, on the other hand, had 'not so much as a knife and a fork…and but one plate' and only hope that 'kinde Providence favour us for the winter'.[14] The nourishment of his post employees largely depended on their access to country victuals.

The acquisition of country provisions often hinged on encountering and cooperating with the natives, who traded food in exchange for brandy, ammunition and tobacco. Although the NWC men were generally better provided for, they also procured country rations from natives, trading textiles, silver trinkets and beads for meat, to the extent that one HBC employee queried whether 'they came here merely to eat, not to get furrs'.[15] Yet the HBC's dependency on native contributions was more pronounced, and the aforementioned officer at Red Lake was concerned that they would face starvation in 1790 if the natives did not furnish them with food. Thus many inland employees grabbed every possible opportunity to acquire food from passing tribes.

Servants at Portland House frequently traded for pounded and dried meat with the passing Southward Indians and the Chipewyan tribe in 1796.[16] It was particularly vital for servants travelling cross-country, and with a limited capacity to store provisions, to make regular contact with native tribes. A group en route from Brandon House to Fort Pelly had no provisions in 1796, so endeavoured to find some natives to supply them with food before they traded with the Canadians. Their furs had already been traded to the NWC, but the HBC employees successfully procured goose meat and also managed to employ some natives to hunt red deer on their behalf. It was quite common to engage natives temporarily as hunters, particularly over the winter, as they were excellent huntsmen and one could easily procure ten times the number of geese that most HBC employees could collectively amass in a day. They were also adept at hunting large animals, as the employees at Buckingham House discovered when they ended up with an abundance of moose meat in 1797.[17]

The significance of the natives' role in maintaining the subsistence of inland employees became increasingly evident in the midst of the fur-trading conflict. It seems that employees developed an over-reliance on their contributions, and that this perhaps discouraged self-sufficiency. For instance, in 1800, the men at Chipewyan Lake spent some time living off the provisions that they had traded from a native, as they had not yet made an effort to construct nets to catch their own fish. This reluctance to develop survival skills was also obvious at Red Lake in 1790; the workforce were poor hunters and inexperienced at both fishing and net-making.[18] One officer was so frustrated by the feeble efforts of his men to procure fish at Trout Lake in 1808 that he exclaimed that the trouble was 'having a Set of Men, the greater Part of whom are as helpless as Children'.[19] While some Orkneymen such as Isaac Batt were considered to be fine beast-hunters, the inadequacy of the Irish employees was noted in 1816, when a superior commented that 'they are totally incapable and would starve in the midst of Plenty'.[20]

In all fairness, it was often no easy feat to supplement the Company rations. Two of the employees stationed at Red Deer River in 1812 were sent to collect moose meat from animals that had been killed nearby. However, the snow was too soft for hauling, so the servants had to carry the animals on their backs, making 'it laborious as well as tedious work to get our provisions brought home at this season'.[21] Their own efforts to fish and hunt were also frequently tempered by seasonal and environmental constraints. Winter was long and hard in Rupert's Land, and while some locations such as Martins Fall could provide plentiful partridges and porcupines, it was more common to struggle to get any provisions at all and encounter many hungry days.[22] As a result, fishing became the chief sustenance for many posts, due to the profusion of rivers and the year-round sustainability resulting from the practice of ice-fishing in winter.

Nonetheless, scarcity was still common. The fishing was so meagre at Isle à la Crosse in 1805 and 1806, due to a flush of water in the lakes and rivers, that the men could scarcely catch one meal a day out of six nets.[23] Besides, the same area could differ enormously in the availability of resources throughout each season and each year. The servants at Pine Lake had poor success with fishing in September 1810, and this continued throughout the rest of the year while there were no rabbits to hunt. One employee believed that 'Provisions of all kinds are scarcer here than I have seen them in any other part of the Country'.[24] Yet they caught ample supplies of sturgeon the following September and continued to fish with success until the end of October, when they got a deplorable catch for that time of year. After the lake froze, few fish were caught under the ice and the situation continued to deteriorate until March 1812 when the master had to resort to distributing the few European rations he had saved, as there was nothing edible to be gained from either the woods or the lake.[25] The servants at Chipewyan Lake experienced similar fluctuation at the end of 1800 and, having managed to subsist on the returns of pike and suckers over the winter, were disappointed to find that fish were very few in the following March. They had no hope of obtaining supplies from the natives and eventually sent two employees to Nelson House as 'we are too many at this place'.[26]

Removal to a more prosperous location was not always possible due to the extreme state of starvation under which some traders already laboured. In such cases the servants could be pushed to radical measures to ensure survival; it was not unusual to eat dogs or animal skins in the fur trade when necessary. George Sutherland was forced to extreme deeds in 1780, eating dogs, shoes, and mittens to subsist, and John Ballenden had to tame his hunger by eating moose skin

and scraps of beaver skins at Henley House in 1812.[27] Regrettable as the circumstances were for HBC fur traders, and usually Canadians too, it was clear that
when country rations were simply unavailable and they were famished, their
native 'partners in furs' were in even more dire straits.[28]

Starvation among the indigenous populations of Rupert's Land was actually
so rife that some turned to cannibalism. The fate of James Clouston, who died
at Capusco, was very unsettling for his young colleagues in the HBC. They were
ordered to return to Capusco and search for Clouston's remains to bury, but were
shocked to find only half a corpse. The boys followed the tracks leading away
from the remains and eventually came across more body parts with a native
family who instructed the servants not to report the incident. The traders, afraid
to camp anywhere near, walked all night and later collected Clouston's remains,
which amounted to broken leg and thigh bones. When one of the natives subsequently died, it was recorded that his death was 'Probably occasioned by his
eating human flesh and that almost raw – the Body of the unfortunate James
Clouston', a deed the cannibals did not deny.[29] Other natives were also suspected
of cannibalism when tribe members disappeared and pieces of their bodies
were later found. One became very ill and the traders believed he had poisoned
himself by eating his father's body, while it was thought that a missing native
girl, last seen in the same cannibal's tent, had also fallen victim to his hunger.[30]

For the most part, the HBC attempted to alleviate the starving condition of
native tribes and the practice of cannibalism should not be overstated. Although
manifesting itself as benevolence, regard for the natives' welfare was as much
about maintaining trade prospects, as it was a genuine humanitarian concern.
The Committee members found it painful to read about the famine among some
native tribes in 1794 and expressed the hope that none of their employees would
refuse assistance to any natives in distress. Officers complied with this policy and
continued to give food to save the lives of those starving, but as one officer at Pine
Lake noted, such support only adds 'to our misery as we must spare them some
out of our scanty pittance which barely keeps life and soul together'.[31]

Additional mouths to feed contributed to deprivation, and the servants
who chose to take native wives and begin families in Rupert's Land faced the
challenge of trying to support them out of their own pocket. Native wives did
help shoulder the burden, as they were adept at hunting and fishing; for instance,
James Spence and 'the old wife' were frequently recorded as rabbit hunting for
the post at Red Lake in 1799.[32] A custom had also developed among the servants
of selling their rations to officers with families. However, such mitigation was
only possible when either country provisions were available or European rations
were superfluous. It was more common to struggle to provide for a family with
as many as three children out of rations such as one fish and some flour.[33]

Unforeseen events, such as the detention of two Company ships throughout the winters of both 1815–16 and 1816–17, could bring whole settlements to the brink of starvation, as the crew and returning servants required support. The complement at Albany had to maintain thirty-one returned passengers from the *Emerald* and *Prince of Wales* ships in 1816 and their arrival was an unwelcome sight. Most of the additional men were consigned to Capusco to hunt geese, where they griped about their rations and threatened to take food by force.[34] The heavy dependency on dwindling rations generated malnutrition and mortality. Officer William Sinclair lost one of the men to fatigue and hunger that year; another two almost shared the same fate, and many others contended with scurvy.

Although scurvy is usually recognised as a seafaring disease, being prevalent in the navy, it was also a common affliction of the nutritionally deficient on land. It affected explorers and the personnel in trading companies, such as the English East India Company, and recurring notations in the HBC's journals verify that the monotonous and scanty diet of servants, protein-based and salty, regularly induced scurvy among employees. In the late eighteenth century, the posts were pervaded with cases of scurvy of varying severity. At Moose, one man was unable to work, while Robert Hog of Churchill River was noted as being ill with the disease in 1792.[35] Commonly, however, scurvy affected more than a couple of men and was actually endemic at the posts; the inhabitants of York Factory were repeatedly afflicted.

In 1789, a scarcity of partridges, rabbits and fish meant that employees at York did not have three-days-worth of fresh provisions. The ensuing scurvy was so virulent that between six and eight men were completely inoperative at any time, making it difficult to carry out the necessary tasks to maintain the post. Later that winter they were grateful that the natives had supplied them with partridges and hoped that this assistance, coupled with their own efforts, would prevent the disease from becoming fatal. Although lemon juice was ordered at York Factory in 1790, the following year Joseph Colen reported that the disease again 'raged with Violence among my People', and resulted in one fatality.[36]

This nutritional disease was evidently a big concern for the Company management, as it was potentially fatal and rendered part of the workforce ineffective. The symptoms of scurvy included swelling of the gums, loose teeth, offensive breath, a swollen body and immobility in their increasingly discoloured limbs, confining them to bed. The disease was also accompanied by 'a kind of putrification' and depression.[37] In addition, for those who survived, the effects could prove long-lasting; William Thompson came to a factory on crutches in 1816, weakened by the scurvy, and it was lamented that James Hutchins, an Orcadian, was not as useful as he could have been, had he not been damaged by scurvy at York Factory.[38]

It was important to curb the disorder, but at this time a lot of ignorance surrounded the condition. The men in Rupert's Land attributed the disease to a variety of factors such as idleness, because the indolent were the first affected, and the 'want of Tobacco', a self-diagnosis presented by the scurvy-inflicted men at Eastmain.[39] The London Committee was not entirely sure of the cause of the disease and in 1790 blamed the poor quality of European provisions and directed the surgeon to examine the beef and pork for decomposition. Only four years later, they attributed the same disease to unsatisfactory cleanliness. They took notice of reports from the officers at Albany Fort that the servants 'keep themselves exceedingly filthy' and concluded that this was obviously the reason for such pervasive scurvy. As a precautionary measure, they advised the officers to fine any men who did not wash 'at least once a Week on Sundays'.[40]

Fortunately the executive soon sought advice on the disorder and followed procedures used by the East India Company and the navy in successive years. Casks containing essence of malt, a highly approved anti-scorbutic, were dispatched to the posts. Officers were asked to provide feedback on the degree of ease and success with which this remedy was used and they reported that it had served the men well at Churchill and York, where the disease had taken a vehement hold.[41] On the other hand, officers at Albany had reservations about its utility as an anti-scorbutic and rather than waste the remaining essence of malt, used it to make beer.

The complement at Moose had equally little use for the treatment as they had only known two cases of scurvy in the previous eight years and attributed their success in staving off the disease to fresh vegetables, exercise and the natural anti-scorbutics found in Rupert's Land.[42] These men seemed to have more knowledge of the disorder, as they availed themselves of local anti-scorbutics such as spruce beer, a native remedy made from the boiled needles and twigs of the white spruce. Cranberries and juniper berries were also readily available to fur traders in British North America, but despite the prevalence of these organic remedies, essence of malt continued to be dispatched to Hudson's Bay by the London Committee, along with concentrated crystallised lemon juice, which although costly, had the benefit of keeping for longer periods than raw lemon juice, and in any climate.[43]

Yet it is evident that despite increased awareness of the nutritional deficiency, insufficient progress was made in tackling it, and the disease remained rife among Company employees. Only a decade after the violent epidemic at York, servants were once again badly affected. John Ballenden reported that the surgeon attended to almost twenty men suffering with scurvy; three died from the disease, and many others were so unwell that they had to cut their contracts short and take the voyage back home. In 1811, William Auld acknowledged the continuing ravages of scurvy, which 'requires now but little to bring it into action', having repeatedly troubled the men for twenty years.[44] Five years later, it was registered that young Scot Stewart Brochie who had long suffered from the illness had died, and Orcadian George Morwick was 'fast going' too.[45]

The worst case arose on another occasion when two Company ships, the *Hadlow* and the *Eddystone*, had become trapped in the Bay in October 1815, due to the early arrival of winter. Having not prepared for the unforeseen – supplies were desperately low – it was stated that if provisions were not passed on from another post, the men could starve. It was determined that 'every exertion should be rendered for the relief of such a Number of distressed fellow creatures who are most of them labouring under the greatest of human calamities'.[46] To this end, malt and essence of malt were sent from Eastmain, and the captains replied that they would be of immense value to the men who were currently ill and would also help safeguard those not yet afflicted. Unfortunately the majority of sailors were so badly affected by scurvy that it looked as if that the disease would kill many by spring, and twelve of this contingent did indeed die.[47]

Although the London Committee and employees made efforts to eradicate scurvy, the unpredictability of the natural environment meant that excessive demands were intermittently exerted on limited rations of food and anti-scorbutics, keeping the disorder active. The Committee's lack of foresight in sufficiently provisioning the posts, in case of such unexpected disasters, only exacerbated the problem. Their inexperience of basic wilderness survival may have led them to overrate the natural food returns of the country, as well as employees' accessibility to, and skill in procuring, such country provisions. Unfortunately, the time-lag in communication meant that the management in London would not hear of the problems that were experienced in the winter of 1815–16 until after they had shipped the following year's supply of provisions. They were therefore unable to avert the subsequent disaster, which resulted when the ships were again detained through the winter of 1816–17.

Disease

Ill-health among the fur traders commonly occurred as a result of malnutrition and a weakened immune system, rather than contagious disease. Unlike various tropical diseases that afflicted sojourners to India and the Caribbean, epidemic diseases appear to have been rare in the fur trade between 1780 and 1821. Although smallpox broke out among the natives in the early 1780s, with devastating consequences, it does not appear to have been a problem among Company employees. It is possible that the spatial distribution of the workforce across the vast territory of Rupert's Land, and the small complements at each post, helped check the spread of such disease.

Infectious diseases were not entirely absent from fur-trade communities, as William Auld informed the London Committee members in 1811 that many types of contagious fever thrived in Rupert's land.[48] Although he did not elaborate on the nature of these illnesses, a condition known as 'the country distemper' was mentioned as a problem in the HBC. Umfreville described this distemper as 'a violent pain in the breast' which 'is supposed to proceed from the cold air being drawn into the lungs; which impeding the vessels from spreading throughout that organ, hinders the circulation, and renders respiration extremely painful and difficult'.[49] Gilbert Laughton was certainly reported very ill with the country distemper for two days in August 1791, and three employees at Albany suffered from violent chest pain during the winter of 1816. One of the men at Albany, James Morrison, was badly taken with violent pain in his chest in December, while William Loutitt died during the winter from a disorder that also afflicted his chest. The symptoms of the third man, Magnus Corrigall who died in January, included spitting blood, which suggests that tuberculosis was also present. Tuberculosis is not referred to directly in the post journals, but Scottish officer John McKay was noted as dying of 'a consumption' (tuberculosis) in 1810.[50] Likewise, allusions to long periods of illness characterised by coughing, weight loss and fever suggests that tuberculosis was a problem in Rupert's Land in both the late eighteenth century and early nineteenth century.

Identifying specific illnesses within the HBC is often problematical as the few medical sources that are available are rarely diagnostic. For example, it was recorded in the Eastmain post journal on 17 January 1815, that Orcadian officer Andrew Moar's seven-year-old mixed-blood son was 'suddenly taken ill with a violent fit of convulsions and continued so the whole day to the great distress of his poor Parents – indeed no Person in their senses can behold the miserable boy without condemning the insignificance of the human race, little can be done by Practitioners of eminence for such an unknown complaint and of course we can do little or nothing'. He died two days later, and unfortunately for Andrew Moar, another two of his young sons died within the following five months, reflecting the high child mortality in the fur trade. However, the last death was considered a 'happy circumstance', as the boy had 'scarcely had a moments intermission from insanity and violent pain for five days'.[51] Thus the medical condition under which the patient laboured was often unknown or misunderstood at the time.

Establishing the incidence of venereal disease is even more challenging. Many testimonies infer that venereal disease was rife in British North America in the late eighteenth century and early nineteenth century. Many European settlers in Canada in 1785 were found to be suffering from syphilis, and traders in the NWC suggest that venereal disease was so widespread in the fur trade that they feared it could really damage business. Alexander Henry noted that out of fifty men residing at Fort George in 1814, nine had been confined to their beds with venereal infections and another eleven traders were affected with the condition, with hardly any being completely free from it. The disease had spread so virulently that Henry was driven to declare that he would deduct employees' wages for the time spent convalescing.[52]

The two trading companies built posts side by side across the country, and both sets of employees partook in sexual relations with native women. It might therefore be expected that venereal disease would be equally prevalent in the HBC quarters. It was mentioned at Cumberland and Hudson House that Magnus Sclator, John Driver, and Robert Davey were sporadically ill throughout the year of 1777 with the venereal disorder.[53] It is not however generally documented as a problem in the Company. One of the few recorded instances of venereal disease was that of Nicholas Spence, who died of the complaint in 1788. It was explained that the disease had been contracted in England prior to entering the service and that he had been in a shameful state when he arrived off the ship. Again, it was insinuated that a couple of Norwegians who were infected with venereal complaints had arrived carrying the disease in 1816.[54]

It is possible that the incidence of venereal disease was higher than that which was explicitly recorded. Omitting to chronicle the prevalence of the disease may have arisen from fear of recrimination: the Committee did not approve of sexual relationships between employees and native women. However, it was not in the interests of the surgeons and officers who recorded ailments to protect the servants from such punishment by failing to document illness, as they also needed fit, active men working for them. Alternatively, the disease may have masqueraded as some other complaint in the documents. Calomel (mercurous chloride), which was a recognised anti-venereal, was certainly listed in both the Churchill and Albany medicine indents for 1796–97, but this evidence is inconclusive as it was also commonly used as a purgative.[55] Overall, venereal disease was probably more common in the HBC than the documents suggest, but medical checks provided by doctors prior to boarding the ship, and monogamous relationships between men and native women in the HBC, constrained the entry, and limited the spread, of sexual diseases in Rupert's Land.

Occupational hazards

At the turn of the eighteenth century, George Gladman, the chief of Moose Fort, reported that on the whole they 'had few instances of sickness, but accidents have deprived us of the services of some of the most useful hands'.[56] The most common cause of death and injury in the HBC was undoubtedly work-related accidents. The *Statistical Account* for St Andrew and Deerness stated that some

Orkneymen in the HBC were killed by accidents on an annual basis. Drowning was one of the most common misfortunes and although it was occasionally caused by swimming, it was typically a by-product of work.[57] Accidental drowning greatly increased when the Company expanded its trade inland in the late eighteenth century, and employees had to venture into unchartered regions by canoe. For this reason, disproportionately high incidences of drowning afflicted Orkneymen who tended to monopolise canoe-related stations.[58]

When the Company moved inland, servants who were often inexperienced in handling canoes had to negotiate rivers and rapids, and as William Auld commented in 1811, the smallest error could result in disaster.[59] Drowning had become such a common occurrence by 1788 that the Company executives sent instructions to the Bay for the recovery of drowned people. One of those was a young lad, Robert Esson, who drowned on the passage inland in 1788, like John Linklater and Orcadian William Sanders of the previous year.[60] Yet even those who were trained in the management of a canoe and had years of experience were not immune to the ordeals caused by rapids or exceptionally high waters. For instance, John Sinclair, whose position of steersman indicated that he must have been a proficient canoeman, also met his end falling overboard while attempting to settle a place near Eastmain in 1793.[61]

Mutilation of a canoe or equipment was another prescription for tragedy. Magnus Garson's oar broke near Nelson House; he subsequently struggled and succumbed in the rapids, and the master of his post later lamented the 'premature death of one of the company's best servants'.[62] The complement at Manchester House also suffered an unexpected accident when they proceeded up a fall and one canoe was cut. The cargo immediately vanished and the life of James Sanderson was saved as he hung onto the wreck, but Archibald Copeland was not seen again after the canoe went down and efforts to retrieve his drowned body failed.[63]

Often servants simply vanished, and the sequence of events that resulted in their death remained unknown. Two Orcadian labourers, Cesar Adamson and Robert Corrigal, disappeared while navigating a canoe on Porcupine Lake in October 1818. This small lake apparently experienced a surge whenever the wind blew. The canoe was later found broken, with no sign of either servant, although Corrigal's drowned body was eventually found in the lake. This type of accident does not appear to have been uncommon, as in 1802 John Thomas reported that he had been out in a boat searching the shores near Moose; he was attempting to recover the remains of his daughter, and the other unfortunate people who drowned the previous day after the canoe had been lost on ice in water.[64]

Following another episode at Snake Hole when a boat went astray, the Company management communicated their regret over the loss of their poor employees but hoped that the accident did not occur out of imprudence. The HBC management often emphasised the need for care, primarily because some accidents were completely avoidable. If the actions of William Budge are in any way typical, it is unsurprising that so many men drowned. After damaging his boat on a journey in 1800, and subsequently repairing it, when his craft became leaky four days later he refused to stop and mend it.[65]

Inattention was a particular risk in the fur trade and often at the root of casualties. Handling firearms was a necessity in the HBC, but due to faulty weapons and careless management it frequently proved hazardous, as two fatalities in the 1790s demonstrate. One employee accidentally shot his gun at another servant without realising that it was loaded; the shot entered his chest, killing him immediately. James Scott was also victim to accidental gunshot when his companion shot him in the thigh in 1793. The accident occurred ten miles away from the factory so the Orkneyman was taken to a tent and examined at the factory the following day. Mr Knight observed that 'a mortification has taken place' and he died a couple of days later, his body 'in such a putrid state'.[66] Gunshot wounds were also responsible for the death of Archibald Graham, a mariner from Stirling who died seven days after an accident with a fox gun.

Although there were fatal incidents as above, gunshot wounds more commonly caused temporary or permanent disability.[67] Archibald Linklater had the ill-fortune 'to blow off his right thumb by the sudden Explosion of a gun in making the Ships signal at Moose' in the 1780s.[68] Likewise, Magnus Kirkness got both his legs shot, immobilizing him for over two months and for some time thereafter, he could not be employed at laborious work or when he was likely to get his feet wet.[69] Others were destined to remain invalids for the rest of their lives. Thomas Whymester was in danger of remaining a cripple after he discharged a gun into his thigh in the mid-1790s; the wound soon healed but the symptoms were unfavourable and it was unlikely that he would regain full use of his leg.[70] Whether these casualties were preventable is unclear, but the recklessness of some servants certainly increased their risk of injury.

Some accidents were the consequences of inebriation, which was apparently one of the most common types of misbehaviour among Company servants.[71] The Company directors recommended sobriety, but the consumption of alcohol was ubiquitous in the fur trade. As well as being a trading currency, it was also utilised for recreational purposes in the remote wilderness of Rupert's Land. Although alcoholism itself rarely caused mortality, heavy drinking was at the root of some deaths in the fur trade.[72]

The combination of alcohol and a severe climate proved lethal for James Slater, who sat on the ice of a frozen river and got intoxicated on rum with a fellow servant in 1816. They became so impaired by alcohol that they were unable to return to their post. His companion eventually crawled back to headquarters but was 'unfit to give any intelligence concerning Slater, so that he lay all Night among the overflowings in the River'.[73] He was found on the ice the following morning without his mittens on and his hands frozen. It was thought that he could lose his fingers, but without a surgeon to summon for assistance, district master Jacob Corrigall could only suggest the application of juniper bark to his hands. Slater died from his injuries three months later.

William Appleby's death in 1789 was also a by-product of excessive liquor consumption. He got drunk, took 'unsanctioned liberties' with a native man's wife at Hannah Bay, and was subsequently murdered by natives. The directors considered Appleby's death to be a cruel result but not entirely unwarranted. They feared the repercussions of this incident, as it undermined efforts to court the affections of the natives and establish a harmonious working relationship. They were right to be concerned, as a breakdown in goodwill was immediately evident when the HBC experienced a decrease in local trade.[74] Orcadian officer John Ballenden hoped that this regretful matter would serve as a warning to all young servants to avoid the habit of excessive drinking.[75]

Yet it is difficult to gauge how many employees actually consumed to excess, or were addicted to alcohol. Between 1815 and 1816, three men out of twenty-two at Moose were noted as being addicted to liquor, while in the Servants' List of 1818–19 seven men were recorded as addicts, among them Orcadians; for instance Peter Craigie from Stromness was 'rather addicted to liquor', as was a labourer from Evie. In other cases, it was not stated explicitly that the employee was addicted to alcohol, but the implication was that their drinking was problematic. James Taylor was considered a 'very refactory, drunken, worthless fellow', while of James Morrison they could say 'nothing in favour of his sobriety'.[76] Additionally, in 1781, Mr Jarvis requested that 'sober men may be engaged his fort having been much hurt by Persons of a Contrary Disposition', while in 1800 tailors were offered a £3 gratuity if they were both sober and able.[77] There are also signs that a large part of the workforce was, if not dependent on, at least preoccupied with alcohol. Servants on inland duty were often coaxed into completing their tasks only by the promise of liquor, and some men at Albany refused to comply with orders in 1812 unless they received 'a pint of grog'.[78]

The Company was justly concerned about the difficulties caused by excessive alcohol consumption, as even the less profound consequences of drinking, such as the neglect of duty, had the potential to injure the fur trade. Employees' drunken antics interfered with the daily business and, for instance, one steersman was reported to be so drunk, troublesome and quarrelsome with his comrades on a journey near Brandon House in 1808, that two servants refused to go any further with him and the voyage was held up for half a day.[79]

The management clearly struggled to control the problem of alcohol abuse. They frequently reiterated that the workforce should not overindulge in drinking, but the liquor allowances available to the men conflicted with this directive. Special occasions such as Christmas, a time of hospitality in the fur trade, were an excuse for the vast consumption of alcohol at the Company posts. The liquor allowance during festivities at Moose in 1793 included a dram of foreign liquor in the morning, strong beer with dinner, and a half-pint of rum each at night. The complement had similar allowances for the whole of the ensuing week, including a pint and a quarter of strong beer for breakfast on some days, and similar rations were being bestowed among the men a decade later.[80]

Festive occasions aside, alcohol remained a considerable feature in the lifestyle of men in the fur trade. At Eastmain, the normal liquor allowance amounted to one pint of beer a day per man, while the men at Nemiskau were given brandy every Saturday night. The Committee permitted further allowances to be issued at each officer's discretion in time of bad weather or particularly hard duties, to motivate and reward servants. On top of official rations, employees could purchase alcohol for personal consumption. Although Andrew Graham testi-fied that in order to prevent immoderate drinking, servants were limited to six gallons of brandy a year and only one quart at a time, some men at Severn purchased seven gallons each in 1807.[81]

Officers had a degree of latitude in alcohol distribution; Jacob Corrigall, a district master at Albany, prohibited any spirits on his excursions. The Orcadian officer had learned over time that the men 'will go on better without any of that article'.[82] However, many other senior employees struggled to tackle alcohol abuse, perhaps because they were susceptible to heavy drinking themselves. Robert Longmoor, a Scottish officer, was 'allwies Drunk', to the extent that the men under his command complained about his behaviour.[83] It was also recorded in 1812 that Mr McCormick, a senior officer, arrived in a drunk state at Albany, using offensive language. He was forgiven as he guaranteed that he would not conduct himself in such an improper manner again. However, it was feared that Mr John Sutherland, the Scottish officer who accompanied him, would persist in such behaviour and there was little hope of his reform. A colleague complained that this set a bad example to junior officers and young employees and he thought that it would eventually result in Sutherland's dismissal.[84]

Officers with alcohol problems were threatened with discharge from the service, and there was a general consensus in Hudson's Bay that this was a just policy. In 1790, the council at Moose informed the directors that any newly recruited officers ought to be sober, as they would not hesitate to send them back on the ship if not.[85] Yet in practice, dismissal was a last resort: both the Company and the senior officers attempted other solutions. For instance, John

Calder, a 28-year-old writer from Edderton had taken to unrestrained drinking, but having promised to moderate his habit in 1816, was allowed to continue his service on a one-year trial. He seemingly survived his probation, as he was listed at Oxford House in 1819. Likewise, James Tait, a district manager from South Ronaldsay, was prone to intoxication and on such occasions let himself and his employers down, leading to his suspension from service in 1818.[86] These cases may have prompted the directors to take a new initiative that year. The Company informed the management at the Bay that it intended to be liberal with their tea and sugar allowance, in the hope that it would dissuade the officers from the consumption of spirits.[87]

Although excessive drinking, like any other debilitating habit or condition, threatened the maintenance of proper authority and discipline, as well as successful trade, the Company often seemed only to pay lip service to the need to regulate drinking. It is possible that the inefficiency, morbidity and mortality which resulted from inebriation were perhaps cancelled out by the perception that alcohol was a necessary compensation and anaesthetic for the harshness of the working environment. The directors wished to curtail excessive drinking, but ultimately it was more important that they had a willing workforce.

Surgeons and remedies

Economic success was the priority of the HBC, and to flourish commercially a competent and healthy workforce was required. In order to maximise the efficiency of the workforce in Rupert's Land, the Company employed surgeons to examine men prior to boarding the ships and assist them on the voyage across, as to some extent the condition in which employees arrived dictated their ability to withstand the physical challenges of Rupert's Land. Additionally, the HBC appointed surgeons to preside at the primary trading posts to treat sick servants and identify malingerers. The high incidence of ill-health in the fur trade meant that illness could easily be used as a device to avoid unappealing duties. Duncan McMillan, a labourer, was apparently prone to 'tricks of feigning himself sick' in 1818, while some servants returned to Moose in 1817, blaming lameness, illness and the depth of the snow for obstructing their journey to New Brunswick.[88] Orkneyman William Craigie was also chastised for simulating illness throughout his year at Churchill in 1812 and had not 'earned his victuals'.[89] The following year, William Stanger refused to embark on an expedition on the grounds of illness. Upon examination, the surgeon revealed that he was actually feigning illness, being as able-bodied as any other man at the factory.[90]

Many surgeons appear to have been highly esteemed in the Company, contributing towards post management, and well-regarded by fellow employees. During a severe outbreak of scurvy at York Factory, it was recorded that its advance was largely impeded by the treatment and care of the surgeon, Mr Southall, and the surgeon at Eastmain also earned praise for his good bedside manner. The surgeons' dedication to employees' health and welfare continued upon the voyage home. For instance, William Leask from Stenness entered the service in 1812 and became very unwell on his return journey in 1820. Rather than continue his voyage to Orkney, Leask was taken to the house of surgeon Dr Stainsby to receive good care and attention.[91]

Yet medical professionals appear to have been in short supply. The ability to procure surgeons was particularly difficult during the war, as the needs of the navy and army drew these professional gentlemen away. It was very fortunate that several Company officers, such as Mr McNab, had originally entered the HBC in a medical capacity and could therefore employ their medical skills when required.[92] The shortage of surgeons in the labour market, coupled with the dual capacity of some officers, may have influenced the HBC's decision not to appoint medical personnel at the inland stations. In 1788, the officers at York Factory notified the London Committee that the business required at least one professional surgeon to operate in the interior, due to the hazardous nature of inland work. Although the officers maintained that such an appointment would bring unanimous satisfaction to the workforce, the Company neglected to institute a surgeon inland and the highest-ranking employee remained responsible for medical care at each of the subsidiary posts.[93]

Even at the factories on Hudson's Bay, where surgeons were permanently instituted, medical care was only irregularly available. The surgeons' sphere was so vast, encompassing everyone at the posts and many of the native populations whose health was equally essential to successful trade, that demand simply could not be met. For instance, when a messenger arrived at Eastmain to get medicines for an Indian woman, the surgeon, Mr McCormick, thought that he should examine her personally. He abandoned the post and undertook a four-day journey to the tent where she lay.[94] Indeed, surgeons were often so busy that ailing servants were shipped around Rupert's Land to obtain medical aid. In 1815, James Rowland, suffering from swelling all over his body, was sent on a schooner from Eastmain to Moose for the doctor's assistance. On other occasions, the alternative was to send a description of the patient's symptoms to the surgeon and wait for his advice.[95]

Despite the absence of uniformly available qualified personnel to treat the servants at all the posts, success in overcoming health problems was equally reliant on the medical supplies accessible to them. There was a variety of medicines listed at some of the major posts, including emetics and purgatives such as jalap, ipecac, rhubarb, and tartar emetic. According to one employee, Edward Umfreville, the servants also made use of natural remedies found locally such as cranberries, raspberries and the herb wishapucca. It reportedly grew in abundance and had beneficial medicinal effects when taken as a tea or a powder and was subsequently used by both natives and Europeans.[96] However, medicines and instruments were not universally available throughout Rupert's Land. For instance, the medicine chest at Albany was apparently short of lancets, an instrument used for blood-letting, and a male catheter. When the management noted that Albany had ordered trepan, amputation and pocket instruments, they permitted them to exchange amputation instruments with the ship if they were out of repair, but refused the pocket instruments, declaring that the surgeon ought to have his own. In addition, while the ships were supplied with medicine chests, each of which contained four trusses, the trusses were charged to the employee who required them on the voyage.[97]

The main establishments reported shortages of essential medicines, but those who suffered most were situated in the western peripheral area of fur-trading territory, and were dependent on York Factory. Buckingham House, Manchester House, and Edmonton House, the posts furthest inland at the time, all complained of scarcity in the 1790s. There was no cinchona bark available at Manchester House in 1792 to treat a servant who was dying of a fever resulting from a gunshot wound. Orcadian William Tomison complained that 'the inland Settlements are very ill supplied with any useful Medicine; which ever will be the case until the Honarable Company takes it into consideration, to have a Box packed up in England, with proper direction for the inland Settlements and then a prudent Person might use them without fear, which I cannot do at present'.[98]

The shortages continued, and Tomison believed that the medical supplies had actually decreased over the years, although he could not comprehend why, as he had always made full use of every medicine in his possession.[99] Yet even the inland posts closer to Hudson's Bay, such as Red Lake, had a dearth of medicine. One employee, Magnus Birsay, had injured himself from a falling stick and the officer in charge had to permit blood-letting as he did not have any remedies to give him.[100]

Owing to the inland shortages, the post employees developed a mutual dependence upon one another, and medicines frequently traversed the miles as and when needed. When two servants journeyed to Edmonton House in 1796 with a supply of medicines, Tomison found the bottles of Turlington's (antiseptic medicine containing twenty-seven ingredients, known as the 'Balsam of Life') quite depleted; the remains of a bottle of hartshorn were frozen and thus ineffective, while the bottle of jalap had perished, being both mouldy and rotten. Tomison could not hide his displeasure at taking delivery of such 'a little worthless medicine-box'.[101]

The servants at Buckingham House also donated some supplies to William Tomison, including opodeldoc and strengthening plaster, but this generosity was to their own detriment, as the following year, in 1797, they were then unable to treat two Orcadian servants who appear to have been suffering from tuberculosis. Benjamin Bruce, whose death was anticipated every hour, and Donald Mowat, who laboured under the same disease, could not be treated, as there were no appropriate medical supplies at the post. George Sutherland subsequently wrote to Edmonton House requesting medical aid in order to help the 'violent cough' of the 'skeletons'. He requested medicines such as opium to ease their discomfort, as well as a blister plaster and spanish flies. He was apparently furnished with these, as although the men at Edmonton House were equally deficient with 'hardly so much rag as would dress a wound four times', they were aware that medicines at Buckingham House were insufficient.[102] In fact, in 1796, Mr Knight had sent a list of medicines required for the posts at Cumberland, Buckingham, Edmonton, Cedar Lake, South Branch, and Jack River, to the management. It was, however, too late for one of the Buckingham House invalids who died; the other poor servant, Benjamin Bruce, remained in very poor health.[103] These were not isolated incidents: similar reports were made from Chipewyan Lake in 1800 when Orcadian servant John Budge was taken unwell in early October. By the end of the month, Budge was reported as being 'at the point of Death having no Medicine to give him'.[104]

Medical shortages were seemingly so prevalent that some of the Scottish employees even resorted to ordering supplies from Britain out of their personal accounts. William Tomison, still disgusted with the dearth of supplies, ordered a medicine chest, while Scottish trader John McKay commissioned two boxes of analeptic pills in 1801 and, five years later, another supply of pills along with a balsam and 'Dr James's Powder'. A further appeal was that the medicines be accompanied with directions on usage.[105] This last request was probably wise, as in some cases the men were probably better served without medical attention, so that they did not have to undergo the rigours of haphazard treatment.

Medical knowledge was rudimentary in the late eighteenth and early nineteenth century and as the most high-ranking servant, devoid of any training, was responsible for medical care at the subsidiary posts, treatment was often poor and experimental. In 1798, when a Scottish servant died, it was considered most likely that the medicines given to him had quickened his death. Apparently that same Dr James's Powder had been administered; this was an approved medicine, but when used improperly could be dangerous. The Committee relayed to the deceased's relatives in Caithness that 'in that part of the world ignorance respecting diseases and the effects of violent remedies are not to be wondered at'.[106] There were some successful treatments administered in Rupert's

Land, such as the application of peruvian bark to William Richs' broken arm. He seemingly found it to be of enormous benefit, as did David Thompson when he broke his leg.[107] All the same, it was perhaps a wise consideration of Orkneymen John Ballenden and Thomas Anderson to purchase personal copies of medical books, such as Buchanan's *Domestic Medicine* and the *London Dispensatory*.[108]

Paternalism, welfare and pensions

Employment in the HBC involved the challenge of survival as much as the trade of furs. Rudimentary efforts were made by the paternalistic management to contribute to the comfort and well-being of their servants. However, because the Company was an enterprise that was managed in England but operated in North America, the directors did not fully comprehend the conditions in which their employees worked.[109] The management often emphasized the need for thrift with regard to provisions, particularly when in 1801 they struggled to obtain adequate supplies for men at the Bay on account of the war. The price of victuals had increased; flour, grain and animal food were so inflated that everyone in Britain was lowering their consumption. As a consequence, the Company struggled to obtain permission from the Privy Council to send factories the usual provisions, such as beef, pork, butter, cheese, hams, and scotch barley. They recommended that everyone in Rupert's Land ought to be as frugal as possible in their consumption. It is unlikely that these words would have brought much comfort to men already incapacitated by light rations and scurvy. Two years later, when the Committee was informed that the contingent at Albany had encountered a period of extreme scarcity, when country provisions were especially hard to come by, the administrators regretted the suffering of the workforce. Still, they resolved that 'it is what every people & Nation on Earth occasionally are liable to – all that can be done, is to deprecate the Evil & bear it patiently when it occurs'.[110]

The directors' inexperience and misconceptions of the hardships of the fur trade occasionally ignited tension among the senior workforce. In 1811, William Auld expressed his frustration with the Committee's naïve perception of life in Rupert's Land and its unrealistic expectations of the amount of time required to train men in handling rapids. He emphasised that they should not compare water transport in the fur-trade territories with that found in Britain, and he asked them to write off the image of 'the spancaly-dressed wherry-man with his plush breeches and his silver badge nor conceive the *descent* of the solitary bargeman at London Bridge with that through the shallow horrors of rocky chasms as at all *synonymous*. Here the slightest mistake is big with fate allow a wrong impulse and the vessel is overwhelmed in an instant.'[111] These physical and conceptual differences of working life in Hudson's Bay had been a long-standing bone of contention with the workforce. Earlier generations of traders had also commented upon it, and James Knight remarked in the early eighteenth century that if the Committee ventured to Rupert's Land, 'they would set a little more Value upon Mens Lives & their goods not to expose all to this Hazard & wee such hardships'.[112]

However, at times when the Committee seemed to be inconsiderate towards its employees' adversity, it was really just expressing its paternalism. Those in charge of the Company had to maintain a delicate balance between the implementation of authority and benevolence; they could not pander to their employees, and wished to instil principles of resourcefulness and conscientiousness. When the Company management had to respond to reports of dissatisfaction in Orkney concerning a high incidence of mortality in 1819, it informed the Orkney agent, John Rae, that it was standard Company practice to investigate such mournful events and establish the root cause of fatalities. Indeed, when starvation and scurvy claimed many lives in 1816 and 1817, the Committee members probed the high death toll and queried the loss of the sailors detained in Hudson's Bay. They concluded that the servants' deaths were poorly accounted for and asked for full statements of all those reported to have died from starvation and exhaustion.[113] Yet the management appeared quick to exonerate itself from responsibility for misfortunes, and stated to the agent, John Rae, that of the deaths, 'several have arisen from casualties' but 'too many have occurred from imprudences which could only be attributed to the individuals themselves'.[114]

Nevertheless, the compassionate facet of paternalism was also perceptible in the HBC. In 1818, the Committee stressed its anxiety that the servants ought not to be subjected to unnecessary hardships. There had been complaints from inland employees claiming that they had not been allowed to purchase blankets to protect them from the tempestuous climate.[115] The executive acknowledged that without sufficient clothing it was impossible for men to keep well, and even if there was a lack of stock, men still needed blankets to ward off the cold and provide them with comfort. Likewise, after a terrible tragedy at Henley House when several lives were lost in a fire, the Committee members expressed their distress over 'the exceeding trouble of Mind and Body that Mr McNab and the Survivors must have undergone'.[116]

Individuals were recognised within the Company, and care was taken to provide for unique needs. When it was decreed in 1790 that James Hudson needed more activity in order to restore his health, arrangements were made to transfer him to the upper settlements. Additionally, the directors were attentive to the tribulations of employees who had returned home. George Sutherland contracted an illness during his service and had to spend time in hospital upon his return to Britain. The Company gave him £20 to cover the medical expenses incurred. In 1801, another servant who was unwell on his arrival home was also reimbursed the cost of his passage across, after a doctor's certificate was produced.[117]

The directors' welfare considerations were actually most evident in their dealings with employees who had retired from service as a result of disability or old age. In 1794, the management had queried Geddes about the provision for the poor in Orkney's parishes. Considering that numerous employees prematurely departed the service as a result of physical handicaps, they determined to award annuities to such workers who had been disabled through illness or accident.[118] Those in need of financial support petitioned the London Committee for a 'small yearly pittance' based on their particular circumstances. For instance, John Flett was granted a pension of £6 a year, commencing in 1820, in consequence of an accident.[119] Another ex-servant who applied for relief, Joseph Johnston, had been completely disabled by a gunshot at Moose Factory in the winter of 1800 and he had no hope of continuing work. The Orcadian sailor was awarded the annual sum of five guineas in 1801 and although it was substantially less than his previous salary of £21, his pension was continued until 1820, when he was sixty years old. Orcadian William Goudie also made a claim for support in 1802, following the loss of his thigh and other injuries during his employment. The HBC secretary believed that the Committee would consent to a generous pension as Goudie's case was so grave and informed the Orkney agent that he could start by paying him £4 or £5.[120]

Elderly servants who had spent the better part of their lives in the Company also qualified for support. David Sanderson requested annual assistance upon leaving the Company in 1817 with over thirty-seven years' service, and duly received £3 per quarter a year as a result of his long service. Likewise James Nicholson, having spent forty-five years in the service, was granted five guineas a year towards his support in 1777. James Grimbester was also given a similar sum upon his retirement and in 1810, after his death, his widow petitioned the Company in the hope that his pension would continue.[121]

The social responsibilities undertaken by the HBC's directors actually extended far beyond providing for aged and disabled servants. The risks of Arctic employment also weighed heavily upon dependent families in Orkney, and in the aftermath of bereavement the executive made some effort to protect those who had been wholly reliant on the income provided by service. One measure undertaken by the Committee in 1796 was of direct assistance to the heirs of Scottish employees who died in the service. The management endeavoured to cover the costs that arose in applying to the Commissary Court in Scotland, if Mr Geddes considered such application to be necessary. The fact that Mr Geddes, the Orkney agent, was specified as the decision-maker suggests that this resolve was primarily designed to help the poor Orcadian contingent.[122]

At the same time, some bereaved wives were also awarded support money on an annual basis. The Orcadian widow of William Craigie was given around £5 a year, and a comparable sum was contributed for the benefit of an Orcadian woman who contacted the Committee after her husband, Hugh Slater, was killed in Hudson's Bay in 1813. Likewise, in 1817, Catherine Loutitt petitioned the Company as her husband, William, had died at Moose that year. The Committee decided that an enquiry would be made into the length of her marriage, her age and the ages of her two children. Following a written report from Rev. William Clouston, a pension of £5 per annum was agreed.[123]

Local investigation into an applicant's circumstances was not unusual as each appeal for financial support was assessed on an individual basis. There was no guarantee that anyone would receive assistance when employment ended prematurely, whether due to ill-health, old age or death, as welfare provision was selective and awarded at the directors' discretion. In 1819, only nine Orcadians, including two widows, a superannuated servant and disabled ex-servants, were awarded pensions.[124] Grounds for assistance were often longevity of service and perceived loyalty to the Company as opposed to severity of disability or financial distress. This was unjust as inexperienced servants were more likely to fall victim to the perils of the fur trade. Additionally, men with a short history of service had met with less opportunity to accumulate capital and safeguard their future, and were thus less capable than long-term employees of sustaining themselves and their families. Therefore despite the management's declaration that they granted pensions with readiness, needy individuals and families often discovered that they were exempt from such support.[125]

Hugh Bakey had been seriously wounded by gunshot at Manchester House in 1791. The shot entered the 'thick part of his right thigh and passed through; and many of the shot went into his private Parts, and made a large wound which makes his Life doubtful'.[126] He made an amazing recovery in that he was able to walk with the aid of crutches, but apparently had not any hope of receiving a pension. Likewise, although Orcadian James Morwick lost his arm in the service, he was told in 1819 that he could not be placed on the pension list as he had not been employed for long enough. Instead he was allocated £20 compensation, which was to be disbursed in the way that would be of most assistance to him, by a local minister. The widow of servant James Finlay was also informed that the HBC's regulations prohibited the payment of pensions to the relatives of short-term employees. As with Morwick, however, the Company directors showed compassion and instructed Mr Geddes to present her with a gratuity of £5 to ease her distress.[127]

A one-off compensatory payment was often allocated to the needy instead of an annual pension. In the first century of the Company's operations, compensation was offered rather than a pension and even then was a rare practice: it was decidedly more prevalent in the HBC's second century. Some resolutions were understandable as sundry servants left the service disabled but still capable of exercising their trade. John Break was a weaver by profession and although rendered lame by an accident in the 1790s, he was still capable of earning a living. To this end, he was awarded compensation of £3, as opposed to a pension.[128]

It was also commonplace for recently bereaved widows to be assigned compensation rather than annuities. This indemnity was usually equivalent to the annual salary of the deceased. David Knarston's widow was presented with £12 in 1798, on top of the balance of £20 already due at the time of his death in the previous year. Similar relief of one year's wages was offered to Margaret Ballantyne in 1807 on account of her husband's death at Eastmain.[129] David Geddes was instructed to inform a Mr Sinclair of this gift of £6, so that he would stop bothering the Committee with his letters petitioning for aid on the widow's behalf. This suggests that although the Company was charitable, it was hesitant to part with funds, and it was often only under pressure that it did so.

It was perhaps the directors' reluctance to offer assistance, coupled with an emphatic understanding of the financial implications of disability or death, which prompted other lower-ranking members of the HBC to offer support to disabled servants and widows. Once aware of a colleague's ordeal, co-workers set up a subscription to raise funds at the posts and contributed as generously as their own funds and obligations would allow them. For instance, in 1809 the complement at Eastmain raised money for the widow of George Banks who drowned that year, and also the family of deceased servant, William Yorston. The two subscriptions amounted to over £60. Similarly, after being deprived of both his frostbitten feet and hospitalised on his return to Britain, John Malcolm was greeted with a pension of £10 upon his arrival in Stromness in 1819, the product of donations made by his colleagues at Moose.[130]

Another amputee, Magnus Brown, divested of both his hands and feet in 1813, was also awarded a subscription raised in Rupert's Land. At Edmonton post alone, thirty-three men contributed sums of money ranging from 5s to £1; and the total donations accumulated at Hudson's Bay amounted to £147 10s. However, as the fund was intended for the purchase of a pension for his life and produced an annuity of only £12 a year, the Committee members supplemented it so that £20 could be paid to Brown each year, and disbursed quarterly.[131] In fact, as former HBC writer Edward Umfreville concluded, it was this munificence displayed by fellow employees that often prompted the Committee to grant pensions. Apparently most of the benefactors of one Orcadian amputee earned less than £6 a year, and the directors, 'actuated by the laudable example set by their servants', then offered the invalid a pension for life.[132]

At times, the Company was a reluctant subsidiser, but its support was suffi-cient for those who were fortunate enough to obtain it. Even the lower-scale pensions were generous and close to the annual salary of a labourer in the Company at this time. Nine Orcadians were given a combined total of £54 3s in pensions in 1819, which was particularly high, considering that in the 1780s, £3 was the total provided for the twelve 'poor' people in the parish of Sandwick and just over £11 was divided among the fifty 'poor' in Stromness.[133] These welfare contributions were not, however, exceptional; the agents of the NWC also took care of old or infirm employees. They provided £100 to be put in a general account from which a maximum of £10 a year was to be given to the men they viewed as 'objects of charity'.[134]

Overall, the selective nature of the directors' sponsorship serves as a reminder that the HBC was above all a business, and commercial matters overrode any paternalistic sentiment. Corporate social provision may have emerged out of genuine philanthropic concern, but it was as likely to have been at least partially rooted in self-interest. Pensions may have enabled employers to remove old and unproductive workers with a clear conscience, but in the first century of the Company's operations, the HBC actually retained some of its workers beyond their point of usefulness, out of charity. This practice, although not absent in the second century of existence, was certainly less evident. It had perhaps been superseded by the more prevalent conferral of pensions and gratuities, and the occasional tendency to employ the sons or grandsons of employees who were dismissed from service as a result of old age or disability.[135] It is unlikely that the HBC's pensions were a ploy to remove worthless workers, as the Company also assisted employees' families, suggesting that welfare support was more likely to have been a gambit designed to assist the recruitment effort, and increase the fidelity of the workforce.

It is clear that employees' well-being remained a secondary concern to the Company's success. For instance, the directors asserted that they never forced servants to continue in the fur trade to the detriment of their health, but one unwell servant, John Valliant, was detained in Rupert's Land. Valliant was suffering from a critical case of scurvy in 1790 and his superiors feared that 'crippled objects' like him would act as a deterrent to potential recruits in Orkney.[136] Again, in 1819, it was considered preferable that decrepit and disabled hands either be sent to the Red River colony or at least continue in the service, to avoid casting an unfavourable impression on their compatriots.[137]

The Committee's fears were not unfounded, and in contrast to views that Orkneymen were particularly hardy and well-equipped for the hardships of the fur trade, the manifold afflictions and miseries that they encountered during their employment did on occasion discourage them from continuing in, or re-engaging with, the Company. Orcadian servant Magnus Kirkness notified his superiors in 1818 of his desire to return home, as he was afraid of developing scurvy. Other men were unwilling to wait for permission to return home and alleviate their hardship. James Lenay from Firth in Orkney absconded from New Brunswick in 1816, despite being contracted until 1820, and told the other servants that it was due to hunger.[138]

Although some Orkneymen, such as Thomas Spence, who went astray in winter and endured eight days without fire, and only thawed snow, oatmeal and raisins for subsistence, were particularly stalwart, there is no indication that Orkneymen in general bore their hardships any better than other ethnicities.[139] It is probable that all servants, like Spence, weighed up the difficulties of service against the ensuing financial reward, and most found that employment in the fur trade remained worthwhile. Illness and mortality were generally an accepted stake in imperial sojourning, and employment in the HBC was not any more hazardous than whaling in the Davis Straits, which was accompanied by the typical Arctic perils of drowning, starvation, scurvy and frostbite.[140] Yet while employees and their families envisaged that physical conditions would be harsh in Rupert's Land, they were not prepared for the physical and psychological onslaught dealt out by fellow Scots in the fur trade. The trading competition between the HBC and the NWC, which elicited some of the worst cases of injury and fatality in the fur trade, is the subject of the next chapter.

FIVE

Competition and Rivalry:
'Fur-Trade Wars'

Roots of conflict

In 1831, Ross Cox, an Irishman formerly in the service of the NWC, published a narrative of his adventures across the Atlantic. He remarked that it 'will undoubtedly sound odd in the ears of British readers, to hear of forts attacked and prisoners taken by commercial companies, natives of the same country, and subjects of the same king'.[1] Cox was referring to one of the most notorious periods in fur-trade history, the competition between the two main trading companies in British North America. The feud between the HBC and the NWC persisted for four decades, far longer than the one decade often cited[2], and was unique due to the shared ethnicity of many of the participants. This era is particularly notable in Scottish history as a time when economic priorities trumped ethnic solidarity, leading to a Scottish civil conflict fought on foreign soil.

Tensions had broken out between the two trading groups in the late eighteenth century, almost from the outset of the NWC's formation, as rival employees encroached on each other's trading patches.[3] Opposition materialised in the form of guerrilla-style campaigns and both parties were soon guilty of sporadic attempts to raid and plunder each other's posts. One of the HBC residences, Manchester House, was pillaged in 1788 and servants of the HBC were equally as troublesome, making threats to seize their opponents' goods and men.[4] Their quarrels became increasingly heated in the next decade, amid reports that a trader from NWC had pulled his gun on HBC's Thomas Isbister in 1795 whereby 'three shot went thro his Coat and sixteen thro the Canoe'.[5] The HBC's house at Ash Fall was then set ablaze after plunder in 1798 and, during the following year, a Scottish NWC trader robbed fellow-Scot and rival trader Thomas Linklater of 180 Made Beaver.[6]

Natives also became unwittingly embroiled in the trading competition at this time, as illustrated in 1790 when a group of natives arrived at Red Lake to trade with the HBC and walked right past the door of the NWC house, refusing to look at the NWC master, Mr Cameron, who 'was so much affronted at them that he turned up his Backside to them'.[7] Such incidents were perhaps inevitable

while conducting trade in the remote wilderness, but several factors, including
the rise of ecological pressures in the fur trade and political changes in the
NWC, contributed to the development of a persistent and increasingly aggressive contest in which intimidation, harassment, and violence became typical
characteristics of fur-trade life.

The beaver was of central importance to the North American fur trade, but
extensive beaver-trapping through the seventeenth and eighteenth centuries
had reduced numbers in some areas of the country. This decline was hastened
following the introduction of steel traps and use of castoreum as bait from 1797
onwards. The subsequent shortage of beaver supplies aggravated competition
between the companies, which in turn fuelled overtrapping. The effects of this
fierce rivalry were evident as early as 1801, when inland traders at Cumberland
House observed that the trade was falling to nothing, fearing that it could not
recover until one of the companies withdrew from the trade or found a new area
abounding with beaver pelts. Further reports of low beaver supplies surfaced
from the Nipigon area, near Lake Superior, in 1804, and a general decline in
the availability of beaver was noted in the older fur-bearing districts between
1801 and 1808. Aside from over-trapping, a beaver disease emerged in the early
nineteenth century, which may have contributed to the partial extermination
of the species.[8]

The effects of beaver decline were far-reaching as the trading companies
made no effort to address the ecological difficulties through conservation, an
endeavour that would have required cooperation instead of competition. As
fur trader David Thompson stated, 'Every intelligent man saw the poverty that
would follow the destruction of the beaver, but there were no chiefs to control
it'.[9] Rather than approach the shortage through methods of preservation and
replenishment of beaver stocks, the trading companies' response was relocation. Trading operations and native trappers became ever more mobile and
gradually moved across the continent in search of new areas of fur. Duncan
Cameron affirmed that the NWC dealt with the growing scarcity by migrating
to new territories each year. This search eventually led to the Athabasca, in the
north-west of the country, where the long cold winters and rich forested habitats
meant that furs of supreme quality could be found in abundance.[10]

Plentiful supplies came at a cost, however, as the new fur-bearing territories
were so remote. New routes and posts had to be established, a greater quantity of
provisions was required and transportation costs only increased with distance.
The NWC was particularly affected by the challenge of the new distant trading
opportunities, as its canoe routes were several thousand miles long and it took
years for furs to be brought back to Montreal, sold in London, and the returns
realised.[11] In comparison, the HBC held a clear advantage with shorter overland

access to the Athabasca district via Hudson's Bay. In order to overcome the difficulties of accessing furs in the north-west, the NWC soon formulated a new objective, to obtain transit rights through Hudson's Bay.

Negotiations began at the turn of the century and Duncan McGillivray, partner in the NWC, wrote to Alexander Lean, secretary of the HBC, looking to form an agreement. The NWC expressed its intention to extend its trade to the north and the west, beyond the Rocky Mountains to the Pacific Ocean, and requested transit rights through Hudson's Bay. They issued a warning that 'if this Overture should be disregarded or should not be productive of the desired effect, the North West Company must then of course prosecute their present commercial views in their Own way & in the manner which they deem most Conducive to their Own Interests'.[12] The NWC had already demonstrated the scope of its determination when it trespassed in Hudson's Bay in 1803, breaching the HBC's Royal Charter, as it tried to oppose the HBC's long-established trade in the area. Consenting to access rights through Hudson's Bay would only bring ruin to the HBC and it is therefore not surprising that the HBC concluded the dialogue in 1806 with the rejection of their plan.[13]

In refusing to give in to their rivals, the HBC had ensured the continuance of intense competition, but the development of political trouble within the rival company added to the probability of an especially violent contest. Personal clashes within the NWC splintered the concern into two groups in 1799, and the seceded faction operated as the XY Company, also known as the New North West Company. The HBC warned its establishments at the Bay that this new company had been formed in Montreal to compete with both themselves and the NWC. They were concerned that their latest rival was particularly ruthless and would, as a result, triumph in the trading contest.[14] The London Committee's concerns were justified as the XY Company fought with a new competitive vigour, but fortunately for the HBC traders, this aggression was largely directed at former colleagues in the NWC. For instance, during a dispute over furs, Alexander Henry from the NWC maintained that the XY traders had advised a native man to kill him.[15]

Fighting between the two factious groups from Montreal actually became so extreme that the imperial government passed the Canada Jurisdiction Act in 1803. It regulated that crimes committed in the interior could be tried in Lower Canada and also enabled the appointment of Justices of the Peace in the inland territories, to promote harmony and reduce crime.[16] The decree was ill-considered, as the Justices of the Peace came to embody men from contending sides of the trading competition who, in the latter years of the fur-trade conflicts, would use and abuse the law to their advantage. As it turned out, the vicious conflict between the NWC and XY Company was relatively short-lived, and only five years after the division of the NWC, the death of its leader, Simon McTavish, prompted the end of infighting among members of the two Montreal companies. In 1804, the XY and NWC formally declared that they wished to terminate their rivalry and in order to conduct a more profitable trade would reunite as one cohesive trading body.[17]

The agreement of 1804 proved to be a crucial turning point in the wider trading competition, as the reunited Montreal traders redirected their hostilities away from one another towards the HBC. The transformation in the trading competition was expeditious as the reinvigorated NWC made rapid headway, extending its operations from Lake Superior to the Atlantic, the Pacific and the Arctic Oceans. In contrast, complaints of waning trade grew vociferous within the HBC as traders were outnumbered by their rivals and faced stronger opposition from the newly strengthened NWC.[18] Yet rather than achieve such dominance through honest competition alone, the NWC had advanced by interfering with the business of the HBC, targeting both natives and rival personnel.

Campaign at the posts

The first strategy taken by the NWC to disable the HBC's operations was rumour-mongering among the natives. Thomas Swain, the HBC master at Chiswick House, observed the effects of this in 1804, when the natives were scared to approach them as a direct result of bad rumours circulated by the opposition.[19] Matters were taken further at Pine Lake, when Mr McBean of the NWC intercepted and harassed natives on their way to conduct trade with HBC men. He threatened 'to cut them to pieces' if they dared to exchange furs with his rivals. Maiming and murder was also declared as the penalty for a group of natives if they carried out business with the HBC at Swan River, and some had this fear reinforced when they were terrorised at the Upper House. The NWC proprietor, Mr Donald, took a child hostage, while the men were taken out of their tents and tied to trees by their arms before being tormented with a horsewhip. This menacing behaviour continued until they promised not to trade their furs with Orcadian HBC employees, Alexander Kennedy and James Gaddy.[20] A further strategy was simply to rob the natives of their furs, and at Nottingham House in the north-west, near Lake Athabasca, the NWC took to 'pillaging any Indian they meet'.[21]

Personnel in the HBC were also directly faced with the foul play of their opponents. In 1806, men from both companies ventured out to trade with natives at Whitefish Lake, but the night before they arrived at the trading place, the NWC members cut their rivals' snowshoes and hid their hatchets, in order to prevent them from continuing. A more ominous approach was taken at Beaver River in the early 1800s, when affiliates of the NWC armed with pistols forcibly removed an HBC servant from a native house, dragging him to the door. Five members of the NWC also entered their opponents' house at Bad Lake in 1806 and stole 480 Made Beaver-worth of furs. Orcadian William Corrigal was threatened with being shot if he resisted the robbery carried out by fellow Scot, John Haldane.[22]

Some posts, such as Red Lake in present-day western Ontario, were repeated targets for attack. Armed thieves from the NWC assailed the servants at the post on two occasions and stole furs along with trading goods, including brandy and cloth. One of the servants was induced to give his opponent gunpowder, while being held at gunpoint.[23] The opposition also struck HBC employees at Big Great River in the Eastmain district in 1806. HBC officer Thomas Alder wrote to his colleague George Gladman at Eastmain, complaining of the NWC's behaviour. He asserted that they had been robbed by their rivals and was concerned that 'Unless men are sent to protect what Trade we have in the Warehouse, 'tis more than probable we shall be robbed of that likewise, it has long been threatened & we (Mr Woode & myself only) expect hourly an attack, many of the Indians also who have given offence to this formidable gang of Ruffians are threatened with severe chastisement, where the business wille ende Gode knows, but if the Spring shoulde pass without bloodshed 'twille be a miracle'.[24]

Thomas Alder actually doubted that Gladman would receive the above letter as the NWC had adopted the practice of intercepting messengers and stealing their packets as revenge. His fears were unfounded in this instance as Gladman received the letter detailing how the HBC servants had been outnumbered and unable to defend themselves against robbery, assault and other ill-treatment. The victims included Orcadian John Crear and William Plowman from Wick, who were beaten and stabbed by a fellow Scot, NWC clerk Alexander MacDonnell, and the men under his command.[25]

Violence actually began to permeate the fur trade during this phase of the competition and armed robbery at Eagle Lake in 1809 resulted in one fatality. Two Orcadian employees of the HBC, James Tate and John Corrigal, recorded the incident. They reported that in September 1809, Scottish NWC trader Aenas McDonall arrived at Eagle Lake with nine men announcing that he had come to 'spill blood'. McDonall apparently seized a canoe full of goods belonging to the opposition and responded violently when HBC traders tried to retrieve it. He struck James Tate, who retaliated with a shove, and McDonall subsequently drew his sword. In the skirmish that followed, three employees of the HBC ended up seriously wounded and one Nor'wester was killed. Casualties of the disturbance included John Esson who was assaulted by a Nor'wester with a hatchet, dislocating his shoulder, and John Corrigal had a pistol held to his chest by Mr Adehmar of the NWC, as he declared 'you Damn rascal I will Blow out your Brains'. McDonall also cut Corrigal down to the bone and then came 'running as fierce as a lion with his sword in his hand', cutting James Tate on the neck. He then pursued other traders wielding his sword, but was shot dead by John Mowat of the HBC, who according to Corrigal committed the act in self-defence.[26]

The account of this incident offered by the NWC differed considerably, in that they claimed that the murder was premeditated and undertaken without any other incitement than McDonall being at the HBC landing place. They reported that three armed men belonging to the HBC attacked him, and a fourth shot him with intent. Reprisal was prompt and members of the NWC took Mowat into custody, declaring that they would subsequently view their rivals 'as Enemies instead of fellow subjects'.[27] In private, however, the NWC appears to have had a more balanced interpretation of the event. George Keith acknowledged that he and fellow NWC traders were too quick to meddle with the opposition and that minor squabbles often descended into grave confrontation.[28]

One of the Scottish HBC superintendents, William Auld, later addressed the NWC proprietors over this sad outcome of the dispute at Eagle Lake. Auld recognised that the incident was simply one of many in which members of the NWC had cruelly treated the HBC and he censured the company for not amending their conduct in the aftermath. He pointed out that their subsequent behaviour in some trading territories such as at Isle à la Crosse had been equally iniquitous.[29] As one of the most strategic positions in the Athabasca, the NWC traders had resolved to force the HBC away from the Isle à la Crosse area by persistent attempts to obstruct the trade and cause injury to the men.

HBC officer Peter Fidler noted that the NWC would do anything to acquire all the furs from Isle à la Crosse, and this included the habitual manipulation of local natives. The trappers had become afraid of the instant beatings and abuse dealt out by the NWC when they endeavoured to trade skins with the HBC men. With this fear established, even a glimpse of a NWC trader was enough to frighten the natives from engaging in contact or communication with the HBC.[30] Obstructing trade in the field was soon accompanied by the impediment of trade at the post through the use of surveillance and intimidation.

Surveillance was often employed in the fur trade, and the NWC had originally used this tactic during its dispute with the XY Company. They built a watchhouse facing the door of their opponent's dwelling and appointed men to watch their activities. The HBC also employed this gambit at Fort Edmonton, building their house within 'musket-shot' of the NWC post. The Nor'westers already had a house to the south of the HBC post at Isle à la Crosse and constructed a second house to the north, adjacent to that of their rivals. It was built only ten feet away from the HBC's stockades, to deter any natives from entering through their door. To ensure that both the natives and their rivals were aware of their surveillance, the NWC sang, shouted and beat sticks on a window.[31]

This strategy with the natives at Isle à la Crosse not only thwarted the HBC's opportunity to acquire furs, but also country provisions. Without supplies from the natives, the HBC servants in this area were wholly dependant on a diet of fish for subsistence. However, their rivals had also sabotaged this means of survival, frequently destroying or removing their boats and fishing nets. The HBC servants were compelled to guard their boats to prevent the NWC from cutting them adrift or setting fire to them and also had to remain vigilant of the nets as they suspected that their rivals were stealing their catch of fish during the night. In this environment where victuals were hard to come by, attempts to deprive men of food supplies were potentially as destructive as outright violence as, without fish, the servants would starve to death.[32]

In addition to thwarting the exchange of furs and trying to starve the HBC into renouncing the trade at Isle à la Crosse, the NWC embarked on a general campaign of harassment. This entailed stealing HBC property, removing their firewood, and cutting down their stockades. Their attempts to immobilise the opposition even went as far as capturing a favoured HBC dog. They had to impound the rest of their dogs in the garden in March 1811 as the opposition was trying to steal them away. Mr Black, a NWC trader from Aberdeen, was actually caught luring away two of the puppies and continued to stalk the dogs, igniting Fidler's fear that they intended to poison them. Aside from hampering daily duties, these measures were designed to harass and annoy the HBC and Fidler confirmed that their rivals did everything they could to cause distress, including firing gunshots at the HBC post and surrounding the house at night, making commotion to disturb the servants.[33]

This psychological warfare was also manifested in the exploitation of native women who were used as 'pawns' by the opponents.[34] The native wife of Andrew Kirkness, an Orcadian HBC servant, deserted the HBC post at Isle à la Crosse following an argument with her husband. Although she voluntarily entered the adjacent house of the NWC, she was so threatened while she was there, that she feared they would cut off her ears if she attempted to return to her husband. Almost a month later, Kirkness, the only fisherman at the HBC's post, abandoned his station in order to reunite with his wife, but he too was allegedly kept a prisoner in the NWC house. Peter Fidler petitioned his rivals for the prisoners' release as he thought that Kirkness would be a good witness to the Canadians' lawless behaviour that winter. He demanded that they be returned immediately and unharmed.[35]

When Kirkness eventually returned, he testified that he had been so badly beaten by Mr John Duncan Campbell that he was unable to get out of bed, and that they had threatened to escort him to Montreal in irons. The NWC had also warned him that if he tried to leave, 'every Canadian in the House would ravish his woman before his very eyes'.[36] His wife had been compelled to state that she did not wish to accompany him and although Kirkness had tried to remove her belongings along with his, a fellow Scot, Mr Black, threatened to beat him within an inch of his life. In the event, Kirkness' wife remained with the opposition, and although she endeavoured to escape and join the HBC men, she was recaptured by the NWC and given to a Canadian.[37]

The primary consequences of such campaigns were as the Nor'westers had envisaged: dispersal and demoralisation. In a letter to John Duncan Campbell, Peter Fidler explained that they had been forced to abandon the post at Isle à la Crosse as two servants had been threatened with their lives and, as the campaign of terror looked set to continue, it was no longer safe to remain in the settlement. The HBC servants were actually so scared of their adversaries that when Fidler asked for the said letter detailing the atrocities to be delivered to Mr Campbell, none of the HBC traders would take it on account of their fear of violent retribution. A few hours after they were coerced into evacuating the post, the NWC burned the HBC house in order to prevent them from returning. The retreating HBC servants were not overly disappointed by this incident as they were so traumatised by earlier events that none of them would be persuaded to go back until the London Committee found a way to protect them from such villainy.[38]

Company policy and reorganisation in the HBC

From the position of bystanders in London, the directors of the HBC had struggled to advise their employees on how best to handle the adverse situations in which they found themselves. Their counsel frequently related to the regulation of their own servants' behaviour, rather than to Canadian antagonism. In 1794, the management had expressed its disapproval of a NWC trader who robbed fur from a native man and warned their employees that anyone guilty of such atrocious conduct would be severely fined. The workforce was instructed to foster the goodwill of the natives and also that of their opponents by avoiding quarrels and refusing to engage in violence. Although the London Committee was concerned to see that discord had increased between the competing traders towards the end of the eighteenth century, they added that it was up to them to stay on affable terms with each other.[39]

The management was not surprised that transgressions occurred in the back country of North America where there was little in the way of legal recourse, but it feared that there was nothing the Committee could do to prevent or alleviate the situation. Reports of hostile incidents and abandonment of posts such as Nottingham House in the Athabasca district, reached the headquarters long after they had occurred, so all that the Committee members could suggest was to send home detailed accounts of misdemeanours and the names of the chief instigators of violence to present to the British government. The directors advised their employees to be utterly truthful in their recounting of events, but they believed that there was barely any hope of redress, given the remote location and nature of the conflict.[40]

The employees of the HBC became increasingly frustrated with this passive approach from headquarters. They faced ongoing pressure from the management to expand trade but struggled do so in such a hostile environment. Posts had to be deserted as early as 1806 because they were unable to compete with their more numerous rivals and the directors would not furnish them with a greater number of men to strengthen their opposition. A growing resentment towards the Committee's lack of intervention became increasingly evident among employees. In 1806 Thomas Alder, the master at Big River, questioned the use of working hard to obtain a profitable trade when a band of armed thugs was then allowed to steal the gains and take employees prisoner without undergoing any punishment. Fellow officer George Gladman agreed that such criminals ought to be held accountable by some law or justice, as it was detrimental to the HBC's business. Aside from apprehension about the Company's success, the workforce also resented its own unjust treatment and suffering.[41]

The events at Isle à la Crosse proved to be something of a watershed and the management began to recognise that its laissez-faire approach was not a sufficient response to the adverse hostility that the NWC brought to bear on the HBC's posts in the lucrative fur-bearing districts in the north-west.[42] This policy change, from one of forebearance to assertiveness, was encouraged by recommendations from William Auld and Colin Robertson and assisted by the reorganisation in the HBC's management team.[43] Under Wedderburn's New System, the HBC rapidly adopted new measures to form a determined opposition.

The Committee had been quite dichotomous in its view towards the trading conflict. On the one hand, it always directed its workforce to abstain from disputes, but on the other, it was frustrated by what it perceived to be a weak effort from its personnel in staving off the opposition. To counter the timorous attitude of the workforce in Rupert's Land, the management advocated a new, explicitly forceful approach. It informed the superintendent of Rupert's Land, Thomas Thomas, that 'as you are opposed to a set of people who proceed upon a systematic plan of violence to prevent the Indians from trading with us, and to deter our people from protecting them when attempting, it is evident than no success can be expected until you are enabled to repel force by force'.[44]

One means of strengthening opposition was to implement a new recruitment campaign that was tailored to meet the growing demands of the fur trade. The Committee strove to furnish the Company with men who were obedient and energetic, and therefore capable of making a strong stand in the face of fierce competition. The directors also sought to reinvigorate the dynamism of existing employees. They believed that if the high-ranking personnel stood to receive direct personal gain from a thriving trade, then they would be inclined to motivate themselves and their subordinates to exert themselves actively in opposition. The Company had moved towards this practice of rewarding and encouraging the personal effort of senior officers since 1806, when it had provided them with a small share in the HBC's profits. Four years later, the Committee expanded this initiative and allocated 50 per cent of the trading profits to be shared among the superintendents, senior officers and traders, in proportion to their rank.[45]

The new vitality of the Company was immediately evident in an official response to the hostilities that had taken place at Isle à la Crosse. Thomas Thomas and William Auld, superintendents of Rupert's Land, wrote repeatedly to the proprietors of the NWC in 1810 and 1811, cautioning against their 'acts of such extreme infamy & savage oppression'. They requested that the partners notify the rest of the NWC that the HBC was no longer following a policy of leniency and that any further assaults on its posts or employees would meet with punishment. The Company would not hesitate in taking legal action as criminal prosecution and public exposure of the NWC traders as malevolent criminals would 'render a service to our species'.[46] Auld was confident that they already had enough proof to ensure the conviction of several NWC traders, which would bring disgrace to the entire organisation, particularly as some of their crimes carried the death penalty in Britain.

The partners of the NWC were acutely aware of their rival's powerful overhaul and were daunted by this development, as in 1810 and 1811 they again attempted to negotiate with the HBC to avoid the cost of a continuing trading competition.[47] Unknown to the NWC, however, two new developments – the institution of the Red River colony in 1811, and the war of 1812 – were on the horizon and would stimulate more aggressive violence between the employees of the two companies, making open hostilities almost inevitable.

Colonisation and the war of 1812

The Red River colony was the pet project of Thomas Douglas, the fifth earl of Selkirk. Originally from Kirkcudbrightshire, Selkirk believed that emigration was the best solution for his countrymen in Scotland, particularly for those in the Highlands who had experienced economic reorganisation and changes in social structure throughout the second half of the eighteenth century. This upheaval had included the consolidation of small-holdings into sheep farms, which generated the displacement of many local inhabitants. Improvement and commercialisation were accompanied by a further breakdown in the clan system, and the response of many was to move abroad. Selkirk was convinced that the Highlanders' unique character, customs, and way of life could be preserved abroad and he argued that emigration was not only inevitable, but was also beneficial to the British empire. It was important to secure the colonies against American expansion, and in his opinion, the settlement of what he perceived to be loyal and militaristic Highlanders would achieve this. The earl stood virtually alone in his pro-emigration views at this time but he successfully assisted the emigration of approximately 800 Highlanders from the north-west of Scotland to Prince Edward Island in 1803, and thereafter turned his attention to the Red River.[48]

The Red River region, depicted in Alexander Mackenzie's published account of his explorations, had captured Selkirk's imagination as a fertile land, well suited to settlement, and he had suggested taking a Highland Regiment to the area as early as 1803.[49] However, his desire to form a colony in the prairies did not actually materialise until 1810 when he gained access to the HBC and his proposal to form a colony were accepted. The broader implications of Selkirk's planned settlement at Red River were huge, threatening the survival of two groups in fur-trade society, the NWC and the Métis.

The Métis were a growing population of people with mixed Scottish, French and native descent, who were progeny of the NWC traders and native women. They lived on the plains surrounding Red River, hunting buffalo and making pemmican, dried ground buffalo meat mixed with berries, which they sold to the trading companies. The construction of a settlement would undermine these activities, as the settlers could disrupt the buffalo hunt, which would interfere with the Metis' livelihood of selling buffalo meat to the NWC; thereby also hindering the NWC's ability to trade in the northwest of the country, as they were dependent on a food supply of pemmican. Likewise, the location of the colony intercepted the NWC's transport routes across the continent, between the beaver-rich territory of Athabasca and their base in Montreal. This could hinder the NWC's trade and, at the same time, offer the HBC a competitive advantage as the colony provided a convenient base from which to conduct rival trade in the north-west. The final bone of contention concerned the availability of, and increased dependency on, food supplies in the region. The NWC employees and the mixed-blood population were often close to starvation and they feared competition for these limited resources. Overall, the settlement was a real sticking-point with the NWC traders, who believed that the colony was really designed to cripple their business and therefore decided to oppose it to the full, 'whatever might be the consequences' as it 'struck at the root' of their concern.[50]

In a surreptitious move, the NWC proprietors began to voice their objections to the colony through anonymous protestations in the *Inverness Journal*. Elsewhere, relations of NWC trader Alexander Mackenzie spread unfavourable rumours about the HBC in Stornoway, where the first band of prospective settlers had congregated for embarkation. This band of Irish, Glaswegian, Highland and Lewis men had been hired as HBC employees to construct the settlement and thereafter remain as colonists. The expedition got off to a poor start as, following on from the NWC's smear campaign, a military press-ganger, Captain Mackenzie, attempted to dissuade the colonists from departing and tried to coax them off the vessel.[51] The ships finally departed in July 1811, far later than intended, and after a long crossing arrived at York Factory in September, too late to commence the long inland voyage to the colony.

The first settlers eventually arrived at Red River in August 1812 with Miles Macdonnell, the appointed governor of the colony. Macdonnell was a Scottish emigrant who left his homeland in 1773, settling in Glengarry, Upper Canada. He attempted to forge a political career and ran for election to the Legislative Assembly of Upper Canada in 1800, but failed to receive the nomination. When Lord Selkirk offered him the appointment as governor of the settlement in 1809, he welcomed the opportunity of a position that offered status, despite the fact that this office put him at cross-purposes with many of his relatives who worked in the NWC.[52] These contrary aims were soon evident on the settlers' arrival at Red River, as the NWC had already begun spreading malevolent reports in that quarter. A Métis interpreter for the HBC, Bostonais Pangman, noted that the NWC was 'inflaming the minds of the Indians against the Colonist and the Hudson's Bay Company's traders'. He feared that if this was not urgently checked, there would be negative repercussions. To thwart any bad outcome, the natives were reassured by the HBC that they could anticipate only amity and goodwill from the settlers and themselves.[53]

As a second party of Irish and Highland colonists prepared to depart from Sligo in the summer of 1812, international conflict broke out between Britain and the United States.[54] The war of 1812 presented Lord Selkirk with an opportunity to raise a Highland regiment and help defend British North America. He intended to provide 1,000 soldiers, on the condition that the regiment and their families were permitted to settle at the Red River colony when fighting ceased. He tried to raise these recruits from the Sutherland estates in Scotland, but faced difficulties in securing financial support so the proposed regiment never materialised. In order to ward off discontent, he eventually had to pay for a small number of the intended soldiers and families to migrate to the colony as settlers in 1813.

The war of 1812 was actually a development of great significance to the fur trade as it also had a direct effect upon the operations of the NWC. Military confrontation was largely centred on the Great Lakes area, which again interfered with the NWC's transport and communication routes to Montreal. This close proximity to the conflict also resulted in military service for some members of the NWC. Shortly after the outbreak of fighting, 200 of its voyageurs took part in an attack on Fort Michilimackinac, at Lake Huron, under a British commander. Some traders became so caught up in these military operations that they were actually supplied with military uniforms; this close involvement with the armed forces may have contributed to the development of a military psyche within the Company.[55]

Perhaps a more important repercussion of the NWC's inclusion in the conflict with America was the cementing of good relations between the NWC and the government of Lower Canada. The partners of the Company were already in favour with the government due to their contributions to the development of a Canadian economic and social infrastructure. They invested profits from the fur trade into other industries and businesses such as shipping, merchandising, and supply, and created embryonic industrial diversification in Canada. In addition, they founded and supported institutions in Montreal including churches and social clubs, and actively participated in the politics of Lower Canada. Assisting in the victory at Michilimackinac merely reinforced the bond between the NWC traders and the government, which was to work in their favour in the later fur-trade conflict.[56]

The second phase of the fur-trade conflict really kicked off in 1814 when the governor of the Red River colony, Miles Macdonnell, undertook some initiatives that impinged on both the Métis and NWC. Relations had remained fairly peaceable at the settlement until this point, but as the colony remained uncultivated and food supplies were consistently scarce, Macdonnell attempted to secure essential rations for the settlers by prohibiting the export of pemmican. He banned the removal of provisions from Red River without his permission for a period of twelve months and posted the proclamation at various NWC posts. To emphasise his command, Macdonnell instructed that cargoes of pemmican should be seized from the NWC posts of Fort Gibraltar and La Souris. According to the NWC, he had apparently 'taken from the Hudson's Bay Company 200 bags of Pemmican & insisted on having an equal number from the North West Company which being very properly refused, He took measures for seizing the whole, in which he succeeded – the servants of the N.W. Co being frightened with a show of Hostility & high sounding words – and not being supported by those who had the Charge of the Department'.[57] In response to this sudden confiscation of provisions, the NWC traders banded together to confront Miles Macdonnell, but eventually compromised and allowed him to take 200 bags of pemmican in order to avoid engaging in hostility.

The NWC discussed the growing friction with the colony during their annual meeting at Fort William in July 1814. The proprietors were confident that any repetition of the recent events would be abortive, as they had decided to defend their property at any cost. They agreed that the wintering men should assemble in case of further plunder and that all of their posts should be fortified in case of violent opposition. The minutes of the meeting indicate that defence was the NWC's priority, but other evidence suggests that in private, some of the men like Alexander Greenfield Macdonnell (the cousin and brother-in-law of Miles Macdonnell) and Duncan Cameron were keen to 'commence open hostilities against the enemy in the Red River'.[58]

What then transpired on 30 August 1814 was the tearing down of the proclamation and the spread of bad rumours about the colony by Macdonnell and Cameron, dressed in military uniform and referring to themselves as Captain and Lieutenant. Miles Macdonnell was not worried about their threats to resist his proclamation, as the settlers had been sent military supplies in 1813 for the purposes of defence, and he now had plenty of well-armed colonists organised – although not necessarily eager – to fight.[59] He felt that his team was strong enough to defeat the local NWC members if they dared to defy his authority.

The settlers certainly seemed to have had the necessary courage as, only a few days after the regimental visit of the NWC, they leapt to the defence of Sheriff Spencer. He had carried out the former pemmican confiscation with the assistance of HBC employees and was subsequently arrested by armed Nor'westers. Both the settlers and servants objected to his arrest and armed themselves, firing a musket at NWC canoes and threatening to 'blow them to pieces'.[60] Cannon were also loaded and pointed at the NWC, while a man stood aside with a lit match. Fortunately, the caution of Mr Macdonnell stopped them from firing.

The pemmican proscription had also incited grievances among the Métis. The HBC had formerly found some members of the Métis to be helpful in countering spiteful reports disseminated by the NWC. However, the ban on the export of pemmican, coupled with a minor dispute between the HBC's Peter Fidler and Bostonais Pangman over some equipment – resulting in the latter's resignation from the HBC in 1814 – helped to alienate the Métis from the settlement.[61] Their relationship with the colony deteriorated further when a second decree was enforced in July 1814, prohibiting the Métis from hunting the buffalo on horse-back. Macdonnell's grounds were just, as running buffalo drove the animals away from the settlement and made provisions both scarce and difficult to bring home, but the proclamation endangered the Métis' means of subsistence and denied them their traditional rights.[62] Their response was to assert themselves as a nation, and although it is not clear to what extent the Métis were tutored by the NWC in their political stance and subsequent organisation as a military group, the connection between the two was particularly strong.[63]

Mental and military preparations for open hostility were occurring among all of the key participants in the conflicts at this time. Both the HBC and Lord Selkirk were attempting to organise some form of military body as a protective measure for the Red River settlement. Rumours had begun to spread in late 1814 of an attack on the colony, and they wanted the British government to authorise troops to be stationed at the settlement. In 1815 Joseph Berens, the governor of the HBC, wrote to Earl Bathurst, the Secretary of State for the Colonies, and expressed his fears over how far some members of the NWC 'may be carried by the thirst of gain, combined with the habit of acrimonious rivalship'.[64]

It was, however, an adverse time to be seeking governmental involvement. The British Colonial Office, established in 1795, badly neglected its commercial interests in British North America. It was a small bureaucracy with a large jurisdiction, and was primarily preoccupied with the Napoleonic wars. It is not clear where the government stood in relation to the Red River settlement. Although it wished to retain the British population, it was not wholly opposed to emigration to British North America, as planned colonisation could help protect British strategic interests from American expansion.[65] However, the Red River settlement had been instituted entirely independently of the Colonial Office, without its permission or approval. In view of that, and the fact that Selkirk and the HBC were engaged in a private quarrel with another commercial company, it is surprising that Earl Bathurst gave the matter any attention at all.

Earl Bathurst directed Sir Gordon Drummond, the Lieutenant-General in Lower Canada, to investigate the legitimacy of reports forwarded by the directors of the HBC in February 1815, that the Red River colony was 'in imminent danger of being destroyed'.[66] The validity of his enquiry was hampered by erroneous communication from Lord Selkirk who had conveyed that the native inhabitants of the Red River area, the Salteaux, were responsible for the threat, rather than the mixed-blood Métis. In addition to this, Drummond was not entirely impartial. The NWC was already highly esteemed in Lower Canada and he considered its employees 'to be persons of the utmost integrity and respectability'.[67] Following interviews with the NWC partners, Drummond, unsurprisingly, recommended that military support was unnecessary and not feasible. In turn, the British government did not sanction military support for the settlement.

Therefore in 1815, the efforts of the NWC and the Métis to annihilate the colony were able to commence. The Métis adopted the role of overt antagonists, harassing and assaulting the HBC and Red River colonists, in much the same manner as the NWC had tormented the HBC servants at their trading posts in the early phase of conflict. With their mixed-blood sons serving as warriors, the NWC was able to assume a more passive stance and gain the confidence of the increasingly disillusioned settlers. They encouraged them to desert the colony, enticing them with the offer of free transportation to Canada.[68]

The subtlety of the NWC campaign was complemented by the aggressive operation of the Métis who led an assault on the settlement in February, holding the migrants and servants imprisoned for six days. By the spring of 1815, the majority of settlers had been impelled by the Métis, and coaxed by the NWC, to leave the Red River colony and relocate to Canada with the assistance of the Nor'westers. Some settlers remained until July, when Governor Macdonnell surrendered and was taken prisoner. The Métis instructed the rest of the inhabitants to leave the colony within two days and to reinforce this order burned their houses and fired on the twenty-eight servants and colonists and their families during the night, with ammunition and arms provided by their NWC allies. Peter Fidler had no option but to lead the remaining migrants away from the settlement.[69]

Conflict continues at the trading posts

Although the tensions had grown to include the Métis, Lord Selkirk, and the settlers, it essentially remained a competition between the two trading companies. Ross Cox reported that 'the infernal spirit of rivalry … attained such a height, that the mildest and the bravest of both parties became in turn the most reckless desperadoes. Force was the only tribunal to which they appealed, and arms their only arguments'.[70] Clashes between individuals continued at the trading posts, and the new assertiveness of the HBC employees only served to fuel tensions. This was evident at Red Deer River in 1813, when Orcadian Alexander Kennedy became involved in an altercation with NWC proprietor, Mr Donald. The latter had tried to prevent a group of Stone Indians from trading with the HBC and, when Kennedy intervened, Mr Donald 'poured out a torrent of abuse … menacing me with his sword'. Kennedy retaliated with a diatribe of his own until Mr Donald 'at last struck me with his sword, which cut me on the back part of the head, & also cut thro' the neck of my coat'. Guns were soon produced and Kennedy fired at his adversary, grazing the inside of his thigh. He dodged an avenging shot and went inside to collect ammunition and stitch his head wound. Mr Donald exploited Kennedy's absence and took all the natives into his own post. Realising that he had only two men with one gun between them, Kennedy, perhaps wisely, let the situation rest.[71]

Continuing skirmishes such as this at the posts and the earlier violence at Isle à la Crosse had forced the HBC to exercise caution in its plans to compete directly for trade in the lucrative Athabasca district. Men like Colin Robertson, a former member of the NWC from Perthshire, who had experience in the field, advised the unseasoned London Committee that trading rivalry would be particularly fierce in the north-west. Robertson warned the directors that the men might have to engage in military activity as the opposition was bound to throw obstacles in their path. He agreed to lead a team into the Athabasca but requested muskets and ammunition for his expedition, as he anticipated that an intrepid appearance might deter their rivals from getting in the way.[72]

The HBC's Athabasca mission proceeded in 1815 and Colin Robertson led the expedition as far as Assiniboia, where he encountered Peter Fidler, accompanied by fleeing Red River settlers. Robertson departed from the Athabascan team and escorted the colonists and servants back to the colony, where he reinstated the settlement.[73] This interference seriously aggrieved the Métis, and as a result, the hostilities soon began to spill over, affecting nearby HBC trading posts around the colony. In one instance, the fury of the Métis was directed at the HBC employees residing at Brandon House. In October 1815, one member of the HBC, John Richards McKay, wrote to Colin Robertson complaining that the Métis 'have got two of the Captains cannon in their war house pointed to us to prevent us from working, they are determined on killing us all … perhaps this will be the last letter you will have from us'.[74] He had received a 24-hour ultimatum from Alexander Fraser, a Métis clerk of the NWC, that they should abandon the country or be killed.

In the meantime, John Clarke replaced Colin Robertson as leader of the HBC expedition into the Athabasca. His group successfully erected Fort Wedderburn and other subsidiary posts near Lake Athabasca. However, their means of support was particularly precarious in this remote part of the country. It soon became clear that despite undergoing preparations for the trip since 1814, the expedition of 1815 was poorly organised and the group was short of provisions. Optimistic hopes that rations could be procured from local natives were rapidly dashed when it became evident that, once again, the NWC had intimidated the natives away from interacting with the HBC. The Nor'westers had generated such fear among the native tribes that they became too frightened to trade with, and hunt for, members of the expedition. To increase their chances of survival, the HBC contingent of over ninety men dispersed across the north-west, seeking aid at Fort Vermillion and the NWC's Fort Chipewyan. Although the NWC eventually saved the lives of some, by offering food on the condition that they sacrifice their trade goods and pledge not to work for the HBC, it was too late for sixteen others who died of starvation in late 1815 and early 1816.[75]

It is unlikely that this news from the north-west would have crossed the Atlantic by January 1816, but the intelligence of the earlier fracas at the colony may have been transmitted, prompting Earl Bathurst to comment that he had heard of 'the violent proceedings which have taken place in the most remote parts of His Majesty's North American dominions, and of the outrages committed by the agents and servants of the Hudson's Bay and North-West companies against each other, it appears highly necessary to adopt some measures for restraining a system of violence which, if persevered in, may ultimately lead not only to the destruction of the individuals concerned, but of others of His Majesty's subjects'.[76] Bathurst instructed Gordon Drummond to tell the companies to abstain from violence and emphasised that the British government was determined to punish anyone who disturbed the peace in such a manner, bringing shame on Britain.

However, the government's earlier disregard of such tensions, coupled with their resolution not to provide military support, prompted discussion between the HBC and Lord Selkirk about the formation of an independent military corps. Selkirk had suggested to Andrew Colvile in 1815 that some HBC employees should be equipped with weapons and that the Company should form a small army to support the officers when needed. He believed there was no harm in organising a section of the HBC as an armed body as the Royal charter seemed to authorise this right.[77]

In March 1816, the HBC Committee sanctioned Selkirk's military proposition, as rumours had grown of an imminent full-scale attack upon the settlement. They instructed Robert Semple, Miles Macdonnell's Scottish replacement as governor of the colony, to form a volunteer corps out of the Red River settlers and Company servants. A secret and confidential letter informed Semple that he was to use this army only for defence and warned that the men should not act as an army under the command of officers. It was emphasised that their conduct must remain within the laws of England. However, an announcement, one month later, that Earl Bathurst had referred the case of conflict between the two companies to 'His Majesty's Law servants', prompted the Company to suspend Semple's orders to form a corps.[78] Yet Lord Selkirk was still troubled by the opposition's conduct in 1815, and was unwilling to abandon hope of arranging a military force to protect the colony. He was aware that some De Meuron soldiers were due to be discharged from Canadian duty in the spring of 1816 and, with no other options available, took the initiative of engaging 100 of these men. On 18 June 1816, Selkirk set out from Montreal with the intention of taking his army, dressed in military attire, to safeguard the Red River colony.[79]

PLATE I. *Beaver and muskrat.* The beaver is the largest rodent in Canada, weighing between 15 kg and 35 kg. The top layer of its coat is long, coarse and oily and the under layer is soft, dense, short, and fine. In long and cold winters the animal's fur thickened, making it more valuable; the search for such prime pelts led the fur trading economy into the northwest region of the Athabasca. The beaver's role in the exploration and development of Canada was such that the animal has now been recognised as a national emblem. (Library and Archives Canada, R9266-2557, Peter Winkworth Collection of Canadiana)

PLATE 2. *Hudson's Bay Company banner.* The HBC used this coat of arms and motto from the seventeenth century onwards. It depicts four beaver, a sitting fox for the crest and two elk on either side. The motto *Pro pelle cutem* means 'skin for a skin' and could be a biblical derivation from the book of Job's Vulgate phrase (2:4). Other interpretations include, 'we risk our skins to get furs'. This would apply to the financial risk of going into the fur trading business and would also be pertinent to the employees who risked their lives in the fur trade. Another possibility is that they wanted the skin, *cutem*, for the sake of the fleece, *pro pelle*, i.e. the beaver pelt was not wanted in its own right, but to provide wool for the felter. (See E.E. Rich, 'Pro Pelle Cutem, The Hudson's Bay Company Motto', *Manitoba Paegant*, Vol. 6, No. 3 April 1961) (Stromness Museum)

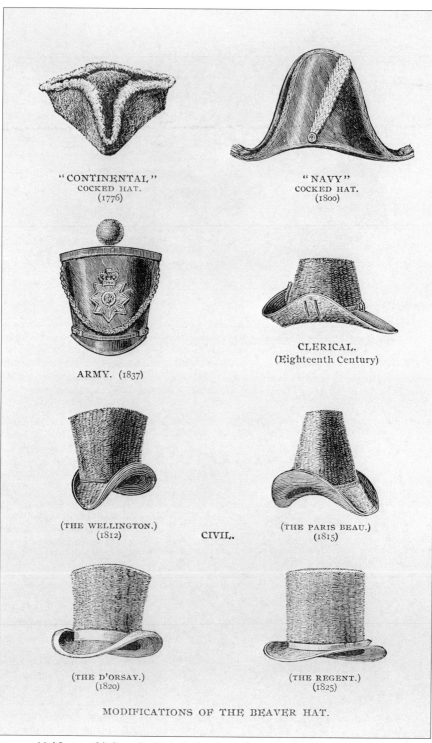

"CONTINENTAL,"
COCKED HAT.
(1776)

"NAVY"
COCKED HAT.
(1800)

ARMY. (1837)

CLERICAL.
(Eighteenth Century)

(THE WELLINGTON.)
(1812)

CIVIL.

(THE PARIS BEAU.)
(1815)

(THE D'ORSAY.)
(1820)

(THE REGENT.)
(1825)

MODIFICATIONS OF THE BEAVER HAT.

PLATE 3. *Modifications of the beaver hat.* Beaver fur is waterproof, supple and holds its shape, making it an ideal raw material from which to make felt hats. The felting process was eased by a procedure called 'carroting', in which the pelt was treated with a mixture containing mercury to make the hair mat more easily. This exposure to mercury caused some hat makers to go insane, giving rise to the phrase, 'mad as a hatter'. British-produced hats supplied the domestic market and were also exported to Europe and the colonies. In the nineteenth century, the fashion for beaver hats was gradually replaced with a trend for silk hats. (Library and Archives Canada, C-017338)

PLATE 4. *Cannon used to signal the arrival of the HBC's convoy in Stromness harbour.* (Austin Ball)

PLATE 5. *Hudson's Bay Company and Northwest Company Forts at Île-à-la-Crosse, 1820.* These posts were situated next to Lake Île-la-Crosse in present-day Saskatchewan, Canada. It was a strategic location, providing access to the Athabasca area. Attempts to maintain a stronghold on this frontier resulted in many scenes of conflict and violence between the two fur-trading companies. The HBC post was abandoned several times during the trade competition, burned down by the NWC in 1811 and then re-established in 1814. (George Back, Library and Archives Canada, Acc. No. 1994-254-1.40R Acquired with the assistance of Hoechst and Celanese Canada and with a grant from the Department of Canadian Heritage under the Cultural Property Export and Import Act)

PLATE 6. *Portaging a canoe.* Travelling and exploring were essential to the fur trade and usually undertaken on the river networks that flowed into Hudson's Bay. There were occasional breaks between the bodies of water, and canoes and cargo had then to be carried by foot across the land. The Methye Portage, near Île-à-la-Crosse, is one of the longest portages, running 19 km from the end of the Churchill River System to the Clearwater River, which runs into the Athabasca river. (Dennis Gale, Library and Archives Canada, Acc. No. 1970-188-1963 W.H. Coverdale Collection of Canadiana)

PLATE 7. *Indian hunters pursuing the buffalo in early spring.* (Peter Rindisbacher, 1806-1834, Library and Archives Canada, Acc. No. 1981-55-68 Bushnell Collection)

PLATE 8. *A hunter-family of Cree Indians at York Fort.* The Cree were among the first members of the First Nations encountered by HBC employees at Hudson's Bay and became some of the earliest traders. They assisted in provisioning and maintaining early HBC posts and became known as the 'Homeguard'. The HBC posts served as a base for these groups and a place to leave children, the elderly and the unwell, when the rest went hunting. They also received medical assistance and imported food supplies when natural sources of food were low. (Peter Rindisbacher, 1806-1834, Library and Archives Canada, Acc. No. 1988-250-16)

PLATE 9. (*Right*) *Beaded pocket-watch holder.* This was taken to Orkney by two of William Flett's mixed-blood children in the nineteenth century. Flett was from Firth in Orkney and entered the HBC in 1782, serving as a labourer at York factory. He retired to the Red River Settlement, dying in 1823 and leaving four mixed-blood children to his native wife, 'Saskatchewan'. At least two of these offspring were sent to Orkney. (Stromness Museum)

PLATE 10. (*Below*) *William Tomison's School, South Ronaldsay, Orkney.* Fur trader William Tomison entered the HBC in 1760 and, after a long and successful career, retired to his homeland of Orkney. He bequeathed funds to establish a school, which was eventually built in 1851, near his former home, 'Dundas House' in South Ronaldsay. The school was closed in the 1960s, but the building still stands and a plaque was erected to mark his generous contribution to Orcadian society. (Charles Rigg)

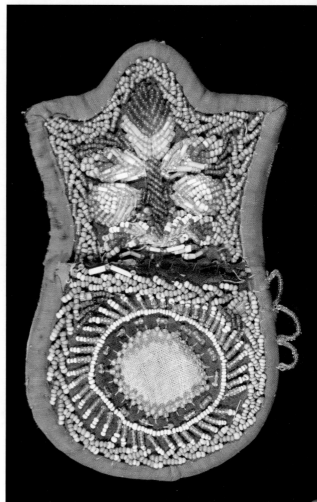

Massacre and retaliation

The following day, as Selkirk began his journey to assist the colony, the most notorious calamity in fur-trade history occurred at Seven Oaks, north of the forks of the Assiniboine and Red Rivers. A group of fifty to seventy armed men, who were largely Métis and led by Cuthbert Grant, the mixed-blood son of Scottish fur trader Cuthbert Grant, bypassed the Red River settlement. It was later alleged that the Métis were actually on their way to meet NWC canoes with provisions, and in order to avoid antagonism with the Scottish settlers, kept a span of two miles between themselves and the colony. However, long-held suspicions of an attack meant that the colony's governor, Robert Semple, with thirty armed colonists, set out to discover the interlopers' intentions. Although a variety of accounts detailing the subsequent sequence of events emerged in the aftermath of this encounter, and each side accused the other of instigating violence, the traditional report is that a gun went off accidentally, from the colonists' side, and general shooting ensued from the Métis.[80] It is indisputable that the incident ended in mass bloodshed in which the governor, twenty-one settlers and one Métis were killed. Rumours suggested that the violence did not end there, as some of the bodies were reportedly found mutilated and scalped, which initiated usage of the term 'massacre' in reference to the incident.[81]

News of the attack spread quickly throughout Rupert's Land, and in August 1816 James Slater, master at Red Lake, informed colleagues at Albany that he had received an account of the colony 'being destroy'd by the Canadians & upwards of Five and Twenty ... being kill'd'.[82] Although the Métis had carried out the assault, the HBC and Lord Selkirk considered the NWC responsible. Their assignment of culpability was not entirely partisan as one native chief, Catawabite, testified that a NWC trader had suggested that his tribe should go to war against the HBC and the Red River colony in 1815, on behalf of the NWC.[83]

Upon hearing of the atrocities, Selkirk detoured via the NWC headquarters at Fort William where many of those who had escaped slaughter had been detained as prisoners. Some of the NWC partners were in residence, participating in their annual meeting, and had not anticipated such a visit. With his military unit in tow, Lord Selkirk presented NWC partner William McGillivray with a warrant of arrest. George Keith from the NWC commented that Selkirk had 'thrown away the scabbard after having unsheathed the sword'.[84] He went on to enter Fort William where he arrested more rival opponents and secured the release of the remaining imprisoned settlers from Red River.

The events of 1816, including the carnage at Red River, starvation in the Athabasca, and revenge at Fort William, were the climax but not the end of many years of tension and conflict. Selkirk was not alone in his determination to make a strong stand against the opposition. When the HBC learned of the proceedings of 1816, they expressed their lament over the 'the melancholy & horrid atrocities which have been committed in the Red River country', the death of Mr Semple, and the distress and loss of life among their men employed in the Athabasca mission.[85] They were clearly disturbed by the reports, but remained chiefly concerned with the injury to their own business interests.

The London Committee resolved that its workforce must now oppose the NWC in the district of the Athabasca with all its might. It was absolutely essential to gain trading opportunities in this area, and in order to succeed, the HBC instructed its employees to form a staunch resistance to further attack. They further explained that 'we approve of your collecting all the force you can for the purpose of defending yourselves & the property of the Company in case of any attack being made. The stronger you are, the less risk there will be of your being attacked, but we cannot too often or too strongly impress upon you the impolicy & illegality of that system of retaliation, which we fear has been practised by our people, as well as by the NWCO, tho' perhaps not to the same extent or with the same violence as by them'.[86] By adhering to the law and refraining from violence outwith self-defence, the HBC tried to ensure that blame would rest with the NWC, and the HBC would not be found culpable.

However, under the NWC's continuing and relentless campaign of coercion in the Athabasca, the HBC servants had few opportunities to make any kind of stand, within or outside the law. The opposition was equally determined to win the trade in the north-west, and rival trader Archibald Norman McLeod had boasted of his intentions to drive the HBC 'from the Country of Athabasca by fair or foul means'.[87] This included masquerading as a Justice of the Peace with fellow Highlander Duncan Campbell and unlawfully taking HBC servants prisoner at Fort Wedderburn in September 1816. The stand-off continued in the north-west, and in 1817 again played out at Isle à la Crosse, a centre of friction in the previous decade. Some members of the HBC were awoken during the night and seized by their armed opponents, commanded by Aberdonian Samuel Black, who claimed to act as such 'for the purpose of preserving the quiet of the Country and to leave revenge for the proceedings of Lord Selkirk'.[88] The HBC employees were then detained as their adversaries raided their stores. These prisoners may have been the men that Ross Cox later referred to in his narrative of the trading conflict, in which the NWC held twenty men captive, some of whom were Orcadians 'miserably supplied with provisions' and all of whom seemed 'dejected and emaciated'.[89]

Rather than offering support to its abused employees, the HBC Committee chastised the efforts of the workforce in defending itself so poorly against such robbery, illegal imprisonment and starvation. They disparagingly commented that 'to suffer such injuries if you have it in your power to prevent it, is a weakness unbecoming any man'.[90] The directors' naïvety led them to query whether the latest outrages might have been avoided through more prescience and activity from its own servants. Without direct experience of the challenges encountered in this far-flung territory, the HBC Committee was clearly unable to guide its employees through the crisis in which they found themselves.

Reconciliation

It was therefore fortunate that His Royal Highness the Prince Regent issued orders to the trading companies in 1817, demanding appeasement. An investigation had been ordered into the tragic events at Red River, and in the interim all violent opposition was to cease, and soldiers were instructed to depart each Company's service.[91] Although the conflict did not die down immediately, it did begin to play out in the courts of law, as opposed to the fur trading territories.

Some NWC partners had been captured during the conflict, and the HBC took advice from Earl Bathurst and transported them to Britain for trial. In September 1817, Orkney agent George Geddes was informed that one of the returning HBC ships had a member of the NWC imprisoned on board. The Committee was anxious that he might be assisted to escape during the vessel's stop in the Orkney Islands. To prevent this, Geddes was instructed to warn the captain not to anchor in Stromness harbour, to ensure that the captive remained in their custody. The prisoner was to be taken directly to London where the Captain would await further instructions from the London Committee, unless the captive had since been demanded by another person under a writ of Habeas Corpus.[92]

A problem with indicting opposing traders in Britain soon emerged. The Colonial Office finally determined that jurisdiction actually lay with the governments in Canada, as the offences were not murder, treason or manslaughter. In addition, because the location of the crime was in territories outwith His Majesty's jurisdiction, they argued that imprisoned traders could not be transported back to Canada under the Habeas Corpus Act of 1679, and therefore must be freed. As prisoners were subsequently released in Britain, some then made their way back across the Atlantic to take legal action against wrongful imprisonment. For instance, NWC partner Duncan Cameron had been arrested by Colin Robertson at Fort Gibraltar in March 1816 and then transported to Britain. He was later freed and returned to Canada to prosecute Colin Robertson for illegal imprisonment.[93]

The repercussions of the conflict were becoming glaringly obvious to those still involved in the fur trade, and it was evident that decades of rivalry had wreaked havoc upon the fur trade and fur-trade society.[94] The Orcadian men held captive at Isle à la Crosse just 'wished they were safe home again' and in contrast to the view that the NWC traders were ruthless bullies and thus unperturbed by the vicious contest, there are indications that they too were disgusted with the extremities of the trading rivalry.[95] Many of the NWC partners had become despondent as early as 1815 when Simon McGillivray observed 'a general wish to retire from the Country'.[96] Some men were averse to continuing in the fur trade due to physical frailty, but others had become increasingly rattled by the aggressive nature of the conflict, and the mounting casualties. One trader, Wentzel, reflected upon the ongoing rivalry in 1820, and surmised:

> How long this contest is yet to continue a subject of regret to every good man is still in the bosom of time, no one knows. The weight of purses may serve to keep alive expenses and loss, and, by that means, lengthen the contest, but, eventually, both parties may find themselves involved in the same ruin, for whichever side preponderates, must remain a long while in possession of the country before they can expect to retrieve their affairs in a sufficient manner to afford them profit … It may perhaps turn out that many of the most respectable traders now in the country will be obliged from age, broken constitutions and other infirmities, to retire before the termination of the existing troubles, or remain to leave their bones in the country where golden dreams attracted them, with the melancholy reflection of having lost their all amongst savage nations and in savage parts.[97]

Fortunately for the fur traders, the termination of hostilities happened sooner than Wentzel had expected. In 1820, the British government sent a formal warning to both companies reiterating that hostilities must cease. On top of this, both companies were in financial straits, and although the NWC suffered more acutely as its money was rapidly consumed through conducting trade in the distant Athabasca, the HBC was £105,000 in debt. As with the union of the XY and NWC in 1804, it was the death of a key figure in the dispute, Lord Selkirk, that really paved the way for a truce. Much of the ill-feeling from 1811 onwards had stemmed from animosity towards Lord Selkirk, and after his death, an amalgamation was decided upon. Most parties agreed that 'it was high time something of the kind took place' and thus on 26 March 1821, the two companies signed a formal coalition agreement, pooling their resources, sharing the profits and operating under the terms of the HBC charter, and under the name of the HBC.[98]

Fur-trade wars?

The fur-trade conflict had endured for forty years and played out in two different phases. In many ways it was unparalleled, due to the far-flung location of Rupert's Land, the ethnicity of participants, and the geographical, techno-logical, and societal scope of the territories in which the traders resided, which shaped the scale, objectives and tactics used in the competition. However, the length of the dispute is reminiscent of feuds in sixteenth-century Scotland, whereby clans became embroiled in clashes over territory and land-holding. Although such vendettas were less prevalent by the late seventeenth century and involved very few clans, it is possible that this heritage, coupled with residence in a land where tribal warfare among the native people was common, influenced the Scottish trade dispute in Rupert's Land.[99]

Clashes in the fur-trade contest, particularly in the early conflict, tended to be sporadic, small-scale and characterised by low-level violence, similar to the guerrilla campaigns employed by Scottish clans in the Highlands and occasionally the Lowlands, and also native tribes in North America. The traders were spread out at posts across Rupert's Land and a small number of individuals manned each post, so that only a few men were involved in each hostile inter-action. The terrain on which they traded and fought was vast, and the form of transportation available, the canoe, impeded swift manoeuvrability. In addition, as the trading posts were widely distributed across the territory, communications between posts regarding hostilities were slow. Therefore, in the first phase of competition, until 1811, the ability of the trading companies to 'make war' was poor.

However, this changed as the hostilities entered the second phase in 1814, as the conflict expanded and the number of participants involved in the struggle, on both sides, was higher. Accordingly, military practice grew in scale and sophistication in relation to the population density, terrain, and weaponry.[100] The population became more localised than previously, and discord became increasingly static and largely centred on Red River, and latterly the Athabasca. At the same time, weaponry and transportation improved as cannon and horses were introduced. Consequently, the ability to commence active, large-scale and organised hostility was easier.

The tactics used by opponents during the struggle often mimicked facets of tribal and clan warfare, whereby raiding, thieving and destruction of property were common, and deaths few.[101] Raiding and plundering were evident in fur-trade rivalry as early as 1788 at Manchester House, and continued to be used as a means of disabling the opposition until the close of the conflict. In the typical fur-trade raid, as in a Native American tribal raid, furs, provisions and trade goods such as alcohol, tobacco and ammunition were taken, and few or no opponents were harmed, despite the assailants being armed. However, these campaigns often had a more enduring and sinister undertone. In the Scottish Highlands of the sixteenth and seventeenth century, where survival was never guaranteed, injury to a rival clan members' cattle and the destruction of crops were as significant as directly killing men.[102] The situation was similar in fur-trade society two centuries later: when rivals destroyed their enemy's fishing nets or the settlers' crops, or prevented access to a means of subsistence via native interactions, they were effectively securing the death of their opponents, as the NWC did in the Athabasca in 1816.

Additionally, following some raids, such as one at Brandon House, the plunderers celebrated for days, as warriors did after tribal raids. In fact, in the later phase of conflict, the Métis and some members of the NWC adopted the guise of warriors during such campaigns. Prior to attacks, they applied paint on the face and body, which were traditionally viewed as tokens of going to war, and during assaults they uttered war-cries and the war-whoop. In May 1816, HBC trader James Sutherland 3rd set out down the river with servants and furs from Qu'Appelle to Hudson Bay. Downstream, he was met by some Métis and Canadians, who according to Peter Fidler had 'their faces all painted in the most horrid & terrific forms & dressed like Indians and all armed with Guns, Pistols, Swords and Spears, & several had Bows & Arrows; and made the War-whoop or yell like the Natives in immediately attacking their enemies'.[103] The band of attackers imprisoned the HBC men for a week and seized their furs. Also, during the aforementioned incident at Brandon House, the HBC's adversaries were dressed as combatants with war-paint, singing a song, flying a flag and beating a drum in 'a little army'.[104]

Another feature of the fur-trade conflict that echoed tribal warfare was the taking of prisoners, and few of the key figures in the competition succeeded in avoiding capture. Although prisoners were not killed, sacrificed or enslaved, there were on occasion elements of ill-treatment, and even torture of opponents. A number of HBC employees were tortured by starvation prior to detention as a means of forcing them to surrender. In addition, some traders were ill-treated while in captivity: two HBC men, John Mowat and John Pritchard, were kept in irons during their imprisonment by the NWC, while others were beaten.[105]

Contrary to many accounts, actions of cruelty were not confined to the NWC traders; the HBC traders were also at fault. The Orcadians held captive at Isle à la Crosse 'spoke in no flattering terms of the treatment they received from their captors; but admitted that such of the NorthWesters as had been made prisoners by their party fared no better'.[106] An example of this is when a group of HBC employees and discharged soldiers acted under the command of HBC governor William Williams and intercepted and ambushed an expedition of Nor'westers at Grand Rapids who were en route to Athabasca in June 1819. The NWC traders were taken prisoner and apparently maltreated by their rivals: Mr Shaw was abused 'in the grossest manner'. Some of the men were held hostage at York Fort where they were detained in a small room with bars on the window, and vermin, dirt and maggots in the bed. Apparently, despite being ill, the captives were refused medicine and given only the 'refuse from the kitchen' as food. One of the prisoners, Benjamin Frobisher, had reportedly been hit on the head with the butt of a gun prior to reaching York Fort and had since suffered dizziness and difficulty in standing. Reduced to a 'mere skeleton' and having been held prisoner since June, Frobisher decided to make his escape in September. Accompanied by two others, Frobisher travelled over 500 miles with little food, and latterly only leather moccasins for sustenance. Unfortunately, as the small party neared the sanctuary of a NWC post, Frobisher died while awaiting relief from the 'last stages of wretchedness'.[107]

The trading companies practised traditional forms of warfare on one another, but it does not necessarily imply that the competition amounted to a war. At no point during the fur trade conflict was an official declaration of war made by either of the parties involved. At the same time, the conflict was between two private trading corporations, not states, and there was not a high degree of military organisation. Although the HBC had considered the formation of a military body, and the Métis were the 'warriors' of the NWC, traders were still focused on their everyday business and work duties. They only formed military units temporarily and as needed, until the latter years of the contest when De Meuron soldiers were employed. There were casualties and one battle, but the feud did not escalate into absolute or total warfare: the majority of fur-trade society was still focused on business, and the traders were not assembled together or deployed as resources to fight in the conflict.

In fact, the extent of the conflict really needs to be kept in perspective. Relations between personnel in the two companies were not consistently hostile and it was not unusual for men from rival posts to socialise together. At Red Lake, which was later a scene of hostility, special occasions such as Christmas were marked by a joint dinner and dance including both groups of traders in the 1790s. High-ranking members of each Company offered one another support when the natives were being troublesome. For instance, Duncan McGillivray from the NWC and Mr Tomison of the HBC held a council of war at Fort Augustus in 1795. This fellowship of sorts was still evident between the fur traders in 1802, when men from both the XY Company and the HBC buried a Canadian man who had been found dead.[108]

Although such cooperation was less evident following the union of the XY and NWC, some opponents continued to offer one another compassion. Colin Robertson was treated almost like a guest during his eight-month confinement with the NWC. Although he was kept in a small shelter, he was provided with liquor, the means to communicate with fellow HBC employees and, in his view, his treatment was as 'liberal as could be expected'.[109] John McNab also received 'much kindness & attention from the Gentlemen of the N. West Company' in 1812, and other HBC servants received a 'very kind reception' from the NWC in 1816.[110] Alex McDougall and Thomas Fraser, master and clerk in the NWC, gave the HBC men rum, potatoes, tobacco and fish when they spent the night near Temiscaming. It was only when they asked for a guide that McDougall became antagonistic, and unsure 'whether he did his duty in not stopping us'.[111] Likewise, an HBC servant, who had formerly wintered alongside two NWC traders, provided them with tea and rum when they were later held captive at York Fort and treated roughly by everyone else.[112]

It appears that the fur-trade conflict was a commercial competition, vigorous and violent, but one that did not amount to an actual war. By 1816, most of the parties were armed, with some in uniform and using military language. This suggests that they were prepared for a war, but one that never quite came. When the companies were militarised and raids became prevalent on both sides, the competition verged closely on war. The situation never deteriorated into a full-scale war, however, due primarily to the trading companies' premise that success in the business of the fur trade was their main priority. It was that objective, in the face of declining beaver supplies, that began the conflict; and the same objective, in the face of financial, material and human ruin, that actually ended hostilities, as the companies had to unite in order to survive.

Entrepreneurial considerations and lucrative ambitions also explain why, despite the marked involvement of Scots on all sides of the contest, Scottish solidarity was jettisoned in the wilderness of Rupert's Land. Although economic success was all-important and rated more highly than ethnic coalescence, this does not mean that ethnic considerations were entirely disregarded in the fur trade. The next chapter addresses the significance of Scottishness and identity in the HBC, and looks at the ways in which this was challenged or reinforced during a sojourn with the HBC.

SIX

Ambiguous Identities, Divided Loyalties and Paternalism: Personal Conflicts in the Fur-Trading Empire

When I am at home, I feel a man from Glasgow to be something like a rival, a man from Barra to be more than half a foreigner. Yet let us meet in some far country and whether we hail from the braes of Manor or the braes of Mar, some ready-made affection joins us on the instant.[1]

Significance of ethnicity

Scottish migrants generally ventured abroad with the hope of improving prospects for themselves and their families, but as Robert Louis Stevenson recognised, overseas relocation did not necessarily imply that Scots had spurned Scotland or their Scottish identities. In fact, he suggests that the desire to preserve their 'Scottishness' was so great that they cast their differences aside. Scots formed one of the largest ethnic groups in the fur trade between 1780 and 1821, and although those in the HBC were itinerants who did not intend to settle permanently, and thus did not have a pressing need to cultivate their ethnic identities abroad, it is clear that even temporary sojourners carried memories of home. Consciously or not, HBC employees transplanted emblems of their national identity across the Atlantic, to the Arctic and beyond, and impacted upon the cultural fabric of the territories in which they resided.

The most overtly Scottish tradition conveyed to Rupert's Land by servants in the HBC was the commemoration of St Andrew's Day. It was observed in 1808, when on 30 November employees at HBC's Brandon House were 'at home doing nothing this day being S'Andrews Day'.[2] Earlier celebrations of this national holiday actually prompted two Scots, one of whom was Orcadian and worked for the HBC and the other who worked for the rival NWC, to bury the hatchet and mark the occasion together. In 1790, James Sutherland dined with rival trader, Mr Cameron, on St Andrew's Day.[3] It is not, however, mentioned frequently in the Company's post journals, possibly reflecting that Scots were seldom of a sufficiently senior rank to commission such a holiday.

These festivities were enhanced by the Scots' love of music and dancing. On a tour of northern Scotland in 1804, Patrick Neill observed that the Highlanders from Caithness and Sutherland danced 'the fling to the music of the bagpipe in the open street' at market day, while Orkneymen were equally fond of music and dancing.[4] This facet of Scottish heritage was openly embraced in the fur trade, and on occasions such as Christmas, served to unite Scots in the wilderness. When James Sutherland entertained members of the NWC, he provided his guests with a festive dinner accompanied by dancing and singing.[5]

In fact, the inclination to express Scottish culture fully was so keenly felt by some fur traders that they went to great lengths to fulfil this, and ordered string instruments to be dispatched to Hudson's Bay. In 1788, James Banks requested a violin to be sent to York Fort, and Orcadian Edward Clouston also ordered a good-quality violin with a bow, case, and a spare set of strings in 1795. The following year, labourer Abraham Harvey from Firth demonstrated his passion for Orcadian fiddle music when he spent half of his previous year's salary on the instrument.[6] This importation of musical apparatus and instruments, including the English flute and barrel-organ commissioned by a couple of Orkneymen, undoubtedly lightened boredom in the desolate sub-arctic environment. More significantly, it also maintained the traders' Scottish identity. The Orcadian musical tradition continued in fur-trade society and passed down through their descendents, to the extent that some music, obliterated in Orcadian society, was actually retained by the Cree descendants of employees.[7]

Scottish dress, paraphernalia and superstitions were also among the medley of cultural manifestations exported into the fur trade. Donald McKay from Sutherland paid homage to his Scottish roots in 1792 by ordering twelve yards of the best-quality Highland plaid in blue, black and green, and in 1795, John McKay purchased a silver-mounted Highland sword.[8] Superstitious notions were also carried across the Atlantic, and one group of servants from the far north of Scotland were, according to David Thompson, 'staunch believers in ghosts, fairies and such like folk'.[9] These beliefs were apparently so ingrained that when the men went on a hunting trip, they actually attributed some lost axes to a ghost, when the guilty thief was in fact a wolverine.

The symbols of Scottishness transplanted by HBC employees tended to be intangible. Their legacies were far subtler than the material emblems exported by their Scottish counterparts in the NWC, which included churches, schools, social clubs and associations. This disparity lies in the differing nature of their imperial engagements. Scottish employees in the NWC were immigrants who had become permanent residents of Canada, and as a result felt an acute need to express, preserve and reinforce their Scottishness overseas. Those in the HBC, on the other hand, were only transient visitors to a forbidding environment, and lacked the same practical means – and more importantly, the need and desire – to deliberately construct a Scottish identity abroad.

Although Scots were prevalent in the HBC, they were not particularly self-conscious as one cohesive ethnic group and were not regarded as such by others in the fur trade. One later observer commented that Highlanders barely identified Orkneymen as being of the same nationality.[10] In fact, Orkneymen were commonly categorised as a distinct group in the HBC. One colleague, Edward Umfreville, referred to them as 'a close prudent quiet people', while the Company management actually described them as a 'quiet, well disposed and easily managed *race* [my emphasis] of people'.[11] The Orcadians' prominence within the fur trade, and their own sense of identity, contributed to their classification as a cohort, wholly separate from 'Scots'.[12] This was not uncommon: national identity, both overseas and in the homeland, was frequently eclipsed by regional and local identities.

Within Scotland there were many divisions based on origin, culture, language, religion and history. Variations between the different regions of Scotland were enormous and, as Stevenson perhaps more aptly stated: 'Scotland ... has no unity except upon the map. Two languages, many dialects, innumerable forms of piety, and countless local patriotisms and prejudices, part us among ourselves ...'[13] The differences between the regions from which the Scottish fur traders hailed would have had a profound effect upon their sense of identity; and particularly for the Orkneymen.

The Orkney Isles were geographically, historically and culturally distinct from the rest of Scotland. In the ninth century Orkney was settled by Norwegians, and despite being ceded to Scotland four centuries later, the Norwegians still possessed some islands until the fifteenth century. This distinctive history, so inextricably linked with Norway, had forged a unique identity among its inhabitants that endured over the years and led to the formation of a cultural barrier from the rest of Scotland. In fact, Rev. George Low observed in the late eighteenth century that: 'In their manner, their genius and the bent of their inclinations the Orkney people differ much from their next neighbours on the mainland of Scotland. Their dress, their language and every attachment is different, more resembling those of the Danes and Norwegians in whose power they were for a long time, than those of the Highlanders of Scotland.'[14]

The Orcadian population had earlier adopted the Norn language, a variant of Old Norse, the language of Iceland. All the place names used in Orkney were taken from this language, and in the first half of the eighteenth century Norn still remained the primary tongue of at least two of the parishes on the mainland. The ancient language had long persisted in Harray where the elderly population retained many words and phrases. It was less well-known in late eighteenth-century Orkney, and Low noted that 'Even the songs, which are commonly longest retained of any part of a language, are now (except a few of the most trifling) altogether lost'.[15] Yet some derivatives remained, and Norn words were often intermixed in Orcadian dialogue. It was reported in the *Statistical Account* in the 1790s that the language spoken in Orkney was English combined with a Norwegian accent, as there were some sounds in the English language that Orcadians could not grasp and so pronounced according to the old Norn dialect.[16]

Norwegian influences aside, Orcadian culture was also marked by some of the characteristics associated with isolated insular societies. As in the Highlands, the inhabitants were staunch in their old customs, and maintained a belief in superstitions and fairies. Folklore was passed through the generations by story-telling, and some of these fables were particular to Orkney or at least the Northern Isles, such as the trows and dows, who were folkloric creatures of short stature and mischievous spirit living in the ancient mounds of the islands. Stalwart traditions included giving a woman in child-birth a knife and bible to prevent herself and the child from being carried away by supernatural beings; and marriage customs encouraged couples to marry in the waxing phase of a lunar cycle, between a new moon and a full moon, to avoid misfortune. The belief in witchcraft was also widespread, but such ideas were abating among the youth, perhaps due to increased exposure to other societies.[17]

Inhabitants of Orkney probably had as much contact with the populace from northern Europe and other countries as they did with mainland Scots, due to the greater ease of communication by sea. Orkney was quite a recent acquisition to Scotland, and it is therefore unsurprising that Orcadians – like the Shetlanders further north – maintained an independent attitude regarding their position within Scotland. This, coupled with unique socio-cultural circumstances in Orkney, fostered an almost separatist mentality among the inhabitants, to the extent that some did not describe themselves as Scottish. Fur-trader James Sutherland 3rd was perhaps typical when he differentiated between the 'Scotch and Orkney people' he came across in Montreal.[18]

Orcadian HBC recruits had an established awareness of their cultural distinctiveness and a strong pre-existing ethnic bond. Their transfer to the wilderness of Rupert's Land not only reinforced those perceptions, but also encouraged them to band together on the basis of their specific, insular, ethnicity. Many new servants were young men in their late teens and twenties who were leaving home, perhaps for the first time. Some of them shared kinship and community ties, as relations and neighbours often joined the Company simultaneously, while others would have at least known someone already in the service. The majority also shared a mutual purpose, the desire to improve economic prospects for themselves and their families. This sense of fellowship was evident among the men when they signed up with the Company. The Orkney agent commented that the 'Orkney Lads from old custom' would not enter into an agreement with the HBC 'without the twelve pence to bind the Contract' with a drink.[19] Once in Hudson's Bay, this ethnic solidarity again came to the fore amidst struggles for better working conditions. Orkneymen bargained for wage increases, collectively refused duty, and threatened to disrupt recruitment in Orkney, as discussed in Chapter 2.

While their commonality, unique origins, and kinship ties had helped form a basis on which to unite, they also carried prejudice, and distanced themselves from some other ethnicities in the HBC. Employees from the Northern Isles interacted with servants from England, French Canada, Lowland Scotland and later on, Ireland, the Hebrides, and Highlands, along with the indigenous populations of Rupert's Land. Diversity of language, dialect, region, and religion would have served to accentuate any awareness of difference as both the Irish and Highlanders spoke Gaelic; the Canadians spoke French, and while Orcadians were protestant, many of the others were catholic. The outcome of such cultural fusions was clannishness, as the barriers between the consortia of Scots in the Company and other ethnic groups, such as the Irish and French Canadians, appeared impenetrable.

Accusations of tribal behaviour and prejudice surrounded Orkneymen in the Company, and some aspects of their behaviour do suggest an inclination towards ethnocentrism, particularly when new, non-Orcadian, recruits were introduced to the HBC. The intense parochialism of the Orcadian faction was evident in 1791 when they subjected the recently-engaged Canadians to hard treatment and refused to cooperate with them, as 'the Canadians were not from their town'.[20] The management was perplexed by this intolerance, but had seemingly grown accustomed to it as they alerted directors that there would be a significant intake of recruits from other locales in 1811, which ought to be considered when allocating them to posts in Rupert's Land.[21]

It was inevitable that despite paying attention to the destination of new servants, men of different origin would eventually encounter one another. Then, when amid recruits from Ireland, Canada, Lewis, Glasgow and Caithness, the 'stupid bigotry' of the Orcadians would rise to the fore.[22] Officer William Auld knew that coaxing the protestant Orkneymen into mingling with the catholic Irishmen would be extremely challenging. They had already suffered 'from the little malicious insults' of Orcadians to the extent that Auld had taken on an Irishman as his own servant in order to shield him from such harrying. He anticipated that two Hebridean employees would meet with similar treatment. However, he hoped that the Irish and 'the Canadian servants being of the same religion' would 'coalesce more readily'.[23]

The management in England and Rupert's Land clearly recognised the clannishness of Orkneymen and the way in which this manifested itself in hostility towards other employees. Fear of ethnic displacement in the fur trade and economic ambition were feasible reasons for wanting to keep others out of the Company, but the directors also felt the need to counter tribal behaviour in the Red River settlement. They tried a new tactic at the colony and intentionally dispersed Orcadians throughout the settlement. There was a large catholic and protestant divide between the French-Canadian and Irish settlers, and the Scottish and English colonists, and they felt that discouraging the formation of discrete settlements in favour of mixed settlement was better for all parties.[24] This desire to mitigate social exclusiveness in the settlement, and not just the labour force, suggests that the Orcadians' behaviour was rooted in more than a need to protect their stronghold in the Company; it is possible that amidst their engagement with fur-trade society, Orkneymen also encountered some challenges that posed a threat to their established identities.

Isolation, integration and country wives

For most servants of the HBC, the original stimulus to migrate was economic in nature, rendering work in Rupert's Land only a temporary deployment. Unlike the Scots in the NWC, these men did not intend to settle abroad on a permanent basis, integrate into a new society, and help build the foundations of a Canadian economy. Most servants had relatives or families in Scotland to whom they intended to return when their contract expired, and this focus on home inhibited their pursuit of cultural assimilation as a deliberate ploy. However, their original objectives and detached attitudes were gradually eroded through contact and communication with native inhabitants in Rupert's Land.

One, albeit inadvertent, instrument of acculturation was the attainment of a native language, which was essential to the trade of furs. Servants' acquisition of a native language was essential for the Company's ability to trade, and it enhanced the development of bonds between employees and native communities in order to secure a trading relationship. To this end, the servants of the HBC were considered useful to their employers only after they had acquired an 'Indian' language. Even traders who planned to serve only one five-year contract before returning home were not immune from such acculturative forces. Robert McIntosh, a 22-year-old Scottish servant, was hired as a labourer in 1818 and was dispatched the following year with the Stone Indians to learn their language. Others, such as Angus McLeod from Uig in Lewis, had elementary knowledge of an indigenous language. He had been in the service for only two years, but since his first language was Gaelic and it was never guaranteed that fellow Gaelic-speakers would abide near him, the acquirement of a native language, no matter how basic, would have enabled him to participate more fully in the fur trade.[25] All bilingual, or in some cases multilingual, servants would hold this advantage and it may not only have assisted in their work duties, but also fostered the growth of relationships with native women.

The Company directors intentionally sought young single recruits from peripheral parts of Britain who were accustomed to remoteness, as the posts in Rupert's Land were far-flung from the urban centres of Canada. Yet there was a difference between the geographic isolation of an island such as Orkney, and the combination of physical and social isolation found at a post in Hudson's Bay or the particularly secluded north-west. Rev. William Clouston lamented that in this 'solitary situation', men were 'cut off from family and friends, and from all social intercourse but with the natives'.[26] Servants obviously had one another for company, and many among them had prior friendships, but given that British women were forbidden from voyaging to Rupert's Land, the isolation of this exclusively male environment must have been bleak.

In response to this segregated lifestyle in the sub-arctic, and the trading needs of both the Company and native tribes, new social customs emerged in the fur trade. Many of the tribes were as eager as the Company managers to form and fortify partnerships, and one common means of doing so was to offer women to traders, temporarily or permanently, as a gesture of goodwill. Some wives were loaned for a period of time before returning to their native husbands, while other women, such as the daughters of tribal leaders, were 'given' to employees. The natives of Hudson's Bay were seemingly aware of the social hierarchy within the Company, as high-ranking employees were held in superior regard, and such customs were initially confined to the senior employees who managed HBC posts and trade. Officers welcomed this social practice as they found social and sexual relief from their solitude, while it also reflected their prominent status within the Company. Although the Company forbade such intimate alliances, the officers would evade the rules respecting their own behaviour, but strictly enforce regulations among their subordinate colleagues.[27]

Towards the end of the eighteenth century, trading operations extended in Rupert's Land and the business spread into uncharted regions where new tribes, eager to join the fur trade, willingly offered women. Small complements of men were dispersed at newly established posts across the country, and this increased their access to women. In addition, recently-promoted post masters may have taken a more relaxed approach to their subordinates' interactions with native women, as the custom grew and became increasingly prevalent throughout the ranks of fur-trade society.[28]

The most intriguing aspect of these affairs is that they were generally not casual, short-lived or profligate interactions, but genuine attachments that developed into durable relationships. Marriage 'according to the custom of the country' became the favoured outcome of these interactions; women married under this arrangement were known as 'country wives'.[29] Although employees of the HBC were not by any means entirely virtuous in their personal affairs, and one observer later commented that 'Scotchmen or Orkneymen who were in the Hudson Bay service ... consorted with Cree women, sometimes giving them marriage and sometimes not', and there were also a couple of instances of sexual assault, nonetheless marriage according to the custom of the country was typical.[30] Owing to the HBC's early proscription of such encounters, and the absence of clergy, these marriage unions were not formally sanctioned or registered, but they were an expression of commitment.[31]

The civil nature of these alliances is really quite striking, and it seems that many employees considered their native partners in the same vein as they would a female companion in their home society. Furnishing women with British presents appears to have come into vogue during the first two decades of the 1800s, and many traders ordered small tokens of affection from Britain, to give to their female companions. Traders commonly purchased items of jewellery, and Scottish officer, Robert Longmoor, ordered 'Hand some Fancy Gold Rings' set with pearl in 1804, while Orcadians George Flett and John Esson commissioned finger rings and earrings. One Orcadian officer, Jacob Corrigal, also made a request for jewellery in 1804, along with a shawl, ribbons, and small needles, specifically for beadwork.[32]

Sewing equipment was actually a popular requisition, as were gifts of lace and cloth. These articles were apparently ordered with the intention of encouraging partners to make their own clothes according to British fashions.[33] In addition, to promote native 'civilisation', Scottish officers such as John McKay and John Sanderson ordered striped stockings, ladies' shifts, shawls of different patterns and gartering, and William Auld ordered a hat specifically for an eighteen-year-old girl. It is not clear what effect such cultural imports had on those women, but the commissions by one Scot for 'gaudy' and 'showy' items, including ribbons, a bridle, saddle and horsewhip, suggest that perhaps a status-conscious trend for ostentatious attire had emerged among the officers' partners.[34]

All of these private commissions were made through the London administrators, demonstrating that mixed-race relationships in the HBC had become less clandestine in the early nineteenth century, and perhaps show a growing acceptance of fur-trade social customs among the directors. Indeed, by 1815, the Committee members explicitly acknowledged country relationships. Their formal policies on domestic unions relaxed and a directive arrived at the posts reiterating that no employee, regardless of rank, was permitted to take a woman as a wife or companion *without consent* from the governor.[35] In fact, the managers may even have realised the extent to which these customs were assumed, as when employees died in Rupert's Land, the directors queried whether the deceased had a wife and family in Hudson's Bay.[36]

The mixed-race relationships undertaken by employees in the HBC differed from some of the inter-racial liaisons that Scots became involved in elsewhere in the fur trade and the wider British empire. Montreal-based fur traders also became involved with native women and while some of these partnerships took the same form as those in the HBC, there was a darker side to these interactions. The low-ranking French-Canadian members of the NWC, and some of the high-ranking Scottish partners, became involved in the trade of women. Trafficking had emerged when indebted natives could not afford to pay their arrears, and women were taken as an alternative form of payment. The Jepowyan (Chipewyan) Indians complained of the Canadian practice of forcibly taking their women from them, who were then kept as slaves and subsequently sold on to other traders. Some Canadians kept as many as three women, and the voyageurs in particular were guilty of then selling their 'country wives', 'either for a season or altogether, for a sum of money, proportioned to her beauty and good qualities, but always inferior to the price of a team of dogs'.[37]

Derogatory behaviour and attitudes towards women were also evident in the British West Indies where mixed-race relationships were similarly endemic throughout the ranks of plantation society. Some Scots 'married a black or brown woman', but the more common encounter was of a casual nature and not necessarily consensual. Slavery was rife in the Caribbean and the managers, many of whom were Scottish, took the right, as owner of the slave and their bodies, to have sexual relations with young females.[38] Unlike the HBC where monogamous relationships became the norm, planters and overseers indulged in liaisons with numerous women. The differing nature of these encounters may explain why the venereal disease that was so rife in the Caribbean, and also the NWC, remained comparatively dormant among Scots in the HBC.

The contrast between the frequently non-consensual and disrespectful encounters in which Scots participated in both the Caribbean and NWC, and the consensual relationships that emerged in Rupert's Land, lies in the historical development of the fur trade. The directors of the HBC had the power to establish laws, government, and colonies in the territory of Rupert's Land, but did not assume any right or desire to dominate the indigenous people. Their sole objective was trade, and the formation of inter-dependent relationships with natives bound by a mutual regard, served trading purposes far better than policies of repression. Of course, with hindsight it is evident that the introduction of weaponry and ammunition intensified tribal conflicts, and that the importation of alcohol and disease had an equally deleterious impact on the indigenous people, but the HBC, from the outset, had wished only to cultivate peaceable relationships and goodwill.[39] It instructed its employees to trade fairly, treat the native people with respect and look after them when they were unwell or starving. The employees of the HBC, unlike those in Montreal, were accountable to this judicious governing body that emphasised morality and encouraged a deferential approach to all native interactions. The HBC's vigilance from London was obviously limited, as the initial development of relationships and marriage customs confirm, but it was also in employees' own best interests to show consideration for the indigenous tribes they encountered, as without native assistance the workforce might potentially starve.[40]

Mixed-blood dependents, split loyalties and settlement

Relationships between employees and native women evolved into a social custom within the fur trade and contributed to the immersion of Scots in the fur trade social sphere. In turn, these mixed-race partnerships helped perpetuate that society as a generation of progeny soon emerged, and by 1822 mixed-race offspring were numerous.[41] Unlike the mixed-blood children belonging to members of the NWC, who formed a separate nation and congregated on the plains of Assiniboia, the descendants of HBC employees did not assume a distinct identity or form a collective settlement. The placement of these offspring invariably presented their itinerant fathers with dilemmas. Their own identities lay neither fully in Rupert's Land, nor fully in Scotland, and therefore the assignment of their children, whether to their homelands, mother's tribe, or HBC posts, incurred a multitude of hardships. Moreover, the subsequent placing of their children could potentially influence the extent to which they themselves further integrated into fur-trade society.

Some members of the HBC sent their offspring overseas to their home societies since, just as did the Scots in the Caribbean, fur traders held Scottish education in high regard. They hoped that a Scottish upbringing would implant the civilised values that fathers feared were not overtly present in Rupert's Land. Progeny were either sent on board the Company ships, under the care of the Captain, or were taken personally by their father during leave from service and deposited with relatives in their home societies. Alexander Kennedy and James Sutherland 3rd dispatched their sons to live in St Margaret's Hope, South Ronaldsay, with the expectation that it would 'be for the good of both ... soul and body to get a little education'.[42] They were not alone in favouring Scottish education and values; John McNab, William Auld and Andrew Stewart also received permission to send their sons home between 1792 and 1821.[43]

This practice helped to facilitate and reinforce strong linkages between migrants, their mixed-blood families, and their former households in their home societies. However, it also fractured fur-trade families, causing emotional hardship. For instance, James Sutherland experienced heartache after leaving his son in Orkney, and reflected that 'I never regretted any thing I ever did in my lifetime as the bringing my Boy Home the thought of being so far separated from him has given me a great deal of anxiety ever since I left him'.[44] In fact, the pain of separation was so immense that several years after leaving his young boy William in Orkney he requested if his brother decided to join the HBC, that he then bring James' son back with him.

If the fathers of mixed-blood children experienced emotional turmoil, such sentiments were much more acute among their wives. Indigenous women were traditionally matriarchal and accustomed to assuming full responsibility for the rearing of their children, so the traders' claim to authority in decision-making could be traumatic.[45] In 1799, Donald McKay left Rupert's Land for Scotland himself, and two years later sent orders for his son William to be sent across with Capt. Hamwell. Despite a dreadful passage, William arrived safely and lived with his father in Sutherland, leaving his half-breed mother alone in Rupert's Land.[46] In another case, Orkneyman William Sinclair actually showed blatant disregard for his wife's wishes and sent all his sons overseas to learn, including his youngest, whom he reportedly sent away without his mother's consent, leaving her overcome.[47]

All traders were actively discouraged from sending their mixed-blood daughters abroad, as the Committee declared that no girls born in Hudson's Bay would be allowed to return to Rupert's Land following a British education. The reasoning behind this was that reassimilation into Rupert's Land would be problematical for them; consequently, mixed-blood daughters tended to be kept in Rupert's Land. One rare exception was the daughter of John Sutherland, who was sent to Scotland in 1799 with a HBC captain, but we know very little of her subsequent fate.[48]

It was fortunate for the mothers of mixed-blood children that the repatriation of children to employees' home societies was not a universally-sanctioned rule. Employees had to apply for permission from the HBC's directors on an individual basis before transplanting their progeny from Hudson's Bay to Scotland. One determining factor appears to have been financial assets. Servants had to prove that they had the economic means to support both the child's maintenance and education overseas, and also had to pay ten guineas for the passage across on an HBC vessel. Thus one labouring servant from Orkney, referred to as Birston, requested permission to take his offspring home, but was not allowed unless his superiors in Rupert's Land could establish that he possessed sufficient property to support them.[49] As a result, few lower-class servants had the option of removing their children from fur-trade society.

There were two remaining options for the children that stayed in Rupert's Land; to reside with their mother and her tribe, or remain at the post with their father where, after 1808, there was educational provision in the form of schools.[50] Some offspring did assimilate into their mother's native tribe and intermarried with natives. However, fathers had paternal concerns about this prospect, particularly for their daughters, as they believed that 'Native women in Attendant [sic] on these young persons seems improper – their society would keep alive the Indian language & with it its native superstition which ought to be obliterated from the mind with all possible care'.[51] Other paternal concerns included the hardship of native life that mixed-blood daughters would endure, such as starvation, and the 'unrestrained discourse of their Indian relations', which 'inflamed' them so that they 'very early give up all pretensions to chastity'.[52]

In an attempt to alleviate some of the privations associated with native life, and to secure a more prosperous future for their progeny, many fathers retained their daughters at the HBC posts and aspired for them to marry members within the HBC.[53] It became the norm in fur-trade society that in the first generation, the mother would be native, and the next generation of her mixed-blood children either inter-married or became the wives of fur traders, until 'the predominant quality would be Scotch'.[54] Yet explorer John Franklin actually criticised the treatment of female progeny in the HBC, because some daughters were given in marriage very young. He observed that this tendency was even more prevalent in the NWC, and that French-Canadian voyageurs in particular took mixed-blood wives as young as ten years old. He blamed Company officers for permitting this corrupt habit in order to encourage the morale of the workforce.[55] However, Franklin overlooked the paternal influence in the emergence of this practice, particularly within the HBC. The fathers of mixed-blood progeny felt compelling pressure to secure the most prosperous future possible for their daughters, in order to spare them the hardships of native life.

In fact, it has been determined that there was an unofficial encouragement from fathers for subordinate employees to marry mixed-blood daughters in Rupert's Land, and that new recruits were susceptible to such customs being imposed upon them. It was certainly common for junior employees to marry the daughters of their superiors. Orcadian William Flett entered the Company in 1782 and took a native wife, Saskatchewan, with whom he produced numerous offspring. One of his mixed-blood daughters, Nancy, subsequently became the country wife of another Orcadian, William Gibson, a canoeman from Rousay who had served at the same post as her father. Although such engagements involved considerations such as the pressure to support a wife and family with provisions and provide for their future, and the dilemma of what to do when the contract ends, it is clear also that the father, junior employee, and mixed-blood daughter stood to derive considerable gain from such alliances, and inter-marriage may have simply reinforced existing Orcadian networks in the fur trade.[56]

Yet, if some relationships were formed under pressure, it is not particularly surprising that further concerns emerged regarding the potential abandonment of such women. Employees were contracted to the HBC for a maximum of five years and thereafter could return to their homelands. The Committee's growing tolerance of country wives only existed within the confines of Rupert's Land and fur-trade society; they did not consider these alliances akin to legal marriage in Britain. Thus the directors of the HBC had dictated that no native women were allowed to cross the Atlantic on their vessels. The captains were under strict orders, reiterated in 1793, 'not to receive, or take on board, or permit, or suffer to be taken on Board, either in Hudson's Bay or Streights, any Indian Esquimaux, Man, Woman or Child, to be brought to any part of Great Britain'.[57] For many couples, a separation was inevitable, whether temporarily when men returned home for an extended visit, or permanently as they retired back to their home societies, and for this reason most unions formed in the fur trade could not be life-long.

Abandonment was a possibility that all country wives faced, but the consequences differed greatly between native and mixed-blood women. Native women tended to reintegrate into their original tribe or thrived under the financial support of their distant partners. Mixed-blood women, however, did not always have the same option of assimilating into a tribe and ultimately faced poverty if abandoned. Some employees endeavoured to protect their daughters from such hardship. William Flett held his daughter's husband to promise a financial bond in case 'he quits the Country' or ceased 'to consider her his wife'.[58] Likewise, in 1818, Orcadian Joseph Spence appears to have formally secured the economic future of his daughter, Sapphira. She married a trader, John Clarke, and had a £200 assignment conferred on her from him, through her father.[59]

Fortunately, it also became common practice for employees with wives and children in Rupert's Land to leave entitlements in their wills, so that after their decease they would not face abandonment and poverty. Such provisions notwithstanding, in the years immediately preceding the union, the Company management was increasingly concerned that not all employees did retain such an attachment or loyalty to their families in Rupert's Land. The concern arose largely from their own viewpoint that families in need of support burdened the Company settlements. A proposed solution was to retain a portion of the servants' wages, £25, to support their wives and children in Rupert's Land. Any persons who chose to marry would be obliged to create such a fund for family maintenance. The proposal was not sanctioned at the time, but an alternative plan was to solve at least some of the problems that fur-trade families experienced.[60]

Lord Selkirk's institution of the Red River colony in 1811 altered the course of many fur-trade alliances, as in the four years before the HBC united with the NWC, the directors arranged for retired servants and their mixed-blood families to settle in Assiniboia. Traders now had the choice of departing the service and returning to their homelands at the end of their contract, or fully integrating into fur-trade society and settling at the colony with their country wives. It offered another option to employees such as James Sutherland 3rd who, as mentioned in Chapter 3, was torn between his desire to leave Hudson's Bay and go elsewhere, and his obligation to his mixed-blood family. Colonisation was not abhorrent to employees and, in fact, the Company observed the servants' welcoming receptivity of the prospect of settlement in 1818. They noted that they were 'glad that the arrangement made for our Servants settling on Red River have given them satisfaction & it is pleasing to us to learn that all the servants in the Northern Establishment consider the settlement of this Country so desirable an object'.[61]

Owing to the problems of competition, the Red River colony took longer to become firmly established than originally anticipated, and their plans for retired servants and families to join the settlement were also delayed. By 1820, however, the directors had requested information from their officers on the character of the men wishing to settle, and details on their history of service and conduct, in order to calculate the amount of land they ought to be allocated. The earliest census of 1827 shows that of the forty-six Orkneymen who had settled at the colony, 90 per cent of them were married and 87 per cent had children. All the children of Orcadian James Spence and his native wife Nosticho resided there, as did the Birston brothers from South Ronaldsay with their respective families. The settlement of couples such as Nancy Flett and William Gibson would have allayed her father's fears of her abandonment when they set up residence alongside him in the colony.[62]

In fact, the founding of the colony really improved the prospects that were available to mixed-blood families. The HBC intended to establish schools at the settlement, and in 1818 the directors ruled that all employees should be encouraged to send their children to the Red River settlement for an education, rather than continue the practice of sending them overseas. This was perhaps an attempt to capitalise on the potential of a mixed-blood labour force, but irrespective of the management's motive, it would have had a positive effect on fur-trade families as it deterred the splintering of families across the Atlantic.[63]

The settlement also instituted in the population civilised ways that the management had never succeeded in inculcating, despite endeavours such as the dispatch of religious books to men who were literate and eager to improve themselves. Those who chose permanent settlement had the opportunity to cement their partnerships through marriage according to the rites of the Church of England. Rev. John West, a Church of England missionary, was employed to provide religious ordinances for the protestant settlers in 1820. The clergyman offered retired employees and current workers an opportunity to formalise their marriage unions. Orkneyman James Anderson, who served as a tailor at Brandon House, officially wed his Salteaux partner Mary, in 1820, while Thomas Halcrow also formally married his Southward Indian wife with whom he already had three children. Even older servants, such as 54-year-old Orcadian James Short, embraced the occasion to legitimise his marriage to his Cree wife in 1821.[64]

Although temporary migration was their intention, for a minority of employees the formation of family ties in Rupert's Land replaced taking a wife and mother from Britain, and emigration became the inadvertent outcome of employment in the fur trade. The establishment of a colony in which families could settle increased employees' physical, social and cultural anchorage to Rupert's Land. Yet even those who had seemingly integrated into the fur-trade social sphere, through a long absence and the formation of country families, still had a connection to their homeland, as the earlier practice of sending home mixed-blood children demonstrates. Many employees retained close attachments to home, and although they were separated from their family and friends in Scotland for a minimum of three to five years, and usually much longer, they were not entirely alienated from their home societies. This was largely due to the paternalistic nature of the directors, who were based at the Company's headquarters in London, and helped counteract acculturative forces by bridging the gap between the servants in Hudson's Bay and their families in Scotland. The ways in which the HBC looked after its workforce and their family members served to maintain, reinforce and sometimes even re-establish bonds across the Atlantic, preventing estrangement.

Communication, separation and Company paternalism

Scottish relatives were physically situated outside the trading domain of Rupert's Land, but were as inextricably caught up in the complexities of fur-trade society as country wives, mixed-blood offspring and the Company's employees. Despite the established belief that the typical profile of a Hudson's Bay servant was young and single, and the fact that the Company did in fact seek those servants, HBC records show that many employees were actually married upon entry to the service, or got married at home during leave from service. Rev. Hugh Ross confirmed in 1797 that numerous married men entered the HBC but, as

Company policy forbade white women from going to Rupert's Land, they had to leave their spouse at home in Orkney until the end of their sojourn.[65]

Although British women were forbidden from entering Rupert's Land in this period, there was one notable exception, a young lady from Tankerness in Orkney. In 1806, the woman who would later become known as Isabel Gunn dressed in disguise as a man called John Fubbister and entered the service of the HBC. She apparently worked in Rupert's Land undetected – although it is hard to believe that her fellow Orcadians were unaware of her ploy – until she went into child-birth in December 1807. Alexander Henry reported on 29 December that

> A very extraordinary affair occurred this morning. One of Mr Heneys Orkney lads came over to my house, who apparently was indisposed and requested of me the favour to allow him to remain in my house for a short time. I was surprised at the fellow's demand however I told him to sit down and warm himself. When I returned into my own room, where I had not been long before, he sent one of my people requesting the favour to speak with me. Accordingly I stepped down to him and was much surprised to find [him] extended out upon the hearth uttering most dreadful lamenta-tions. He stretched out his hand towards me and in a pitiful tone of voice begg'd my assistance, and requested I would take pity upon a poor helpless abandoned wretch, who was not of the sex I had every reason to suppose, but was an unfortunate Orkney Girl pregnant and actually in Childbirth.[66]

Two years after giving birth to a son, James, Isabel was forced by the HBC management to return to Scotland with her young child and went on to live a deprived life in Orkney.

Gunn's motive in joining the fur-trading company is unknown, but rumours suggest that she may have followed an Orcadian lover into service. Her experi-ence was anomalous, as the traditions of migration within Orcadian society meant that local families were generally accustomed to, and accepted, a tempo-rary separation from their lovers, spouses and offspring. It was simply part and parcel of the sojourning experience. However, service in the fur trade entailed a lengthier departure than the other temporary employments with which Orcadians were familiar, and some employees and their families really did struggle with absenteeism. Those who suffered from extreme angst, or found the strains of separation unbearable, had no option but to turn to the Company in the hope of alleviating their misery by, for example, permitting an early return, or obtaining an update on their loved one.

Newly-weds and those sundered for the first time were perhaps more inclined to grapple with the adjustment to life alone. Wives who had been separated from their husbands for only a short time frequently petitioned the London Committee requesting the premature return of their spouse. The wife of John Inkster appealed for the early departure of her husband from Rupert's Land in the 1790s and in 1801 Orcadians Margaret Mainland and Anne Rendall urged the directors to send their spouses home on the next ship, despite their absence of only one year. Even wives who were accustomed to long-term separation, such as the spouses of John Stickler and William Cromartie, employees who had worked in the HBC for over twenty years, were not immune to the traumas evoked by separation. They petitioned the Company in 1806 to authorise their husbands' leave from service.[67]

Pressures of absenteeism and homesickness were not by any means confined to the Scottish families who were left behind. Some of the servants struggled to cope with their own extended departure from their homelands, and those who lived unhappily sometimes begged to return home. James Annald from South Ronaldsay had been in the Company for only one year when, in 1793, he informed the management that he desired to go home to his wife and family. Likewise, long-serving employee, James Halcro, was criticised for pining after his Orcadian family. The 41-year-old assistant trader from Orphir had first served in the Company in 1789, but was berated by his superiors in 1812 for 'doing no Service to the Company' because he 'is only waiting for the comfort of himself & Family'.[68] It is possible that the burdens of hard labour and, perhaps, failed expectations of service, may have heightened employees' homesickness. Yet these instances probably reminded the Committee why it preferred bachelors, who would more easily adapt to their placing in Rupert's Land.[69]

In contrast to the Company's first century of operation when spouses were habitually allowed home in order to maintain morale and prevent marital problems from spiralling, these later entreaties were denied. The directors explicitly refused the appeals of both wives and employees for an early return, and insisted that the servants honour their contracts. One Orcadian wife was reminded in 1801 that her husband had committed himself to five years' service and therefore would not be allowed to return home until his agreement expired in 1803.[70]

The managerial response to marital appeals may have seemed indifferent, but from their perspective as business administrators, the family woes of employees were often burdensome and time-consuming, and threatened to interfere with the successful running of the Company. Aside from the expense in ferrying men back and forth across the Atlantic, the Company was chronically short of servants during the Napoleonic wars. Granting any appeals for early retirement from service would set a precedent that could not be maintained. They asserted in 1796 that if 'the wishes of the Mens wives were to be complied with the Company would loose half their servants'.[71]

Yet on very rare occasions, despite a firm resolve not to gratify family appeals, the Committee members did relent and sanctioned the return of men before their contracts had expired. In 1802, Mary Kirkness asked for her Orcadian husband to return home, and this appeal was forwarded to the Orkney agent, David Geddes, who was instructed to enquire into the legitimacy of the circumstances. Although it is not clear what formed the basis of Kirkness' request, the Committee resolved that if Geddes found her representation to be genuine then they would reluctantly allow her husband home by the next ship, if he so desired.[72] In another case, Andrew Linklater was permitted to return home in 1789, this lenience owing to requests from both his parents, but the managers could not resist adding that such generous treatment was not due to his conduct in the Company, which had not entitled him 'to any favour from the Board'.[73] These allowances may have been made in situations where a family member was gravely ill as, for instance, when the father of Thomas Halcrow petitioned for his son to return home for one year in order to see his ailing mother. This concession was only permissible on the condition that Geddes found the plight to be genuine.[74]

In fact, considering that the HBC was a corporation, the attention devoted to family affairs was actually quite remarkable. The humane nature of the managers was frequently evident in their interactions with employees' families. They offered paternal reassurance to discomforted wives such as Mrs Ballenden – who married John Ballenden in 1796, a year before he re-entered the service – and reminded her of the anticipated remuneration.

> if you will permit me Madam, to give you my opinion on the Matter I think it the very best Measure that can possibly tend to the future Comfort & Happiness of you both – The addition which Mr Ballenden will be enabled to make to his present Income by the time his Agreement is expired, cannot, in these distressing times be a matter of indifference to either of you, & therefore let me earnestly recommend to you to wait patiently until the period arrives ... that you may meet each other with, at least, some better prospect of you being then more comfortable than your present finances will admit you now to be that you are both of you reconciled to the short absence of each other.[75]

The HBC's managers also tried to keep communication flowing directly between employees and their family members in Scotland. The Company ships travelled to Hudson's Bay once a year, and the directors permitted servants and their relatives to exchange letters, news and packages via the vessels. They informed Scottish relations outwith Orkney that their dispatches ought to reach the Company headquarters before April each year, as the ships departed in June, while Orcadian families sent their parcels on board the vessels when they arrived at Stromness. The Company directors made great efforts to ensure that these transmissions remained fluid. When the HBC's vessels did not stop at Orkney in 1810, the Committee was eager to prevent disappointment among its servants in Hudson's Bay who expected their usual correspondence. To this end, the directors authorised Geddes to purchase a fishing boat or small vessel to carry the letters and keepsakes from Stromness to the Company ships at Stornoway.[76]

The ships usually reached Rupert's Land in September, and the arrival of a packet of letters from friends and family at home was always pleasurable news to employees.[77] Following the receipt of Scottish correspondence, the servants soon wrote their letters home in response, and these interchanges enabled employees to preserve their interest in family, community and local affairs. James Sutherland, who had a mixed-blood family in Hudson's Bay and eventually settled at the colony, upheld his interest in Orkney through such traffic. His Orcadian family forwarded newspapers, presumably imported from the mainland, but in 1817 he noted his disappointment at receiving only a few months' worth. In his subsequent reply, Sutherland reminded his family not to forget and to 'send me it as frequently as possible' and then included a bill for the payment of more newspapers.[78] His family would have received his letter a couple of months later when the inward-bound ships arrived in Orkney and the letters they carried were posted at Stromness.

In fact, the directors' role as brokers between employees and their British families was far-reaching, particularly when direct personal communication had broken down. On occasion, families in Scotland were disappointed at not receiving any word from their menfolk in the Arctic. Relatives were well aware that the fur trade was a dangerous employment and that life was uncertain in Rupert's land. Bad news often took a long time to be conveyed across the Atlantic and, for instance, it was four years after the death of his son that Alex Sutherland from Clyne was given absolute notification of the son having been 'among the unfortunate party that were murdered at the Red River' in 1816.[79] This delay in communication often resulted in fears that a relative might have died in the service. In such circumstances, the London Committee served as a rallying point for concerned parents and spouses, anxious to know the well-being of their loved ones. Robert Stewart from Glasgow was worried about his son Andrew, as he had sent him a package but had not received any news since. The Committee was able to assure Mr Stewart that his son was well and that he would have received the goods and letter, but as he was situated in a remote area of Rupert's Land, he would not have had time to reply before the ships departed. The management offered similar comfort to the wife of Peter Allan, who wrote to the directors in 1796 because she was convinced that her husband had met with an accident.[80]

In some instances, the break in communication was the result of an employee's abrupt departure from service. The impulsiveness of their conduct and subsequent failure to forewarn their relatives in Scotland of their plans, left families distraught. Yet the directors ensured that even the families of these ex-employees were not left in the dark, and assisted them in their endeavours to regain contact. One servant's father had heard no word from his son for two years and was very relieved when the Company informed him that his son had only deserted the Company. He said that he was 'very happy to hear of my son being alive'.[81] An Aberdeenshire man also communicated his concerns about an employee in 1818. The managers were able to report that the employee in question had quitted their service in 1817, and that 'the last accounts we had of him were that he was seen on his way to Temiscaming in one of the Canoes of the NW Company'. Although the servant had entered the employment of the HBC's rivals, the Committee still advised the inquirer that a letter directed to the agents of the NWC would undoubtedly reach him.[82] Mrs E. Norquoy from Orkney also made contact with the Company in 1820, and related her disquietude. She believed, from a lack of communication, that her brother was dead. The managers were able to relieve her distress and inform her that her brother had in fact simply retired from the service and relocated to the Red River colony.[83] These examples illustrate the potential difficulties of transatlantic communication that were encountered by men who had removed themselves from the paternalistic sanctuary of the Company, yet it also proves the efficacy of prior Company membership in sustaining overseas connections.

Of course, informal communication networks also operated across the Atlantic. When James Sutherland wrote to his brother in St Margaret's Hope in 1825, he included only essential news, as he informed him that Mr Kennedy was going home and 'will give you all the news respecting me'.[84] He was presumably referring to Alexander Kennedy, who was also from South Ronaldsay and went on leave to Orkney that year. Although this method of conveying news across the Atlantic would have served illiterate Orcadians particularly well, informal networks also created difficulties. Some of the tidings transmitted to Orkney were only hearsay, and thus inaccurate. Orcadian Margaret Ballentine had learned that her husband, James Howie, had died in Hudson's Bay and was convinced that he had been eaten by natives. The Committee notified her that this was absolutely not the case, but by that point her belief was so ingrained that they had to offer her repeated assurance.[85] Therefore, although returned employees were of some utility as a link between fur-trade society and Scotland, particularly to the Orcadian contingent, the directors remained central to the transatlantic information network, as they possessed bona fide intelligence.

Overall, it is clear that the Company management recognised that its workforce and their dependants laboured under a particularly complex set of social and emotional circumstances. Their overtures successfully facilitated contact and communication across the Atlantic, and provided some much needed comfort and reassurance to those left behind. There was a vestige of self-interest in this benevolence, as from the managerial perspective it probably helped to boost morale among the workforce and thus maintain participation rates, as well as raise the Company in public estimation. Yet the amount of consideration shown towards employees' families in Scotland was exceptional, and the directors' humanity extended well beyond the scope that would be expected from a corporation.

Employees' families, identities, and attachments are also a focal point in the next chapter, which examines the profits of the fur trade, and the ways in which they were repatriated and invested. In this sense, Company paternalism also remains significant, as the directors were instrumental in the process of remittance and investment, and in looking after the economic well-being of servants and their dependants.

SEVEN

Remitting the Profits of the Fur Trade

A business relationship: the HBC and Orkney

The initial connection between the HBC and the Orkney Isles developed in the early 1700s and was solely commercial, as the Company ships stopped in Stromness harbour to purchase supplies for their long voyage across the Atlantic. The vessels continued to call in at Orkney on their outward-bound journey throughout the eighteenth century, and this regular custom boosted the local economy. Farmers benefited from a ready market for beef, poultry, butter and vegetables, and by 1814 the visit of the HBC ships had created an annual fair in the Orkney Islands.[1] From this market, the local HBC agent was able to obtain necessary provisions for the vessels, which in 1812 included fourteen barrels of local potatoes for the passengers of the *Eddystone*. In 1819 the new Orkney agent, John Rae, was instructed to take on board fresh beef and vegetables, and two years later, good quality, kiln-dried oatmeal. This seems to have been a preliminary trial, as the twenty bolls of oatmeal were to be shipped across the Atlantic on board the *Prince of Wales* and *Eddystone* and, if met with satisfaction at the posts, would be re-ordered from Orkney in larger quantities.[2] The HBC's entire annual order of provisions was considerable, but there was a negative consequence of its reliance on Orcadian supplies; non-HBC boats making the same passage struggled to purchase enough refreshments in Stromness because the HBC bought up all the local supplies before they sailed for Hudson's Bay in June.[3]

These commercial exchanges between the HBC and Orkney were on a far smaller scale than those carried out in England, where the Company provided a market for a variety of merchandise, including bricks, stationery, cheese, combs, guns, beads, shoes, hats, and linen, all of which were exported to Hudson's Bay.[4] Yet the impact on Orkney was more concentrated, and as Rev. William Clouston noted, the money paid out by the HBC agent in Orkney 'tends to quicken the trade of this little place'.[5] He estimated that £2,000 to £3,000 a year entered the local economy as a result of the transactions between the Company and Orkney. However, only a small proportion of this capital entered Orcadian society through the purchase of provisions; the bulk of cash entered the community through the employment of local men in the fur trade.

It had taken decades for the initial mercantile contact between the HBC and members of Orcadian society to evolve into the profound working relationship evident in the late eighteenth century, but this development had a significant impact on the Orkney Islands. Temporary migration from Scotland to Hudson's Bay was stimulated by economic motives, and substantial sums of money entered Orkney through personal remittances from employees in the HBC to members of Orcadian society, and the payment of wages to men on their return home. In accord with Clouston, it seems that £2,500 was the minimum amount entering Orkney though repatriation each year. In 1797, Geddes paid ninety Orcadian servants' wages and bills in Orkney, amounting to £2,543 19s 5d, exclusive of any advances paid prior to embarkation. Three years later, when the participation of Orkneymen peaked, the balance of wages alone owing to Orkney servants totalled £4,831, exclusive of any remittances. Of course, the amount diminished in correlation with the decrease in Orcadian participation, but in 1814, wage packets and bills paid in Orkney amounted to over £3,300, while in 1820, £2,667 was paid out directly to employees and their families.[6] It is important to remember that these wages and money orders did not include the numerous funds retained in servants' Company accounts or directed by Orcadian employees to savings accounts and investments in Britain, some of which entered Orkney at a later date.

Financial commitments

Many servants in the HBC worked to provide for the economic needs of their family household and entered the Company with financial commitments in their home societies. Individual obligations varied according to the personal make-up of each employee's family, but one officer advised the Committee in the 1790s that the majority of employees had families on the breadline. Many of these impoverished men entered the service in order to relieve their wives and children from destitution, and in these cases, temporary migration to Rupert's Land seems to have evolved as a domestic sustenance strategy.[7] Some Orcadian servants, such as George Banks who died in the service in 1809, were their family's only support. Other employees, without wives and children, also held considerable responsibility. Many worked to provide for their parents, siblings and distant relatives and, in such instances, the servant was often the sole breadwinner.[8]

Those without such obligations in their home societies, and perhaps some with, often acquired other familial commitments in Rupert's Land. Native wives and families incurred fewer expenses than Scottish families, but outfitting children and provisioning country wives and offspring with factory goods were considerable costs. The Company directors had sanctioned the support of native families belonging to officers, despite the fact that it was a costly burden on the Company. However, they decreed that all corporate support to those family members would cease once a servant had died or retired from the Company. Therefore many employees with mixed-blood dependants faced considerable pressure to accumulate sufficient economic resources to secure the future of their families.[9]

Servants also had numerous expenses of their own, which they had to meet during their service. The Company supplied accommodation and basic provisions, but despite recruitment propaganda, which had pronounced that there were no opportunities in Hudson's Bay to spend wages, other necessities had to be purchased.[10] Adequate clothing was essential for the men who laboured in the freezing Arctic climes of Hudson's Bay. The directors did not bear the cost for the outfitting of British employees; servants had to equip themselves with clothing. They either purchased these items before departing their homeland, from ships' stores or at the factories in Rupert's Land. The men who entered the service of Lord Selkirk in 1812 were granted gratuitous equipment, and the clothing tickets issued to them offer an indication of the outfit that was required during a sojourn. Alex Miller was entitled to a hat, 'Coat, Jacket and Trousers, Flannel Waistcoat and Drawers, two Shirts, two pair of Stockings, two Handkerchiefs, and a Blanket'.[11] Other necessary goods included needles, paper, thread, soap, knives, and twine. It is therefore not surprising that 19 per cent of the annual wage of Orcadian servants at Severn post was spent on goods in 1807.[12]

Financial responsibilities did not end with the termination of employment in Rupert's Land, or a short visit home; both came at a price, contrary to the claims of the contract that promised a free passage. Until the 1790s, all employees who did not hail from London had to pay for their own travel costs from Gravesend to their home societies, and the journey from London to Orkney was expensive.[13] After the 1790s, although this cost was eliminated, employees still had to pay for their own beds on the voyage home and, during the war-induced labour shortage, also had to pay five guineas for the voyage across the Atlantic if going on leave, or re-entering the service.

Constructing a mode of remittance

The London Committee members may not have realised the extent of their employees' cumulative financial responsibilities, but they were aware that many families relied upon service in the HBC as an essential source of revenue. The management developed various mechanisms to help the servants meet their financial commitments and ease the process of remittance. Although some of the Company's regulations were formed under the guise of paternalism, ulterior motives often prompted such measures, which ultimately infringed upon employees' autonomy.

The traditional method of transferring wages and savings from employees in Rupert's Land to their families in Scotland was complex. At Hudson's Bay, employees endorsed bills that were payable to the ships' captains, who then collected the servants' wages on their return to London in September. The captains were given instructions on whom to pay the money to and subsequently disbursed the men's accounts in Orkney on the outward-bound journey the following year. The long delay experienced by the poverty-stricken Orcadians, desperate for an income, was a great inconvenience.[14] Any remaining money was retained by the captain and presented to the servants when they arrived in Hudson's Bay.

This mode of payment was beset with problems for both the Company and the servants. The directors had no means to control their employees' financial dealings, resulting in indebtedness to the Company and private trade at Hudson's Bay.[15] It was an equally unsatisfactory arrangement for the workforce, due to the lack of security in remitting via the captain, particularly as the Company claimed no responsibility for the safekeeping of their funds while they were in the captain's possession. In the early 1780s, the death of a captain was accompanied by the loss of all the servants' property in his custody, highlighting the precariousness of this method of transmission.[16]

The managers elected to develop a new method of payment that was safe and convenient for their employees and that also restricted unregulated activity at Hudson's Bay. They aspired to uphold their decree that 'no Captain or Officer of their ships shall sell or barter any Slops, Liquor, or other Articles with the Company's Servants', and in order to do so, decided to stop remittances from 'passing through the hands of the Captains'.[17] Upon seeking the advice of Andrew Graham, an ex-officer located in Edinburgh who was familiar with the people in Orkney, the Company instituted a new system in the mid-1780s that offered servants an alternative method of dispatch.

The most significant change was the removal of cash from the remittance process. All transactions in Rupert's Land were to be conducted on a credit and debit system, so that employees could continue to take up factory goods and order sums of money to people and financial institutions in Britain, without handling any cash directly. Liaison agents, Andrew Graham, and subsequently David Geddes, were then appointed to arrange the payment of the balance of wages due to returnees, in cash, in Orkney, and also the support money directed to employees' relatives. Prior to embarkation, servants were required to leave notice with the agent of any orders that they had given to their wives and families to receive a portion of their wages during their absence.[18]

The directors also implemented some guidelines to support their servants in the management of their accounts and prevent them from becoming overdrawn. An annual limit was imposed on all money orders, regardless of whether they were directed to members of family, the Company agent, or a bank account. The directors declared that they would not allow any of the workforce to purchase goods at the post and draw bills that together amounted to more than two-thirds of their annual wages.[19] They also told their chief factors to inspect all of the servants' drafts, regardless of to whom they were addressed, approve them, and then enter them into the factories' books. The chief factor was to signify his reasons for permitting each remittance and to sign each order to ensure that the bills were sensible and genuine. This rule was to put a stop to gambling and decadence amongst the servants; any of the men who partook in gaming would find the drawback to their transgression as their money orders would not be paid.[20]

Restrictive regulations applied only to the lower-ranking servants, as the directors believed that the officers might wish to invest their salaries to good advantage, such as into bank stock. The management emphasised that the limitations placed on servants' accounts were not designed to prevent men from equipping themselves with adequate clothing, or from easing economic domestic pressures at home. They claimed that it 'originates in our attention to the Welfare of our Servants by curbing extravagance, and providing that they may not be exposed to Poverty and evil Courses when they come over'.[21] Altruistic reasoning aside, it was clear that by limiting the amount of European goods in each servant's possession, the opportunity to participate in private trade diminished, and prescribing expenditure reduced the likelihood of indebtedness to the Company.[22]

The directors thought that their servants in reduced circumstances, and their households in Orkney, would welcome this system, particularly as this method did not incur any cost, such as postage, and they would receive their money in cash. Employees were assured that all drafts would be fulfilled in Orkney or wherever else required. Although the Company had not forbidden its employees from remitting via the ships' captains, and indeed, some continued to transmit their wages in this manner, most of the Orcadian servants were appreciative of the new way in which they could send allowances home to assist their families.[23]

Remitting wages: putting theory into practice

Despite the efforts of the Company directors to construct a dependable mode of repatriation, it was inevitable that some problems would emerge in implementing mechanisms for the transferral of wages over such a distance, and through a variety of channels. Servants, intermediaries, and administrative staff had the potential to cause obstacles to the flow of money. The consequences were particularly severe for employees who had financial responsibilities in their home societies, and the intended recipients who anticipated essential financial support.

For a start, the ongoing reliance on the Company ships was a major drawback to easy repatriation. The details of servants' accounts and instructions for remittance carried on these ships and any deviation from the vessels' standard timetable caused a time-lag in dependants' receipt of money orders. Unpredictable weather – such as in 1817, when an early winter at Hudson's Bay brought ice – could detain the ships in the Arctic. This meant that families did not receive their designated stipend until the following year.[24]

While delayed ships were sometimes to blame for obstruction in the transmission of funds, the carelessness of employees was perhaps the most common barrier to remittance. Employees often dipped into their intended funds during their sojourn and, although their insolvency was the product of a variety of factors, it was usually self-inflicted. The father of James Mowat was informed in 1820 that he would not receive any support money from his son because he had taken up more goods during his sojourn at Hudson's Bay than his wages would allow.[25] Of course, servants had to spend a portion of their income on essential factory goods, but some also indulged in unnecessary purchases such as tobacco and alcohol. In 1817, one Orcadian wife was refused any subsidy from her husband's account as his balance was so low and it was noted in his character reference the following year that he was 'frequently in the habit of getting intoxicated', to the point that he had been suspended. Perhaps the directors' statement that 'few sober men' can spend at Hudson's Bay was more accurate than their assertion that there was no outlet for expenditure in Rupert's Land.[26]

Extravagant purchases, such as musical instruments and silver watches, also consumed valuable funds. The private commissions record numerous requests from long-term servants for silver watches, which cost almost the equivalent of the annual labouring wage at the time. For instance Nicholas Spence, a boat-builder from Stromness, bought a watch costing £5 in the 1790s. The upkeep of these was also expensive and employees had to fork out for repairs at considerable expense: the accumulated cost of just over forty men getting watches cleaned and repaired was £66.[27]

Overspending in Hudson's Bay was certainly a common obstacle to solvency and the payment of domestic debts, and another was misbehaviour. Servants who deserted the service, or contravened rules, were punished in their pockets. For instance, when James Johnston smuggled and stole at Hudson's Bay in 1815, his remittances were not paid in Orkney, for the sake of public example. Likewise, penalties were imposed on employees who refused to undertake unwelcome work duties. In 1801, Alexander Gunn was fined £10 at York Factory, along with another three Orcadians, for refusing duty. In view of the fact that his wages were £16 at the time, the fine was quite substantial. However, the Committee, believing 'excessive Punishments as well as too lenient ones have their Evils', reduced the fine to the lesser, but still significant amount of £4.[28] In addition, William Flett Snr was fined £20 in 1795 for impudent behaviour towards his officers and refusing duty. He was fortunate that his long service was well-regarded by the Committee who eventually decided to reduce the fine.[29] Perhaps it was due to this clemency that servants did not appear overly troubled when fined by officers. Those who refused to undertake their duties at Albany in 1812 were threatened with punishment, but scoffed at the notion of a fine, and the men were later docked the entirety of their wages.[30]

The other misdemeanour that merited firm action was desertion, and the management was resolute that no payment would be made on the accounts of deserters. The circumstances of these men were perhaps so dire that the consequences of their conduct did not occur to them, or they may simply have been unaware that the penalty for their behaviour would rebound upon their dependants at home. Four families in Islay were refused any money to alleviate their financial difficulties, due to the conduct of their spouses and sons. They had been in the habit of receiving £15 bi-annually, but since their men had deserted the Company service in 1815, it was decided that they would get nothing more.[31]

It is clear from the correspondence written by family members of two Irish deserters in 1817 and 1818 that such behaviour caused both emotional and financial anguish. One father begged the HBC to remit him a portion of his son's wages, which he was 'entitled to get … during these two last years' and added that 'If my son knew my distress I would not be long wanting'.[32] In a last attempt, he enquired as to whether the Company would take another son into the service. The mother of another deserter and a self-proclaimed 'distressed widow' echoed his troubled sentiments when she informed the Committee that she was really upset with her son as 'his wages was my chief support'.[33]

Employees' irresponsibility was a significant bar to successful remittance, but there was also considerable scope for malpractice and fraud from the inter-mediaries who were involved in the repatriation process. In 1790, the officers at York Fort received a number of grievances from Orcadian servants over the captains' failure to pay their remittances at home, as promised. William Oman had sent one guinea to Jennet Oman through the hands of Captain Tunstall but she, like many others, did not receive her allowance. The non-payment of these remittances meant that employees' wives and children were 'left in great distress and destitute of every support'.[34] It was fortunate that officer William Tomison was on leave in Orkney, and heard of the suffering of several households in

Stromness, including the families of employees, John Flett, Alex Flett, James Murray and Robert Sinclair. He was able to relieve their relatives' discomfort by advancing them a combined total of £8; however, the rest of the families would have remained terribly deprived. In response, the management expressed their disapproval of servants continuing to remit via the captains and instead advocated the services of the Orkney agent.[35]

The employment of an agent in Orkney had been intended to secure the property of the workforce, and under the management of David Geddes this was generally the case. However, in 1813, when the administration of Company business in Orkney passed to his son, George, the servants' financial affairs became less secure. Some servants, already in arrears, were led into further debt by the actions of Geddes, who permitted extravagant advances on their wages. In 1816, he offered employees more than their annual salary in advance. For example, William Dickson was given £30 when his wages were only £25 and at least another two servants, William Manson and George McDonald, got into debt in 1818 as a result of his excessive advances.[36]

Furthermore, in 1818 George Geddes went bankrupt. The repercussions were profound for both Orkneymen in the HBC and their loved ones at home. The Committee were sorry that employees' relatives would once again experience problems in receiving their remittances from Hudson's Bay and they were also concerned that these people still had interest to claim on money being held by George Geddes.[37] Although domestic households suffered, the real devastation fell upon servants in Rupert's Land who had mistakenly entrusted Geddes with their savings. The HBC informed officers at the Bay that upon hearing the news of bankruptcy, the men might try to return home to recoup their money. This was to be averted by reassuring servants that the Company had taken the matter in hand and was better placed to deal with the crisis than the employees themselves would, on their return.

It is clear that employees were distraught at the news, as five Orcadian servants wrote to the directors querying the state of their accounts and desperately claiming that the document authorising Geddes to receive their wages was a forgery. However, they shot themselves in the foot as the management pointed out that the signatures on the written queries matched those on their letters of authorisation to Geddes.[38] Despite these false assertions, the Company attempted to assist the servants and sent out affidavits and powers to gain their authorisation to act on their behalf. The claimants were also instructed to inform the directors of the amount the ex-agent owed them, as Geddes' property had been put under sequestration. They each named a person who might act on their behalf and invest any money recovered, either in the Company's hands or in such security as they thought advisable, but by 1821, the Company was still awaiting news on whether the sequestration would allow anything for the 'poor fellows' at Hudson's Bay.[39]

Although the Committee members were sympathetic towards these distressed servants, managerial obduracy also proved to be a significant obstacle to remittance, as the directors were pedantic about the execution of their rules for repatriation. Employees who wrote bills that did not comply with the administrative requirements, which included getting their money orders signed by a superior and entered into the account books in Rupert's Land, were informed that their remittances could not be met. In 1793, a bill from an Orcadian servant to his wife was not entered in the books, so the directors informed the Orkney agent that he was only to pay it, when presented to him, if signed by an officer at Hudson's Bay.[40]

Some families were not afforded any relief, because their benefactor had failed to comply with the stipulation that any instructions for support money were to be left with both the HBC and the intended recipient in Orkney. Allowances to family members would not be paid if the Company did not have a signed letter or order from the servant on whose account the demand was made: sons and spouses intermittently failed to leave such an assignment. For instance, William Longmoor from Edinburgh had a son in the HBC who annually remitted £6; however, in 1787 he was notified that it could not be paid as his son, Robert, an officer in the Company, had left no instructions to that effect. Although the Committee tended to assume that a servant had simply overlooked the drafting of an assignment and took the time to inform the employee that a family member had requested money, Orcadian mothers and wives such as Jean Irvine and Margaret Odie, who were anticipating support money in 1818 and 1820 respectively, were often left without.[41]

Yet in some cases, the servant from whom money was requested simply did not want anyone to receive a payment on his account, perhaps due to the formation of competing responsibilities in Hudson's Bay. The husband of Janet Tate in Stromness wrote to the Committee from Albany factory in 1820, instructing them to pay her no more than £12 a year, and only after the following year was up, as he had left her enough money to sustain her for two years. He stressed that 'any bill that may be drawn on me do not accept till you hear from me as I am determined not to pay any money but what I give an order for'.[42] Likewise, Thomas Mainland informed the Committee in 1795 that a £7 claim on his account from his wife was not sanctioned.[43]

Overcoming problems

Failings in the system of remittance frequently emerged, and the London Committee endeavoured to tackle the various difficulties, paying particular attention to the problems that directly affected the corporation, such as debt. Yet although the HBC was more concerned with maximising its profits than with assisting employees who were in financial need, at the same time the directors were not unmindful of the plight of families whose impoverishment was a consequence of the Company's administrative failings.

A sceptical view may be that although the Company officially discouraged debt, in reality it may have been to its advantage that servants were in debt, particularly to the HBC, not least in times of labour shortage. George Simpson echoed this sentiment in 1823, when he commented on a reluctance of servants to renew their contracts but indicated that this was acceptable as a number were already hired and 'bound by their heavy debts'.[44] Yet debt did not necessarily tie a servant to further service. Some Inverness men served only three years and then returned home while still in arrears. Edward Fraser returned £15 overdrawn but 'possessing more honourable principles than are generally found in persons of his Class of life ...squared his account'.[45] The HBC's concern was that not all employees held such scruples. In addition, employees' arrears frequently 'occasioned some disappointment as well as dissatisfaction for the service' in Scotland, which was detrimental to recruitment.[46]

It was in the best interests of the Company to overcome the problems of indebtedness, and in 1800 the directors really endeavoured to crack down on the number of servants in debt. Many employees had managed to evade the rules and draw unapproved money orders despite being overdrawn, and in 1800, over thirty such irregular bills appeared, not entered in the account books and drawn by servants in arrears.[47] A practice had also emerged among the inland servants of drawing for the entire balance of their wages. According to the officers in Hudson's Bay, the servants did this to thwart punishment, as without credit they could not be fined for refusing to undertake unwelcome duties. It was clear that although the Company had imposed a limit on expenditure, and dictated that all bills must be signed, these regulations had proved ineffective. The managers commented that this practice had crept in over time, and when some were paid by Geddes, it put the Company to significant loss. The directors had insisted in 1801 that if the agent had paid anyone too much, then he must try to reclaim it, even if the servant had already departed the service and returned home.[48]

In order to overcome this, the Committee decreed that the 'Country Bills' must wait to be paid until the servants' accounts had been examined.[49] Imminent drafts and irregular bills were then deposited at the London headquarters until the accounts from Rupert's Land had been regulated. The directors wanted to confirm that servants had not purchased more goods at Hudson's Bay than their wages would allow. This merely aggravated the difficulties that servants had in remitting, as overdrawn servants and those without enough money to meet their assignments would not have their bills honoured.[50] Such was the case of Orcadian Peter Knight, who drafted an order for £7 to his wife Ann in 1809. It was not discharged as he was in debt to the Company. The following year, another twenty-six employees did not have their remittances complied with in Orkney, in consequence of their insufficient funds. This was not confined to Orcadian employees; the father of Hector McLean from Inverness was not afforded any allowance in 1820 because of his son's indebtedness.[51]

A delay in disbursement also occurred, as families had to wait for the ships' arrival with account details, which were then checked in London, before being granted a remittance. This meant that the Company refused to honour payments, such as that of William Ross who was left a £5 order by his son Alex in Rupert's Land in 1820, until they received confirmation that his son's assets met the assignment.[52] Therefore the system that had been designed to overcome delays and ease the process of remittance had actually come to slow down the transfer of funds.

However, the directors were not entirely pragmatic, and despite drawing up guidelines for the management of servants' accounts, and professing that they would be strictly adhered to, the Committee and the agent occasionally utilised their discretionary powers. They ensured the well-being of employees' dependants, and in some cases, this was in conjunction with the servant. For instance, in 1783 John Cox, a carpenter, permitted the Company to bestow support money on his family, from his account, as the directors 'think necessary and their necessities require'.[53] In addition, the management occasionally permitted families an advance on an anticipated remittance. Trifling sums were awarded to the wives of employees, on the condition that these were not forgotten and later deducted from the money orders sent by their husbands.[54]

The HBC also offered financial assistance to families that were in dire need, without an endorsement from the employee whose account would be affected. Unsanctioned assistance was offered to needy relatives when the ships were detained in Hudson's Bay. Isabella Bews was annually transmitted the sum of £15 from her husband and was awarded the equivalent amount of support money when the *Prince of Wales* failed to arrive in 1812.[55] Likewise, wives who suffered as a result of their husband's debt or carelessness were sometimes given subsidies. When William Loutitt was overdrawn by £3 in 1799, the directors authorised the Orcadian agent to use his discretion in helping the family, as his wife in Orkney might be in need of some financial support. In 1818, they also permitted Marian Sinclair from Kirkwall, wife of Peter Sinclair, a carpenter, to be given £12 a year from her husband's wages, despite his arrears. This allowance was granted because of harsh family circumstances but would be stopped if her husband, Peter, spent more than £10 a year on factory goods, until he recompensed the Company.[56]

On some occasions the Company actually went to great lengths to ensure the financial welfare of its employees' dependants. An example is the saga of David Sanderson and his wife Barbara, which is systematically documented in the Company's official correspondence between the early 1790s and 1811. Although it is not certain that David Sanderson entirely abandoned his wife, she interpreted it as such, and persistently badgered the Company managers for financial aid from 1794 onwards. The directors eventually demanded that the Orkney agent 'give Barbara Sanderson some money to stop her mouth & prevent her presenting the Committee with her letters', and she was subsequently furnished with £10. They also suggested that she apply to her spouse for an annual bill, but this seemingly was not sanctioned. In 1802, the directors went as far as to confirm the Laws of England, which required a husband to assist his wife if he was in a position to do so, unless divorced. To this end, they addressed Sanderson in 1805 while resident in Hudson's Bay and intimated that his wife needed support money for the upkeep of herself and her child during his absence. They pressurised him to remit a portion of his wages, stressing that it was his legal obligation. He was commanded to acquaint them with the amount he would allow her for annual maintenance and to 'make that proper Allowance for them which you can afford'. The directors were successful, as Sanderson did grant an allowance, but his wife relentlessly drew bills that exceeded the limit prescribed by her husband. The Company Secretary warned her in 1811 that her husband had notified them that she had 'fully sufficient to support yourself & Daughter if you make a proper use of it'.[57]

The tumultuous affairs of the Sandersons serves as a reminder that the servants did not always share the directors' concern for the well-being of their dependants, and that such interference was not always welcome. It is certainly clear that the Committee took considerable liberties in permitting its agent to make the occasional advance to family members without the consent of the employee.[58] Yet it is likely that most employees would give their permission if they were aware that their relations were in financial straits and would ultimately appreciate the assistance offered to their families. Certainly some servants, such as Archibald Currie from Islay, were unperturbed to find that his account was not as high as expected on his departure from service. In 1818, he understood the fact that his family had been advanced extra money from his wages in consequence of the adversity they had experienced in Islay, in the years since he left them.[59]

Although the directors probably based their paternalistic intrusion on the conviction that it was both welcome and necessary, they seem to have had underlying motives for offering this aid. In fact, it is clear that their support did not emerge from compassion alone, as the directors advised the Orkney agent in 1796 that such assistance could ease the future recruitment of new hands.[60] Furthermore their generosity had definite limits. When George Geddes took advantage of the discretionary powers in 1818 and gave out £230 unsanctioned support money to the relatives of servants, the Committee changed its policy. Any person who required support and did not have an order from their relative, countersigned by an officer at Hudson's Bay, would be considered for relief only if the request was accompanied by a testimony from a Parish Minister or elder confirming their hardship.[61]

Sustaining households

Despite the challenges and obstacles to remittance that some servants and their families faced, for the most part employees successfully conveyed support money to their relatives in their home societies. Even the worst cases mentioned above, such as Peter Knight, who failed to send back money due to his indebtedness in 1809, successfully repatriated a total of £89 to his wife, Ann, between 1813 and 1819. In fact, at least 41 per cent of the eighty-three men stationed at Edmonton post transferred their wages to households in Orkney during this time. The aggregate sum amounted to less than £350, however, which suggests that perhaps Rev. John Malcolm's remark that HBC employees were 'able to remit a trifle to their families', was well-informed.[62] Yet considering that the Company believed family support was a key incentive for service, and the men noted that without financial assistance their households were often on the breadline, it is possible that the above figure does not offer an accurate depiction. The number of men who remitted to dependants may have been underestimated, as the enumeration included only bills that specified the recipient as wife, parent, sibling, or to someone bearing the same surname; many employees sent money to women bearing different surnames. In addition, 65 per cent of men at Edmonton also remitted money to the Orkney agent between 1813 and 1818, amounting to £1,405.[63] Some of this money may have also entered private households during an employee's absence, as the agent not only saved the men's wages but also provided families with local goods in Orkney, which were then charged by the agent as cash advanced.[64] Accordingly, it seems that a greater share of the profits of the fur trade entered private domestic economies in Orkney than the above figures suggest.

Examination of the servants' accounts at Moose, Eastmain, Albany, Edmonton, and Churchill posts also suggests that there were no particular trends or patterns in the remittance behaviour of Orkneymen as a group, or even individuals. However, it is clear that some members of the HBC worked with the sole purpose of providing subsistence for their families in their home societies, as many of the money orders specifically stated that they were to their wives and for support during their absence.[65] These remittances were regular orders, and of such a size that they could have constituted a vital portion of the household income.

For instance, John Spence, a labourer from Birsay, earned £72 17s 8d at Moose, over a period of six years, 83 per cent of which was remitted to his wife. Likewise in the early 1800s, William Irvine, a labourer from Stromness, released funds varying between £5 5s and £6 6s to his wife on an annual basis; and another labourer, Nic Bews, made yearly payments to his wife and children in Kirkwall from 1805 until his return to Orkney in 1809. Out of his annual salary of £10, Bews remitted sums of £8 to £9 2s, aside from one payment, which was only £2 2s. While there was no apparent explanation for the smallness of the latter allowance, the varying sizes of some remittances can be explained by the wage rate. For example, William Scolla from Kirkwall also made regular remittances to his wife between 1796 and 1799. He served as a tailor at Eastmain, and when his wages were £8 he sent back just over half his salary; and when his income increased to £15, he again transmitted over half his salary, but amounting to a far larger sum.[66]

In contrast to the remittances dispatched to wives, those directed to parents tended to be less frequent and insubstantial. Peter Flett dispatched £2 to his mother every second year during his tenure at Edmonton between 1813 and 1819, while Charles Stanger made four remittances to his father between 1803 and 1809, which alternated between £1 and £2.[67] It is possible that the allowances sent to wives were intended to cover a broad outlay, including the support of children, rent, and perhaps education, whereas parents, who were possibly widowers, required less substantial provision.

In addition to difficulties in determining the amount of money that was applied for family support, few sources shed light on the direct impact of such remittances on household economies between 1780 and 1821. The clearest indication of the importance of remittances in this era can probably be gauged from the distressed response of dependant family members who did not receive their anticipated allowance, as previously noted. In addition, a horde of undelivered letters dating from 1830 confirms that the transmittal of support money to families in Orkney was often instrumental in sustaining struggling household economies and alleviating crippling poverty. It is likely that repatriated wages had a similar impact in the preceding decades, and that the stream of money eased the financial burdens of renting a dwelling-house or farm, and ensured basic family welfare through the provision of food and clothing.

The correspondence from the Orcadian father of an HBC employee, William Wilson, reflects the positive effects that remittances had on relieving poverty in 1830. Wilson entered the Company in 1826 when both his parents were in poor

health and struggling to meet essential costs. His father divulged that he was
unfit to pay the rent, and that William's siblings faced an equally hard struggle
as they could not make a living for themselves in Orkney. It was left to William
to provide a lifeline for his family and he honoured this sense of duty by sending
£5 a year to his parents in Orkney. His father noted that the 'Littel that I have
recived from you is bine A verey great help to me' and 'I hope the Lord will bliss
you on account of your former Kindness and hopes you will continue it as I
niver was in more nide'. In a second letter, also written in 1830, Wilson's father
acknowledged receipt of another remittance of £4 and to being in desperate
need when he received it. His acknowledgement that 'Sheurlie it is the Lordes
doeins that has provided such a wey of help for us', shows that although the
payments may appear small, their impact on domestic economies was huge,
and they may have made the difference between domestic self-sufficiency and
dependence on the local poor fund.[68]

Yet some remittances suggest that a number of household economies were
not wholly reliant on the earnings provided by HBC service. Thomas Loutitt
sent only one bill of £5 1s to his mother in Harray over a five-year period and
William Ballenden made only one payment of £4 to his father in eight years.[69]
In these cases, remittances seem to have served as an irregular top-up for family
income, or to ease the burden of unexpected domestic expenses. This may have
been the case for Oman Norquoy who was able to transfer £4 of his wages to his
sister in 1814 in order to bear the cost of his mother's funeral expenses. Likewise,
when James Sutherland requested that his brother should take his mixed-blood
son back to Rupert's Land in 1817, he wanted to ensure that they were both well-
equipped with proper clothing. He directed his brother to go to Mr Geddes if
he was short of funds to purchase clothes and the agent would supply him with
the necessities from the funds in Sutherland's account.[70]

These remittances serve as a reminder that although a portion of employees'
wages flowed through the hands of the Orkney agent to family members and
dependants in Orkney, crippling poverty and family support were not the sole
incentives to serve in the HBC. Employees who remitted in this manner were
mindful of the economic difficulties that family members could endure in their
absence, but their own aspirations for personal betterment were often the driving
force behind their sojourn. To this end, larger portions of the servants' salaries
were either retained in the hands of the Company, the care of the Orkney agent,
or sent directly to financial institutions in Britain. This afforded servants the
opportunity to accumulate capital during their sojourn, offering them better
prospects on their intended return.

Savings and investments

In 1841, Rev. James Anderson of Orphir reflected upon the earlier tradition of temporary migration from the parish and observed that the main goal of employment for a servant in the HBC had been 'to save as much as might render [his] future days at home, easy and comfortable'.[71] Servants who aspired to hoard their wages had a variety of means through which to do so. Of course the most straightforward mode was to economise as far as possible and leave their earnings intact in their personal Company accounts. The HBC's regulation that employees could only draw upon two-thirds of their wages would have proved advantageous to those seeking to save money in this manner. Their balance was tallied at the end of a contract, and either paid to the employee in Orkney if he had departed the Company, or carried over into the new ledger if he remained in the service.

One HBC scheme, conceived in 1812, furthered their ability to accrue capital in this manner. The directors resolved that servants who left their annual wages in their Company accounts would receive the 'beneficial privilege' of being rewarded with as much as 5 per cent interest on their balance.[72] The Committee's intention in offering this incentive is unclear, but it was perhaps intended to encourage employees not to overspend, and thereby relieve the directors from the encumbrance of servants' debt. It is also likely that the HBC was sincerely keen for its workforce to reap as much from service as possible, in order to maintain morale and perhaps earn a reputation in recruiting sectors as a lucrative employment. Yet another possibility, which is suggested by the timing of this measure, is that the HBC wanted to delay the payment of wages, as it needed, and benefited from, the extra short-term money. The financial problems created by the Napoleonic wars reached an all-time low towards the end of the first decade of the nineteenth century and had prompted the Company to borrow around £500 to £1,000 from its committee members, at a rate of 5 per cent interest.[73] Although the workforce totalled a fairly meagre 432 servants at this time, many of them had several hundred pounds in their Company accounts, and the extra money would have been of considerable advantage to the HBC as the Retrenchment System initially got underway.

In any case, employees who sought to garner their wages undoubtedly benefited from this gesture. Between 1813 and 1819, Thomas Loutitt from Harray received wages of £18 a year. In addition to remitting money to his mother, and buying factory goods in Rupert's Land, he managed to accumulate over £100 on his account, and retain it for at least three years, adding almost one year's salary to his account through interest. Likewise, Thomas Patterson from Kirkwall gained over £15 in interest on his account in the same time, while Robert Kirkness from Harray saved his balance of £97 4s 6d in the HBC's hands and gained £9 13s 10d in interest over five years. Several other Orcadians enjoyed similar gains.[74]

Many servants' accounts snowballed in this manner, before being sent to other financial bodies to safeguard or accumulate further. Aside from remitting funds to the Orkney agent as previously mentioned, numerous employees intermittently deposited their takings with the private Scottish bankers, Sir William Forbes, J. Hunter and Company in Edinburgh, formerly known as J. Coutts and Company, via the HBC agents. This trend probably arose from existing connections between the firm and the HBC, who used them for transactions with Andrew Graham, and latterly the Geddes family, in order to conduct Company business in Scotland.[75]

The Servants' Account Books illustrate that a small but significant number of Orkneymen at Edmonton post remitted money to Sir William Forbes' bank between 1810 and 1819; the fifteen employees repatriated funds to the bank altogether totalling £687 12s 2d. It seems that their ability to set aside money was unrelated to their station within the HBC, as Orcadian labourer, Robert Thompson, saved £48 in Sir William Forbes' bank, while another unskilled worker, George Flett 2nd, deposited £96 between 1815 and 1818, and semi-skilled worker, James Whitway, an interpreter, banked £82 in 1813. The saving trends of servants at Churchill confirm this, as Thomas Halcrow, a blacksmith earning £30-£32, put away £90 in Sir William Forbes' bank between 1815 and 1819, while colleague William Tait, a labourer and steersman from Ronaldsay, banked £73 in the same time, despite earning considerably less.[76]

These savings were intended to secure the future of employees in the HBC, but they also served as a safety net during service. Despite the durability of employment in the fur trade, changes could occur within the Company that affected the financial security of servants, and consequently there were occasions when employees had to dip into their private saving funds. For instance, Magnus Spence from Birsay entered the HBC as a labourer in 1783, was upgraded to the position of canoeman in 1788, then to a steersman and linguist in 1791. Until 1814, he served in that capacity and earned £30 a year, but in 1815, he was demoted to a labourer earning £20, and the following year held the position of steersman at £15. It is possible that his financial commitments to his native wife and family could not be sustained on the equivalent of 50 per cent of his earlier salary, hence his bill on Sir William Forbes for £145 in 1817.[77] George Robertson experienced similar amendments to his terms, and suffered from a reduction in salary from £30 to £20 in 1815. He also had a family in Hudson's Bay and spent £21 annually on factory goods alone, perhaps prompting his withdrawal of £387 from his savings in Sir William Forbes' bank in 1818 with the realisation that his wages alone were no longer sufficient to support them.[78]

It may have been this temptation to draw upon savings in a bank account that prompted other servants to make longer-term investments, which were less readily accessible and more likely to burgeon. Several employees invested their resources in funded property, and this trend was encouraged by the HBC Secretary, Alexander Lean, who acted as their agent in purchasing stock. He offered monetary advice and practical assistance 'in employing, to their advantage what Money they may have to spare'.[79] Although Orcadian servants were considered to be naturally cautious, some such as George Short and James Banks trusted in Alexander Lean's knowledge and goodwill to identify which of the stocks would best serve them, being most profitable and secure.[80] When Lean happened upon an opportunity to purchase funded property in the 3 per cent consolidated annuities of the Bank of England, he invested money on the servants' behalf.

In 1792, Alexander Lean bought property for Scottish servants, George Short, James Tait, James Banks, William Flett and Robert Longmoor. They each purchased annuities of around £100, which equates with approximately £6,000 today; and Robert Longmoor was simply incrementing his existing funded property of £566 4s 11d. It was a nerve-wracking venture for some servants but Lean sent bank receipts to reassure the apprehensive investors like James Tait that their investment was safe.[81] The following year another four Scots, as well as one of the above men, again invested in shares of between £100 and £150. Originally Mr Lean had not charged for his role in the undertaking, but as stock purchase increased in popularity he began to take a commission, so that inclusive of brokerage fees, the cost of these annuities ranged between £77 and £115.[82]

Stockholding became so prevalent among the HBC's workforce that the directors boasted that 'there are very few, if any of the Company's Orkney Servants, after their first Contract is expired, who are not in the Habit of accumulating the fruits of their Industry & placing it in the public funds of the Bank of England'.[83] Although this was rather embroidered, many other employees did take advantage of this opportunity. In 1798, at least sixteen Scotsmen, all but two of whom were Orcadian, had assets in the 3 per cent consolidated funds, altogether totalling £6,000. Likewise, between 1802 and 1813, twenty Scottish servants at Albany post ordered a total of £1,382 14s 10d to Alexander Lean, to lay out for their benefit in the funds.[84]

Many Scottish officers acquired property in the Bank of England during their service, including John Sutherland, John McKay, Jacob Corrigall and Andrew Moar. Edward Wishart from Orphir, who was a canoe-builder and trader, had also invested in £375 worth of property by 1797, and James Tait bought £105 worth of stock in 1792 when he worked as a summer master. He came to hold a total of £468 of stock in 1798.[85] Both men had worked for over nineteen years in the service and, like the other officers, enjoyed decent salaries and thus probably had a reasonable amount of disposable capital.

Yet investment was an opportunity available to men in all ranks of the Company. James Banks, a 43-year-old labourer from South Ronaldsay, invested in the funds in both 1792 and 1793, culminating in £255 of property, which is worth over £14,000 in present-day values, while William Rich, also an Orcadian labourer, had amassed £150 worth of stock by 1798. After at least fifteen years in the Company as a labourer and steersman, George Short had purchased a total of £138 5s 4d in the 3 per cent consolidated funds. In fact, the station of servants appears to have had little effect upon their ability to invest money. The length of service appears to have been more significant, as for instance, each of the sixteen employees who held stock in 1798 had worked for somewhere between nine and twenty-eight years in the fur trade.[86]

Those who purchased stock in the Bank of England had the potential to accrue economic gains through their investments. The advantages came to fruition in two forms: dividends and appreciation. Servants who had enough disposable capital to make an initial investment, regardless of the amount invested, soon received remuneration as the HBC received annual dividends on their behalf. Dividends were often retained in the hands of the Company Secretary to accumulate with time, and when supplemented with wages, were reinvested. Orcadian officer, Alexander Kennedy, opted for this method of capital accrual, and periodically reinvested his dividends, along with earnings from his Company account, into funded property in the Bank of England. The amount of property bought on his behalf was never less than £25 and up to £125, so that by 1818 he had a total of £625 in the 3 per cent consolidated funds.

Alternatively, the dividends could be given to whoever the servant appointed to receive them. In some cases the annual dividends corresponded to the annual wage that many lower-ranking employees received and could act as a financial security for their families. In 1797, James Tait received as much as £14 interest on his stock of £468, while James Johnson received £2-£3 on his smaller investment, the equivalent of many annual remittances.[87]

There were risks to such investments, as appreciation was not a guaranteed outcome. Some servants such as John Petrie, who died in 1787, left a bank receipt of £100 in the 3 per cent consolidated funds, but in the four years since he purchased the stock, his funds had decreased in value to £74.[88] Fortunately for the stockholders, the Company Secretary, Alexander Lean continued to act as financial adviser and made recommendations to unseasoned stockholders on when to sell their property. He kept an eye on the stock market, and in 1795 was able to advise Scots such as William Flett, George Ross and James Banks, who wished to sell their funds of between £100 and £255 each in the Bank of England. He informed them that the stocks were rising and if peace followed, they might recover the price at which they bought them.[89] Three years later, Lean also suggested that another stockholder should wait to sell his funded property, as it would significantly rise in the event of peace. He noted that the government was creating a plan to produce a similar effect if the war should persist. When peace finally arrived in Europe in 1815, Company employees were notified that their funds had risen, although not as much as was anticipated.[90]

Employees seem to have embraced the various methods of capital accumulation available to them, to the extent that the Company might not have been exaggerating when it claimed that all servants could save money through service. Whether servants held accounts with Sir William Forbes' bank in Edinburgh, property in the Bank of England, or simply retained their wages in the Company account or in the hands of the Orkney agent, they were able to amass profits from the fur trade. Although some availed themselves of their financial reserves before the end of service, the majority of savings eventually entered Orcadian society, whether temporarily or permanently, to the benefit of individual servants, their families, and local communities.

Personal ambitions: agriculture and land ownership

Employment in the HBC was only ever intended as a transitory undertaking, and most employees envisaged an eventual homecoming to brighter prospects. Reports in the *Old Statistical Account* suggest that Orkneymen intended returning to their homelands to set themselves up as farmers. Indeed, local ministers assert that many Arctic sojourners had reaped sufficient wealth to achieve this ambition. They indicated that after an absence of eight to ten years and having made some money, HBC servants were able to rent farms upon their return.[91] Although it might be expected that Orcadian tradesmen who often earned substantial amounts in the fur trade, would set up independent businesses on their arrival in Orkney, the *Statistical Accounts* imply that even they established themselves as farmers.[92]

However, those who managed to stave off debt during their service and accumulate funds for their return to Orkney often found that their fortunes were short-lived and that several years after their homecoming, they were again faced with poverty.[93] The inexperience of returnees in agriculture was problematic, and although the years spent cultivating canoe and trade skills assisted their advancement within the Company, they were a useless accomplishment in Orkney. Many of those who returned to work as farmers found 'their skill in that line not improved by their absence, and their habits frequently not calculated to make them successful'.[94] Critics observed that through 'ignorance and want of industry, the emigrant' was again 'reduced to poverty, and must give way to another of his own tribe'.[95]

Ex-HBC servants may have genuinely failed as farmers but this kind of criticism, often emanating from Rev. Francis Liddell, who held anti-emigration sentiments, was probably fuelled by their seemingly negative impact on the broader agricultural community in Orkney. Temporary migrants were accused of contributing to a high turnover of farmers, as upon their return to Orkney they were 'enabled to overbid the honest industrious farmer'.[96] Those who had temporary arrears were displaced by the comparatively wealthy sojourner, which meant that most farms were over-rented. In addition, frequent changes in land-holding prevented essential improvements in Orcadian agriculture.

However, it is erroneous to assume that the unfortunate affairs of some early returnees, portrayed in the 1790s, represent the experience of all Orkneymen in the HBC. The prosperity of returning sojourners has been seriously under-estimated. Although homecomers commonly aimed to set up as renting farmers in the 1790s, there appears to have been a gradual change in their perception of betterment. This development is confirmed in the *Register of Seisins*, and it shows that some new landowners were employed, or previously employed in the HBC.[97]

Many fur traders who served in the Company between 1780 and 1821 used their revenue and repatriated savings to gain access to the property market. Virtually all of the Scottish employees in the HBC who invested in landed property gravitated to their native homelands and local communities. By 1800, several traders had purchased land, and this trend increased throughout the first two decades of the nineteenth century, with ten HBC employees acquiring land in Orkney between 1810 and 1815 alone. At the same time, some traders who had gained an early footing on the property ladder expanded their property domains. This tendency towards land purchase was such that, by the mid-nineteenth century, ex-employees in Harray were termed the 'Peerie lairds'.[98]

It is not surprising that some of the new landed Orkneymen were among the HBC employees who had risen into the highest ranks of the Company, including Alexander Kennedy, James Clouston, James Kirkness, and James Tait. William Tomison, late governor in the HBC, and thereafter residing in South Ronaldsay, also attained extensive property upon his retiral from the fur trade. He bought land in Grindelay in South Ronaldsay in 1805, the Pabdale lands in St Ola in 1815, which included dwelling-houses and a kailyard, and in 1822 also gained twenty acres of land at Linn Cottage and Linn Breck in St Ola, along with three tenements of land or dwelling-houses on the outskirts of Kirkwall. Officer Adam Snodie, with his wife, also reaped the benefits of sojourning, and in 1819 bought a dwelling-house, smiddy, and byre, with a piece of ground in the village of Stromness.[99]

Remarkably, investment in landed property was not restricted to the officer class in the HBC. Many employees who became registered landowners did serve in the managerial stations of the Company, but a significant number worked in the semi-skilled and unskilled low ranks. In 1789, after sixteen years' service as a tailor at Severn Fort, Thomas Flett and his spouse Margaret Sinclair bought land, in life-rent and fee, in the town of Holland, South Ronaldsay. Another landowner, John Crear, entered the HBC in 1792 at the age of seventeen and toiled as a labourer and unskilled canoeman until 1813. His savings from the latter ten years of his service amounted to over £200, and he bought land in Stromness upon his return to Orkney in 1813. Two HBC labourers, John Brough and James Slater, also acquired property in Orkney. The former purchased land in Rendall in 1818, and the latter bought his property in his home parish of Firth in 1810, prior to his promotion to officer.[100] This confirms that station was not the definitive factor in achieving betterment.

Applying the fruits of the fur trade to landed ambition held many appeals, offering social status as well as economic security to individuals and their families. Land was generally a secure form of investment, and it could be further utilised to attract loans, or later sold to accrue further capital.[101] Some Orkneymen who formerly worked for the HBC sold their landed property onto their Orcadian counterparts upon their return home. They seem to have either assisted their former colleagues onto the property ladder, or perhaps taken advantage of their new-found wealth. William Linklater entered the HBC as a labourer in 1783 and rose through the ranks to the position of trader in 1797 and inland master at Churchill in 1800. He bought half of the lands of Gairth in Stromness in 1798 and later acquired '3 Penny land' in Sandwick, which his wife sold with his permission to retired HBC officer, James Clouston, in 1829.[102] Likewise, HBC employee, John Loutitt Jnr, sold two small houses or tenements of this land to his colleague, John Crear, in 1813, as mentioned above.

When the first Orkney agent, David Geddes, died, his son George became heir to considerable landed property. He, in turn, disposed of some of this land to his former colleagues in Hudson's Bay. James Johnstone, a boat-builder, purchased lands from George Geddes in his home parish of Stenness in 1813, and John Howiston who had worked in the low ranks of the Company as a labourer and middleman since 1798, bought land in Sandwick, on disposition by George Geddes, in 1816. He departed from the Company in 1815 and directed a bill of £52 8s 3d to George Geddes that same year.[103] In fact, it is possible that some employees may have become land speculators, as William Tait who bought a dwelling-house, quay and piece of beach in Stromness in 1821 was involved in at least another five land transactions between 1815 and 1830.[104]

The hazards of the fur trade unfortunately meant that some HBC servants did not live to enjoy the rewards of their hard work. William Sinclair from Harray, who was Chief at Oxford House, took a return trip home between 1814 and 1815 and invested in the lands of Eastquoy and Meadow in Harray. He subsequently returned to Hudson's Bay, but less than three years later died of dropsy at York factory. Another employee, James Robertson, suffered a similar fate. He entered the Company in 1781 at twenty-two years of age and, serving as a labourer and steward, worked hard to achieve prosperity. On a brief visit to Orkney between 1805 and 1807, he bought land in North Unigar and Scarwell, both in the parish of Sandwick. He did not occupy this property but continued in the workforce for another two years, until his untimely death in the sub-arctic region of Churchill after twenty-eight years' service.[105] Perhaps the only consolation in such misfortune was that these gains were often transferred to relatives in their home societies.

Family inheritance

The benefits of employment in the HBC filtered through to families in a variety of ways. Aside from the remittance of support money, some servants also ensured that their relatives would be looked after in the event of decease and made arrangements to bequeath their financial gains to dependants. Although the fortunes made in the HBC were generally not grand, some employees' estates did provide a comfortable inheritance for their families, and included land, stock and savings.

Orcadian officer John Ballenden entered the service in 1770 and served for thirty-two years, rising through the ranks to the position of chief factor, and retired from the Company with substantial riches. By the time of his death in 1817, he had accrued £5,000 in the 3 per cent consolidated funds of the Bank of England and also had a share of capital stock in the Commercial Bank of Scotland, valued at £150, from which he received six-monthly dividends. This funded property provided an ample legacy for his wife and six children in Orkney. He also bequeathed the land used by him and his family as a dwelling-house with grounds and other buildings, to his wife in life-rent and children in fee, along with another tenement of land possessed as shops in Stromness.[106]

Another Scottish employee, James Sutherland, also bequeathed a stock-pile of invested property to his family; upon his premature death in Rupert's Land in the 1790s, his brothers in Caithness received £1,050, the equivalent of almost £60,000 today.[107] The HBC emphasised Sutherland's affluence during their recruitment campaign in Caithness in 1805 and boasted that his family had received substantial property between them. The fact that the Company highlighted it suggests that this kind of prosperity was exceptional rather than the norm. In fact this appears to have been the case, as many estates, particularly of Orkneymen, were valued under £300.

Legacies tended to be modest, and for instance, John Howiston's endowment to his brother Thomas Hourston, a farmer in Firth, consisted solely of his landed property, which his brother inherited in 1820.[108] Ailing employee James Robertson likewise made a will in which he bequeathed his landed property in Sandwick to his Orcadian relatives, and the land passed to his nephew in 1822.[109] He also accumulated £400 worth of stock in the 3 per cent consolidated funds of the Bank of England, and requested that any money owing to him be placed in the consolidated funds with his other capital, and the interest would thereafter be used to provide annuities for his family.

This was not an unusual occurrence; employees often requested that their assets be retained in a financial institution after their death and used to provide annuities to family members. For instance, Orcadian Magnus Twatt ensured the continued financial security of his mother and sisters by sanctioning an annuity of £10 to be paid to his mother, and thereafter his sisters, from his funds in Sir William Forbes' bank.[110] These bequests were reminiscent of the remittances sent from Hudson's Bay, and it is possible that servants simply sought to ensure the continued subsistence of their relatives after their death, rather than leave them vast fortunes.

Although Scottish fur traders bolstered the private domestic economies of Orkney, their overall impact on Scotland was diluted by competing responsibilities formed during their service in the HBC. Most traders remitted their wages and savings back to Scotland during their service, but the profits of the fur trade were not always contained within Britain, and employees' funds often entered Rupert's Land at a later date. Long-term employees were more prone to have mixed-blood families, and at the same time were more likely to have amassed substantial profits from their sojourn. Thus it seems that some of the greatest riches of the fur trade were sent back to Rupert's Land.

Servants with attachments in Rupert's Land were more liable to make wills than those without; they were well aware of the poor outlook facing their progeny once paternal financial support was no longer available to them. In fact some employees, such as James Sutherland from South Ronaldsay, felt considerable pressure during their tenure to earn enough money to take care of their mixed-blood families. Sutherland had entered the service in 1797 and hoarded his assets in the public funds throughout his career. Yet even after twenty-eight years' service in the Company, he wrote to his brother expressing his concerns that, 'I now begin to wish to have a settled abode, but when that will be I have not yet determined, nor will the money I have as yet enable me to support myself and provide for my numerous family in the way I would wish'.[111] He continued working in the Company, and by the time of his death in 1834 had stashed a massive £7,000 stock in the Bank of England, the majority of which he left to his eight mixed-blood children in Rupert's Land.

Alexander Kennedy also made sure that his native wife Aggathas would be taken care of during his life and in the event of his death. He had reassured her in 1829 that he would take care of her and their children and to 'be assured that as long as I live I shall never forsake you nor forget you'.[112] He arranged for her to receive the annual interest of a share of his property in the Bank of England for her life, and also bought an allotment of land in the Red River settlement in 1830–1831; 'Widow Kennedy' was listed as the occupant in 1835. The nine mixed-blood children of Alexander Kennedy also fared well, receiving shares of his funds in the 3 per cent consolidated funds and the 3 per cent reduced annuities in the Bank of England.[113]

In a similar vein to the men who provided for their Orcadian relatives, some servants with mixed-blood families arranged for their capital to be retained within Scotland and for annuities to be sent to the HBC for the use of their family members. For example, James Gaddy, who entered the service as a labourer in 1793 and progressed through the ranks to the position of assistant trader and interpreter, made a will in 1818 in order to secure the future of his four mixed-blood children in Rupert's Land. Gaddy left instructions for the annual interest of his bank savings in Scotland to be paid to the HBC so that his children in Rupert's Land could obtain necessary goods from the Company. He stipulated that the shares were to be allocated by the governor at York Factory, and then at the age of twenty his offspring were to receive the remaining funds in cash, along with his landed property in Kirkwall.[114] At least another five executors of Scottish employees' estates, including the representatives for Hugh Sabiston and John McKay, paid annuities totalling £70 to the HBC in 1818, for the use of the deceased employees' children remaining at Hudson's Bay.[115]

The confidence that these men placed in the directors was typical of the HBC's employees; most servants with mixed-blood dependants consigned their whole property, or at least a portion of their assets, to the charge of the London Committee. Benjamin Bruce entered the fur trade as a young man in 1789 and served in the capacity of labourer, interpreter and assistant trader during his 34-year career. During his tenure he remitted his funds back to Scotland where he held a bank account with Sir William Forbes. Bruce also possessed land in his home society of Orkney, but as he spent his adult life working for the Company, he did not have the opportunity to occupy it before his death at Isle à la Crosse in 1823. He granted full power to the directors of the HBC, upon his death, if not already done so by his brother, to sell his house and land in the parish of Walls in Orkney.[116] The proceeds of the sale, along with the rest of his property, which was valued under £300 in 1826, were to be divided by the HBC among his five mixed-blood children whom he had fathered during his long tenure in Rupert's Land.

Similarly, William Flett Snr who was originally from Firth in Orkney transmitted all of his money to the Company in faith that the HBC secretary would disburse the annual interest accrued on his funds to his mixed-blood family at Red River. Flett had worked in the service for forty-one years as a labourer, steersman and master, before retiring to the Red River settlement with his wife Saskatchewan in 1823, and dying soon thereafter. His legacy of £365 14s 1d in the house of Sir William Forbes & Co, and funded property in the Bank of England, were transferred to the HBC and the interest was paid annually for 'the sole use and benefit of my reputed wife Saskatchewan and my four reputed Children' at Red River.[117]

These endowments were always disposed of in the form of provisions from the Company's trading posts rather than cash, which was not used at posts in Rupert's Land at this time and would have served the wives and children no purpose. When James Spence Senior from Birsay became so unwell at Buckingham House in 1795 as to have no hope of his recovery, he made a will in favour of his wife and children, specifying that his family should receive £20 a year in goods, on production of a certificate that the children were still living. Following his death that year, after twenty-two years' service, his stipulation was adhered to, and the family was often given provisions by William Tomison. However, the HBC was unsure about the exact quantity of goods that had been dispensed, noting that if the children had been paid too much in goods, the directors ought to recoup the money from the executors. Nonetheless, the allowance, which amounted to just over £1,000 a year in modern-day terms, was still being paid for Spence's children in the northern district in 1816.[118]

Yet some traders had neither the foresight nor the desire to make a will with entitlements for their family in Rupert's Land. In such instances, the Company management took the liberty of reminding British families of the deceased servants with offspring in Hudson's Bay, that the children required financial support. When James Sutherland from Caithness died in the 1790s, his Scottish relatives were advised that the mixed-blood children in Hudson's Bay were generally better off than the poorest class of children in Britain, so a small annual allowance paid to the HBC would be sufficient to provide them with necessary rations. They mentioned that this method of support had been undertaken by several employees' descendants.[119] As with the native family of Spence, £20 was recorded as the allowance bestowed upon Sutherland's children at York Factory.[120]

Many long-serving employees had formed country marriages and families in Rupert's Land but, despite their integration into fur-trade society, their attachments to their homelands remained strong and they tended to look after the needs of their family members on both sides of the Atlantic. Some of the servants mentioned above also bequeathed money or land to their family members in their home societies. For instance, James Gaddy left two rooms of his landed property in Orkney to his sister Catherine Dick, while James Sutherland left £400 to his brother John in South Ronaldsay with whom he had corresponded during service. Alexander Kennedy was equally mindful of his Orcadian siblings, granting the farm at Braehead to his two sisters, along with £300 each. In addition, his first will had made provisions of £400 for his brother-in-law and £100 to his niece.[121]

Community considerations: education and poor relief

In fact, their attachments to home were sometimes so strong that some of these long-serving employees endeavoured to provide for their local home communities in Orkney as well. In stark contrast to Rev. Francis Liddell's depiction of returnees as idle, debauched and sacrilegious, some Orcadian fur traders bolstered the wider society of Orkney and utilised their gains to effect social change in their home communities.[122] These patrons contributed to the development and maintenance of educational institutions in Orkney. William Tomison entered the fur trade in 1770, served for almost fifty years, and during that time rose to the position of chief factor at York inland. Tomison 'acquired a considerable fortune in Hudson's Bay Company', totalling £10,500, which is the equivalent of more than £500,000 in today's terms. As early as 1785 he declared that he had 'more money than he should live to spend' and in the 1790s manifested a desire to improve educational facilities in his homeland. To this end, he drew on his earnings whilst still working in the fur trade to pay £20 each year as a salary to the schoolmaster in his home parish of South Ronaldsay.[123]

Following his retirement from the HBC and return to his local community, Tomison continued to explore ways in which he could promote education in South Ronaldsay. He conceived of, and implemented, a plan for his trustees to fund and run a fee or charity school in the south parish of South Ronaldsay, which was suitable for the education of poor children. In a Deed of Mortification in 1829, he left funds amounting to half of his estate for this purpose, and after twenty years of capital accumulation, his trustees were either to improve the existing school by enlargement, or to build a new school, along with a school-house and suitable accommodation. Tomison stipulated that natives of Orkney and particularly those bearing his surname should be given preference as students. He also left very specific instructions regarding the recruitment of teachers and bound his trustees to advertise for staff in the Scottish newspapers, inviting candidates to compete for the vacancy.[124] This stipulation suggests that he genuinely cared about the standard of education provided in Orcadian schools. Tomison's Academy was eventually built in South Ronaldsay in 1851 and apparently drew people to Orkney for education, coming to be 'one of the glories of our Island'.[125] The fund was thereafter utilised for the payment of teachers' salaries and maintenance of the school.

The generous donation of Magnus Twatt, who died during his HBC service, was perhaps even more noteworthy. He endowed a school in his home town of Kirbister in Orphir, which is particularly remarkable because, unlike Tomison, his position within the Company did not guarantee colossal wealth. Twatt originally served in the lower ranks of the HBC as a labourer, canoeman and carpenter, and then progressed to the station of occasional master before his death in 1801. During his thirty years of service, Twatt accumulated funds in Sir William Forbes' bank in Edinburgh, and in 1796 bequeathed £700 of this money for schooling. The sum of money was laid out on landed security, and the interest was to foot the bill for a school and schoolmaster for teaching the children of the parish of Orphir.[126]

Another local HBC servant, James Tait, founded a second school in Orphir. He served as a labourer in the Company from 1778, but worked his way up the ranks during his career until he became an occasional master and trader at York inland in 1794. He continued in that position until he left the Company in 1812 and returned to Stromness. Tait shared Tomison's aspiration to encourage education in Orkney and to this end, he stated in his will of 1830 that out of his fondness for the district of Petertown, Orphir, he was going to leave £100 for that purpose. The money was given to the minister of the parish to be applied for 'the benefit and encouragement' of the schoolmaster, and a request was made, similar to Tomison's, that favour be given to 'the Youths of the name of Tate in case of application for gratuitus instruction'.[127] The sum of money was lent on landed security and a new school was instituted in 1839, while the teacher received the interest as a salary. Tait also left £100 to encourage education in Stromness and fur trader, Henry Inkster also left £50 for this purpose in 1841. The latter instructed that the money should be invested securely and the interest should be used on occasion to endorse the education of under-privileged Orcadian children.[128]

It is possible that despite their own success in the HBC, these employees were aware of the detriment that many of their Orcadian colleagues laboured under as a result of their poor literacy and inadequate education. Moreover, the emphasis made by some of these patrons that the educational institutions should specifically serve the poor of Orkney suggests that they themselves may have come from impoverished families who struggled to finance their education. In fact, three of the above benefactors also bequeathed money to the poor of Orkney. Magnus Twatt designated that the surfeit from his estate should be distributed annually to the poor people in the parish of Orphir. Likewise, William Tomison bequeathed £200 to the local destitute in South Ronaldsay, while Henry Inkster donated £8 to relieve pauperism in the parish of Orphir and another £8 to assist the impoverished in Stromness.[129] He also endowed the Stromness Church Missionary and Bible Society with £24, half of which was to be used for missionary purposes, with the rest to go to the Edinburgh Bible Society.

Overall, it is apparent that despite the wealth of a few of these retired employees, the fortunes made in the HBC were generally not vast, particularly in comparison with the great riches that Scottish sojourners often incurred through temporary employment in the American tobacco colonies, Caribbean sugar plantations and India. These men had gone into enterprises in which the pursuit of opulent wealth was ubiquitous, and many returned to Scotland affluent, able to flaunt their prosperity through extensive land purchase and improvement.[130] In contrast, the fur trade was not hailed as a money-spinner, and HBC employees were rarely renowned for their wealth. Scots destined for the Arctic did not harbour grandiose materialistic objectives, but equally, they did not share the disappointment often experienced by those involved in the American, Caribbean and East India trade. Instead, they carried modest and attainable ambitions which were often realised, and it is clear that, in their own way, these humble profits were far-reaching, benefiting members of the Company, their families in both North America and Scotland, and the local societies from which they hailed.

EIGHT

Conclusion

Between 1780 and 1821, the HBC was engaged in a dynamic attempt to address its mercantile potential; but rivalry from the NWC, the competitive labour demands of the Napoleonic wars, a shortage of beaver supplies, and obstructed markets in Europe created a taxing climate, and one in which the contribution of Scottish labour, and Orcadian labour in particular, became increasingly paramount to the success and fortitude of the Company. And if the first century of the HBC's operations was difficult, the period after 1779 presented some particularly acute challenges.

In the 1780s, when the Company made a determined effort to move inland, the growing recruitment tradition, in which the Company turned to Orkney as a source of labour, became more structured, and subsequently formalised. The convenient location of the Orkney Islands, and the abundance of its cheap labour supply, meant that Orkneymen were prime labour for the inland endeavour; in fact, the HBC's commercial expansion was wholly enabled by their enlistment. However, the recruitment scheme became so decisively orientated towards this wellspring, that its increasing dependency on this source proved to be something of a handicap when faced with a backlash of public opinion, and rivalries for the islands' manpower during the Napoleonic wars. Although this instigated a slight deviation from habit, and recruiting agents were directed towards the Highlands and Shetland Isles, the Company continued to seek and encourage Orcadian recruitment.

The most significant turning point in the HBC's recruitment campaign occurred after the institution of the New System in 1810, when, in addition to struggling with the problems caused by the British-French conflict, the Company had to contend with the intensification of trading rivalry with the NWC. A new recruitment practice was ushered in, and a decade of experimentation ensued. The search for energetic, obedient and driven servants to make a firm stand against the Nor'westers broadened the recruitment sphere throughout Scotland, introducing more Highlanders, Lowlanders and Western Islanders to the Company, as well as Canadians, and other Europeans. Although the new strategies often posed a threat to the continued prominence of Orkneymen, and the influx of non-Orcadian recruits resulted in the belief that the Orcadians' hegemony had expired, this was not the case. Both Orcadians, and Scots more generally, gained and retained a remarkable foothold within the Company, and the Orkney Isles continued to provide not only the fall-back labour supply, but also the crux of the recruitment effort, right up until the merger.

Considering that the challenges posed by inland residence had served to deconstruct the management's long-held stereotype of Orkneymen as submissive, obedient and tractable, it is even more remarkable that the HBC's dependency on Orkney endured. The perceived foibles of unfitness and insubordination were attributed to shoddy recruiting by the agents and mismanagement in Hudson's Bay. However, the introduction of men from other locales showed that they all had shortcomings. In fact, juxtaposed with other recruits, the cheapness, convenience, experience and apparent loyalty of Orkneymen rendered them invaluable to the concern.

While Orkneymen were of vital and persistent significance to the HBC, equally the fur trade offered a crucial lifeline and avenue to betterment for many Orcadians. It is clear that domestic prospects were limited, fruitless, or undeveloped in Orkney during the late eighteenth century, and that endemic hardships were periodically exacerbated by famine. However, a versatile temporary migratory tradition meant that members of Orcadian society who laboured under crippling poverty, as well as those who were moderately comfortable and simply sought to improve their lot, had access to numerous opportunities for improvement. The decision to enter the service of the HBC in particular appears to have been a considered one, and based on a variety of factors: recommendations from those already involved, the prospect of fixed wages, stable long-term employment, and considerable scope for advancement of station and enhancement of salary.

Although most employees entered the HBC in low-ranking positions, any servant who wished to achieve a higher status within the Company, and was willing to learn new 'country' skills, could usually realise his ambition. The opportunities provided by inland expansion meant that uneducated and unskilled men were not debarred from advancement into the officer ranks, and although employees who possessed an education had superior prospects, many Orkneymen rose from labouring positions to stations such as trader, clerk, and district master. These opportunities for promotion diminished following the establishment of the New System, as education and social status became imperative, and the implementation of patronage was restricted, but it is important to remember that they had not been abolished. The high value placed on the country skills in which Orcadians excelled, such as fluency in a native language, and trade, meant that Orcadians continued to rise within the Company, despite their apparent lack of officer quality.

It has been suggested that when career prospects were curtailed, fewer Orcadians saw service as a favourable undertaking. However, the earning potential, which was available throughout the ranks, ensured that the Company still provided the avenue to improvement that most men sought. In fact the material success of employees who worked in unskilled labouring positions suggests that the terms in which advancement is viewed ought to be reconsidered, as many Orkneymen of a lowly status successfully utilised their service with the HBC to acquire funded or landed property in Britain. It is probable that the return of men who had achieved their modest ambitions was the most persuasive factor in recruitment. They demonstrated the realistic outcomes that service could provide, such as supporting domestic households in their absence, safeguarding their own future by investing in stock or land, and also securing the future needs of their dependants.

Yet men continued in the service only while the HBC remained more attractive than other employments, and particularly those in their homeland. Home was important to most employees in the HBC, and remained central throughout their sojourn. Servants brought their Scottishness into the fur trade through the transplantation of ethnic symbols, traditions and customs, and stamped their mark on fur-trade society. Although employees celebrated their national origins, it is also clear that inhabitants from regions like Orkney had formed their identities according to their distinct local roots, and the localised origin of the majority of the HBC's recruits was highly significant in shaping their encounter within the fur trade.

Orkneymen were bound together by common origin, a shared history and cultural heritage, pre-existing affiliations which were carried into the fur trade. Orcadian servants were further united in the HBC by mutual purpose, while some also shared strong kinship ties and bonds formed around local parish associations. This nexus was a source of cultural and social solace in Rupert's Land; it underlay friendships and festive celebrations. The links which were formed prior to entering the Company seem to have been reinforced by the shared experience of working in the fur trade. Inter-marriage in Rupert's Land, or simply struggling together against the hazards of the fur trade and the hardships of separation from home, strengthened the attachments of employees to one another. Orkneymen were a unique grouping and this was conspicuous to others in the fur trade in both positive and negative ways. Employees' financial contributions were vital in easing the privation of dependants who had lost their breadwinning spouse to mishaps, and their colleagues who had abruptly departed the service as a result of disability. Yet the Orcadians' overt demonstration of some of the less positive ethnic traits associated with Scots abroad, including cliquish tendencies and rivalries, serves as a reminder that some of the HBC's stereotypes were not just simple ethnic-based generalisations, but were actually legitimate observations.

It is clear that Orcadian webs were of practical utility, and although the vertical structure of the HBC and the infrastructure of Rupert's Land meant that Orcadian coteries and networks were not blatantly visible in the Company, their subtle operation could be detected within the Scots' endeavours for advancement. Most recruits entered the service in low-ranking positions, but some Orcadians with connections in the Company, whether family, friends or the recruiting agent, gained access to hard-to-obtain positions. The ways in which employees were able to influence the London Committee meant that these ethnic bonds were also of utility to the men who had entered the Company in the lowest ranks. Although Scottish patronage was not essential to career success, it was a constructive mechanism for advancement to those who could obtain it, and recommendations, salary increases, and occasionally promotions materialised out of Orcadian networks.

Furthermore, Orcadian solidarity was effectively utilised to enhance the bargaining power when haggling over contracts and wages in Hudson's Bay. Although ethnicity was not the driving force behind these actions, the disproportionate presence of Orkneymen in the Company meant that their identity offered a useful and natural alliance which facilitated such combined initiatives. The Orcadian network transcended Rupert's Land and, as the HBC eventually realised, incorporated former employees and servants' relatives in Orkney. When word of low wages, harsh circumstances, and poor management reached the Orcadian community, these supporters added some influence to the crusade for better wages, by rumour-mongering and discouraging recruitment. The impact of these collective undertakings was a significant and serious concern to the HBC, particularly as one such combination had contributed to the need for recruitment in Caithness and Shetland in the early 1800s.

Yet not all of these campaigns were designed, as the Company believed, to increase wages. Some resistance emerged out of genuine concerns regarding the conditions in Rupert's Land, as the environment in which sojourners in the HBC sought to better their fortunes presented as many risks to their welfare as it did opportunities for advancement. Scurvy, starvation, frostbite, fatigue, disease, gunshot wounds and canoe accidents produced numerous injuries, disabilities, and hardships, as well as claiming many lives. The wide dispersal of posts stretching across Rupert's Land occasioned the need for long journeys on snow-ridden ground or in canoes, to secure food supplies, trade supplies, medicine, and to establish new posts. This meant that employees' attempts simply to ensure their own survival were often negated by the hazards encountered while undertaking these tasks.

In addition, despite the established view that Scots, and Orkneymen specifically, were well-suited to the rigours of the fur trade, they were no more prepared for the challenges that they encountered in Rupert's Land than their English, Irish or French-Canadian counterparts. Irrespective of whether they were seasoned to hardships, hunger, and water-related activities in Orkney, the physical environment of Rupert's land, the nature of their occupations, and the wilderness in which they operated meant that all employees, regardless of ethnicity, were susceptible to the hazards of the fur trade. In fact, Orkneymen were perhaps more vulnerable to such dangers, due to their disproportionate employment in laborious and canoe-related occupations.

The challenges presented by the nature of the work and the climate of Rupert's Land were further exacerbated by the hostile nature of relations between the personnel in the HBC and the NWC. The rivalry between the two concerns emerged in response to commercial competition in the wilderness, and at no point was the contest entirely passive. Robbery and intimidation were evident in the eighteenth century, but opposition became more aggressive after 1804 as a consequence of depleted beaver supplies, a change in the internal dynamics of the NWC, and failed negotiations over transit rights through Hudson's Bay. Imposed starvation, beatings, harassment, intimidation and imprisonment became the standard fare delivered by Scots in the NWC to their counterparts at the HBC's posts.

Opposition became more violent after 1811; the war of 1812 and the institution of the Red River colony broadened the scope of animosities, while the HBC's increasingly tough stance exacerbated existing tensions. The NWC feared that the operations at the settlement, combined with further displacement induced by the war of 1812, would devastate their syndicate. Thus the small-scale attacks, which prevailed in the previous three decades, proliferated into mass group violence as the NWC initiated, and their mixed-blood offspring implemented, plans to destroy the largely Scottish-occupied settlement. The British and Canadian governments' failure to understand, and thus suitably address the conflict, led to the escalation of fighting and the notorious battle at Seven Oaks in 1816. Although the settlement was often the focus of hostility in this era, HBC employees also continued to be embroiled in the rivalry in the Athabasca, where hostage-taking and abuse were rife. The degree of organisation in the latter years of the conflict, the huge mix of Scottish participants, the violence, and loss of life, suggest that the conflict could have amounted to a Scottish civil war fought on foreign soil, but the companies' prioritisation of commerce prevented this development.

It is clear that the HBC struggled for survival throughout much of the fur trade's competitive era and it is thus surprising that so much attention was awarded to employees' working and personal lives during this period. The administration was guided by paternalistic principles, and the directors sought to uphold this ethic in all areas of the fur trade. They recognised that employees had not entered the business from a social vacuum, and that many had families in Scotland. In fact, they also seemed aware that these relatives were as affected by sojourning as their loved ones who served the Company. Thus the London Committee assumed social responsibility for its employees and their Scottish dependants, and eased the burdens of separation, bereavement, anxiety, abandonment, and financial distress. Their willingness to act as intermediaries linked the spheres of 'home' and Rupert's Land, and assisted the servants and their relatives in retaining a connection. This paternalism also manifested itself more obviously through the delivery of compensation, pensions, and support money, and the HBC's benevolence was significant in the lives of men who had been disabled through work in the fur trade, the widows who had lost their bread-winning husband, and the families who did not receive an expected remittance due to debt, neglect, or administrative delays.

It is clear that the Company was often a valuable source of comfort, relief and assistance to the workforce and its dependants, on both sides of the Atlantic. Its emphasis on cooperation and kindness, rather than subjugation, was one precursor of the development of fur-trade society, as it encouraged the growth of congenial alliances between its personnel and the indigenous people in Rupert's Land. In fact, the directors' humanity appeared to be far-reaching, as although they disproved of their employees entering into the 'country marriages' that subsequently emerged, they undertook initiatives to alleviate some of the difficulties caused by the indeterminate state in which these men found themselves; the prime example being the Red River settlement, which offered a base for mixed-blood families to remain united in Rupert's Land.

However, it was often the Company's actions, or lack thereof, that placed servants, widows, and impoverished wives and parents in Orkney in the position where they required such intervention. Their regulations forbidding white women entry into Rupert's Land, and native women into Britain, increased the ambiguity and distress of employees who had split loyalties. Likewise, the directors' failure to adapt their health and welfare provisions to the new demands exerted by inland service, in much the same way that they failed to modify their recruiting scheme, contributed to the high incidence of disability and mortality in the fur trade and the accompanying need for social support. Increased European provisions, anti-scorbutics, and medicinal supplies could have mitigated the perils of Rupert's Land, but the directors' inexperience of working life in a remote, inhospitable location, prevented this from happening. In addition, had the Company been less stringent about some of its rules for remittance, many employees could have supported their families independently, without the assistance of the HBC. Therefore, for most, the HBC's interference proved to be a mixed blessing, as although the directors could offer comfort and reassurance, they also imposed restrictions and regulations, which curtailed the autonomy of employees and their dependants.

In fact, welfare provision was almost tantamount to a reward for perceived loyalty to the Company. Many of the directors' undertakings appear to have been related to general recruitment concerns, rather than individuals' misfortunes. On occasion, the directors explicitly acknowledged that ulterior motives underlay their overtures, and that they were really designed to encourage recruitment in Orkney. This motive also underlay their endeavours to settle their employees and mixed-blood families in Rupert's Land. It is unclear whether such measures did boost enlistment, or even increased fidelity to the Company; particularly as unfavourable reports, some of which may have reflected the inconsistencies in the Company's paternalistic attitude, often made their way across the Atlantic. As in most businesses, commercial considerations were at the vanguard of decision-making and eclipsed paternalistic concerns; this was to become most true in the years after the merger of the HBC and NWC.

In many ways, 1821 was a watershed year in the history of the HBC; the union of the two companies brought an end to an era characterised by trading rivalry and expansion, and was followed by a complete reorganisation of the fur trade. Yet the long-standing temporary migratory movement fostered by the HBC was to endure. This diaspora had been truly remarkable as generation after generation of Scots, and largely Orkneymen, uprooted themselves from their homelands and migrated temporarily to the territory that now forms vast swathes of Canada, and adapted to work in sub-arctic lands. It was an initiative that required real mettle. These men were the life-force of the company that developed and shaped western Canada, making them true men of spirit and enterprise.

Scottish and Orcadian Participation in the HBC, 1789–1819

Year	No. of employees in HBC	No. of Scots in HBC	Scots as percentage of total no. of employees	No. of Orcadian employees	Orcadian employees as percentage of Scottish employees	Orcadian employees as percentage of total HBC employees
1789	308	222	72.07	217	97.74	70.45
1800	524	425	81.10	418	98.35	79.77
1812	432	301	69.67	290	96.34	67.12
1816	528	328	62.12	266	81.09	50.37
1819	624	423	67.78	319	73.50	51.12

Notes

Compiled from HBCA: A.30/4, A.30/10, A.30/11, A.30/15, A.30/16. Some employees on the list were of unknown origin, but their place of origin was identified through correlating information (including name, age, date of entry and station) in the Servants' Contracts, A.32. Tabulation excluded employees who were listed but had a line through their name indicating that they were deceased or had returned home.

Regional Contribution of Scots to the HBC, 1789–1819

Year	Highland employees			Lowland employees		
	No.	Percentage of Scottish employees	Percentage of total HBC employees	No.	Percentage of Scottish employees	Percentage of total HBC employees
1789	3	1.35	0.97	2	0.90	0.64
1800	4	0.94	0.76	3	0.70	0.57
1812	9	2.99	2.08	2	0.66	0.46
1816	41	12.5	7.76	8	2.43	1.51
1819	66	15.2	10.57	13	2.99	2.08

Year	Western Isles employees			Northern Isles employees		
	No.	Percentage of Scottish employees	Percentage of total of HBC employees	No.	Percentage of Scottish employees	Percentage of total HBC employees
1789	0	0	0	217	97.74	70.45
1800	0	0	0	418	98.35	79.77
1812	0	0	0	290	96.34	67.12
1816	13	3.96	2.46	266	81.09	50.37
1819	25	5.76	4.00	319	73.50	51.12

Notes

Compiled from HBCA: A.30/4, A.30/10, A.30/11, A.30/15, A.30/16. Some employees on the list were of unknown origin, but their place of origin was identified through correlating information (including name, age, date of entry and station) in the Servants' Contracts, A.32. Tabulation excluded employees who were listed but had a line through their name indicating that they were deceased or had returned home.

Notes

CHAPTER 1

1   Edward Chappell, *Narrative of a Voyage to Hudson's Bay in His Majesty's Ship* Rosamond *containing some account of the north-eastern coast of America and of the tribes inhabiting that remote region* (London, 1817), p.5.

2   Chappell, *Narrative of a Voyage*, p.13.

3   David E. Mitchell, *Lords and Proprietors: A Reader's Guide to the Hudson's Bay Company Charter* (Toronto, 2004), pp.4–20.

4   Ibid.

5   Michael Payne, *'The Most Respectable Place In the Territory': Everyday Life in Hudson's Bay Company Service York Factory, 1788–1870*, Studies in Archaeology, Architecture and History, National Historic Parks and Sites, Canadian Parks Service, Environment Canada (Ottawa, 1989), p.28; Michael O'Leary, Wanda Orlikowski, JoAnne Yates, 'Distributed Work over the Centuries: Trust and Control in the Hudson's Bay Company, 1670–1826', in Pamela J. Hinds and Sara Kiesler (eds), *Distributed Work* (Cambridge, 2002), pp.27–32; Edith I. Burley, *Servants of the Honourable Company. Work, Discipline, and Conflict in the Hudson's Bay Company, 1770–1879* (Toronto 1997), pp.1–2, 245.

6   J. M. Bumsted, *Lord Selkirk: A Life* (Michigan, 2009), p.185.

7   Mitchell, *Lords and Proprietors*, p.15; Glyndwr Williams, 'The Hudson's Bay Company and The Fur Trade: 1670–1870'. *The Beaver* (Autumn 1983), pp.6–7; O'Leary et al, 'Distributed Work', pp.27–32.

8   NAS: RH15/14/41, Thomas Bannatyne, Charlton Island, to Anna Bannatyne, 1684; E. E. Rich (ed.), *Minutes of the Hudson's Bay Company 1679–1684: First Part, 1679–82* (London, 1945), pp.251–77; E. E. Rich, *The History of the Hudson's Bay Company, 1670–1870*, vol. 1 (London, 1958), p.498; Burley, *Servants*, pp.64–5; Jennifer S. H. Brown, *Strangers In Blood: Fur Trade Company Families in Indian Country* (Vancouver, 1980); pp.24–5; K. G. Davies (ed.), *Letters from Hudson Bay 1703–1740* (London, 1965), p.361.

9   Davies (ed.), *Letters*, pp.22–3, 116, 129, 162, 165, 184–5, 199, 214; *OSA*, vol. XX, St Andrews and Deerness, p.265. Rich, *History*, p.499; Brown, *Strangers*, pp.26–7.

10 Olaf D. Cuthbert (ed.), *A History of The Orkneys Introduced by A Description of the Islands and Their Inhabitants by George Low* (Orkney, 2001), p.85; *OSA*, vol. XX, St Andrews and Deerness, p.265; vol. XVI, Sandwick and Stromness, p.442.

11 Williams, 'The Hudson's Bay Company', pp.8–9; O'Leary et al, 'Distributed Work', pp.33–5; Mitchell, *Lords and Proprietors*, p.15.

12 Richard Glover, 'The Difficulties of the Hudson's Bay Company's Penetration of the West', *CHR*, vol. 29, no.3 (September, 1948), p.240; Glyndwr Williams, 'Arthur Dobbs and Joseph

Robson: New Light on the Relationship between Two Early Critics of the Hudson's Bay Company', *CHR* (1959), p.132; Williams, 'The Hudson's Bay Company', p.13; G. Woodcock, *The Hudson's Bay Company* (Toronto, 1970), p.78.

13 O'Leary et al, 'Distributed Work', p.44; Williams, 'The Hudson's Bay Company', p.37; Woodcock, *The Hudson's Bay Company*, p.87; HBCA: A.11/116, fo.114; A.6/13, fo.76.

14 Brown, *Strangers*, p.28.

15 Dennis F. Johnson, *York Boats of the Hudson's Bay Company: Canada's Inland Armada* (Calgary, 2006), pp.3, 19, 27, 30, 39.

16 Harold A. Innis, *The Fur Trade in Canada: An Introduction to Canadian Economic History* (Toronto, 1970), pp.9–22.

17 Innis, *The Fur Trade in Canada*, pp.28, 113.

18 J. M. Bumsted, 'The Affair at Stornoway, 1811', *The Beaver* (Spring, 1982), p.53; Woodcock, *The Hudson's Bay Company*, p.100; Williams, 'The Hudson's Bay Company', p.44.

19 Studies that specifically remark on Scots in the HBC include: J. Storer Clouston, 'Orkney and the Hudson's Bay Company', in *The Beaver* (December, 1936); Philip Goldring, 'Lewis and the Hudson's Bay Company in the Nineteenth Century', *Scottish Studies*, 24 (1980); Carol M. Judd, 'Mixt Bands of Many Nations: 1821–1870', in Carol M. Judd and Arthur J. Ray (eds), *Old Trails and New Directions: Papers of the Third North American Fur Trade Conference* (Toronto, 1980); Brown, *Strangers*; J. M. Bumsted, *The Scots In Canada* (Ottawa, 1982), p.6; E. A. Mitchell, 'The Scot in the Fur Trade', in W. Stanford Reid (ed.), *The Scottish Tradition in Canada* (Toronto, 1976); John Nicks, 'Orkneymen in the Hudson's Bay Company, 1780–1821', in Judd and Ray (eds), *Old Trails and New Directions*; T. M. Devine, *Scotland's Empire, 1600–1815* (London, 2003); Michael Fry, *The Scottish Empire* (Edinburgh, 2003); Marjory Harper, *Adventurers and Exiles: The Great Scottish Exodus* (London, 2004). For a full historiographical discussion see Chapter One in S. Rigg, 'Scots in the Hudson's Bay Company, c.1779–1821' (PhD thesis, University of Aberdeen, 2008).

20 See Appendix 1a: 'Scottish and Orcadian Participation in the HBC, 1789–1819' and Appendix 1b: 'Regional Contribution of Scots to the HBC, 1789–1819'.

21 Ibid.; HBCA: A.6/13, fos.1–13; A.32/1–4; OA: D31/22/1, Servants' Contracts and Passengers Lists.

22 W. R. Scott, 'The trade of Orkney at the End of the Eighteenth Century', in *Scottish Historical Review*, vol. 10, no.4 (1912–13), p.361; *OSA*, vol. XX, p.265.

23 Quoted in Burley, *Servants*, p.64 (see also pp.3, 69–71); Brown, *Strangers*, p.27; Rich, *History*, p.499; Devine, *Scotland's Empire*, p.200; A. Fenton, *The Northern Isles: Orkney and Shetland* (Edinburgh, 1978), p.596; Sylvia Van Kirk, *Many Tender Ties: Women in Fur-Trade Society in Western Canada, 1670–1870* (Winnipeg, 1980), p.11.

24 Cuthbert (ed.), *Low's History*, p.14; Richard Glover (ed.), *David Thompson's Narrative 1784–1812* (Toronto, 1962), p.17.

25 Fry, *The Scottish Empire*, pp.97, 101, 106.

26 Ibid.; Bumsted, *Lord Selkirk*, pp.181–233.

27 Stephen, *Masters and Servants*, p.269; Brown, *Strangers*, p.34.

28 A. J. Ray and J. B. Freeman, *'Give Us Good Measure': An Economic Analysis of Relations between the Indians and the Hudson's Bay Company before 1763* (Toronto, 1978); D. Francis and T. Morantz, *Partners in Furs: A History of the Fur Trade in Eastern James Bay 1600–1870* (Kingston and Montreal 1983); Stephen, *Masters and Servants*, pp.302–5.

CHAPTER 2

1 HBCA, A.6/13, fos.73, 156d.

2 HBCA: A.5/2, fos.61, 120.

3 HBCA: A.5/2,, fo.61; A.6/14, fo.10; A.30/4, fo.11; A.11/117, fos. 37d, 59d; A.30/4; A.6/13, fos. 149d, 153d, 156d–157, 160.

4 HBCA: A.11/117, fos.21d–22, 37d, 59d; A.11/45, fo.157; B.121/a/4, fo.45d.

5 Sir John Franklin, *Thirty years in the Arctic regions, or, The adventures of Sir John Franklin* (New York, 1859), p.19; Glover, *David Thompson's Narrative*, p.9; HBCA: B.3/a/119b, fo.5.

6 HBCA: A.11/117, fos.21d–22.

7 HBCA: A.11/117, fos.22, 126d; B.59/b/10, fos.3d–4.

8 HBCA: A.6/13, fos.2, 39d, 157; A.6/14, fos.13, 28, 73; A.30/2, fo.21; A.5/2, fo.50d; A.30/4, fo.15; B.121/a/4, fo.17d; Burley, *Servants*, p.30.

9 B.121/1/a/4, fos.17,51; A.11/117, fo.61d.

10 HBCA: A.11/117, fos.21d–22; C.1398, fo.59d; Burley, *Servants*, pp.73,110.

11 HBCA: A.30/4, fos.14–15; A.6/16, fo.70d.

12 HBCA: A.5/2, fo.68d; A.5/3, fo.73; A.6/13, fo.41; A.10/1, fos.87–94.

13 HBCA: A.5/3, fo.82; A.6/13, fo.41; A.6/14, fo.2d.

14 HBCA: A.5/3, fo.80d.

15 HBCA: A.6/14, fo.28–28d; Isaac Weld, *Travels through the States of North America and the Provinces of Upper and Lower Canada, during the years 1795, 1796, and 1797* (London, 1799), pp.182–3.

16 HBCA: B.121/a/4, fo.51d.

17 HBCA: A.5/2, fo.161d; A.6/14, fo.28d; Burley, *Servants*, p.76.

18 HBCA: A.11/117, fo.56d.

19 HBCA: A.5/2, fo.137; A.5/3, fos.54d–57d.

20 HBCA: A.5/3, fo.132d.

21 HBCA: A.5/3, fos.69, 73, 80d, 95d, 100d.

22 Devine, *Scotland's Empire*, p.293.

23 OSA, vol. XIV, Birsay and Harray, p.325; vol. XV, South Ronaldsay and Burray, pp.311–12.

24 HBCA: A.5/3, fo.107d; A.6/15, fos.49d, 56d; A.6/17, fos.129, 133d; B.135/a/82, fo.65d.

25 HBCA: A.5/3, fo.90d.

26 HBCA: A.1/47, fo.32; A.5/3, fos.146, 149d.

27 HBCA: A.5/3, 126d,143d–144, 146, 149d; A.1/47, fos.93d,112.

28 HBCA: B.159/a/3, fos.11–11d; B.59/a/74, fo.14d.A.10/1, fo.89; A.6/15, fo.99; Burley, *Servants*, p.13.

29 *OSA.*, vol. XIX, Orphir, p.407; vol. XIV, Firth & Stenness, pp.133–4; vol. XVI, Sandwick and Stromness, p.464.

30 HBCA: A.5/3, fo.151; A.6/15, fos.54, 65d, 109d,130d.

31 HBCA: A.6/15, fos.49d, 133–133d; A.5/2, fo.50d.

32 HBCA: A.6/16, fos.35, 42, 91d.

33 *OSA.*, vol. XVI, Sandwick and Stromness, p.442.

34 Burley, *Servants*, pp.78–9.

35 HBCA: A.11/117, fo.56d.

36 Marjory Harper, 'British Migration and the Peopling of the Empire' in Andrew Porter (ed.), *The Oxford History of the British Empire, vol 3, the Nineteenth Century* (Oxford, 1999), p.76; James Horn, 'British Diaspora: Emigration from Britain, 1680–1815' in P. J. Marshall (ed.), *The Oxford History of the British Empire, vol. 2, the Eighteenth Century* (Oxford,

1999), p.32. Also see Amicus, *Eight Letters on the Subject of Earl of Selkirk's Pamphlet* (Edinburgh, 1806); R. Brown, *Strictures and Remarks on the Earl of Selkirk's Observations* (Edinburgh, 1806); Alexander Irvine, *An Inquiry into the Causes and Effects of Emigration from the Highlands and Western Islands of Scotland, with Observations on the Means to be Employed for Preventing It* (Edinburgh, 1802); Ian McGowan (ed.), *Samuel Johnson & James Boswell Journey to the Hebrides* (Edinburgh, 2001), p.173; A. J. Youngson, *Beyond the Highland Line: 'Three Journals of Travel in Eighteenth Century Scotland'* (London, 1974); Andrew Mackillop, *'More Fruitful than the Soil': Army, Empire and the Scottish Highlands, 1715-1815* (East Linton, 2000), pp.190-201.

37 *OSA*, vol. XVI, Sandwick and Stromness, p.444.
38 *OSA*, vol. XIX, Orphir, p.406.
39 *OSA*, vol. XVI, Sandwick and Stromness, pp.444-5.
40 Chappell, *Narrative*, p.245.
41 HBCA: A.6/15, fos.136-141; A.6/16, fos.40-45d; A.5/4, fo.21d; B.59/b/14, fo.1d; B.135/a/82, fo.41d.
42 HBCA: A.6/16, fos.45d-46; A.5/4, fo.32.
43 HBCA: A.5/4, fos.109, 115; A. 6/16, fo.144d.
44 HBCA: B.49/c/1, fo.2d; B.135/a/90, fo.11.
45 HBCA: A.5/4, fo.102d.
46 HBCA: A.5/4, fos. 94, 102d-107d; A.1/48, fos.62, 72d, 78, 81.
47 HBCA: E.41/3, fo.83-5.
48 HBCA: A.5/3, fo.121d; Burley, *Servants*, p.77-8.
49 HBCA: E.41/3, fo.88.
50 HBCA: A.6/16, fo.50.
51 HBCA: A.10/1, fo.51.
52 HBCA: A.10/1, fos.41, 48; A.6/16, fo.160; A.6/17, fo.17d.
53 HBCA: A.6/17, fo.51d.
54 HBCA: A.5/3 fos.80d-82, 130, 139, 140d.
55 HBCA: A.1/48, fos.120-120d; A.5/4, fos.135-137d; A.6/17, fo.23; B.49/c/1, fo.2d.
56 HBCA: A.1/48, fo.120d; A.5/4, fos.136d-137d, 143d-144; A.6/15, fo.141.
57 Burley, *Servants*, p.70; HBCA: A.32/13; A.1/48, fos.120-125; C.1/416, fo.8; C.4/1, fo.17.
58 HBCA: A.1/48, fo.122, A.1/49, fos.5-10, A.5/4, fos.156-156d; A.6/17, fo.66.
59 HBCA: A.6/17, fos.98, 125-134; A.1/49, fo.26d.
60 HBCA: A.1/49, fo.70; A.5/5, fo.48d; Williams, 'The Hudson's Bay Company', pp.37-44; Bumsted, 'The Affair at Stornoway', p.53; Woodcock, *The Hudson's Bay Company*, p.100.
61 HBCA: A.10/1, fos.87-94.
62 HBCA: A.6/17, fo.67; A.36/1a fo.20d; A.32/5; A.5/3, fo.140d; A.5/5, fo.31; A.5/4, fo.134; A.16/111, fo.71d, Glover, *David Thompson's Narrative*, pp.108-9.
63 HBCA: A.1/48, fos.35d-36, A.6/16, fo.225.
64 HBCA: B.198/b/4, fos.9-9d.
65 HBCA: A.5/2, fo.69; A.5/4, fo.170d.
66 HBCA: A.10/1, fos.87-94.
67 HBCA: A.6/18, fo.175.
68 HBCA: A.11/118, fo.29d.
69 HBCA: A.6/18, fo.176.
70 HBCA: A.1/50, fo.7.
71 HBCA: A.6/18, fo.27; A.5/5, fo.32, 40d; A.10/1, fo.89d.

72 WL: John MacLeod Papers (Transcript of original letters supplied by the Public Archives of Canada), pp.2–3; J. M. Bumsted, *Fur Trade Wars: The Founding of Western Canada* (Winnipeg, 1999), p.53; HBCA: A.5/5, fo.32d.

73 HBCA: A.5/5, fos.32, 37; A.5/6, fo.87d.

74 HBCA: A.32/40, fos.113–14; A.32/41, fo.1; A.32/42, fo.103; A.32/45, fo.247; A.32/56, fo.270; A.32/58, fos.57, 278; A.67/9, fo.1; A.5/5, fo.40d; A.6/18, fo.25–60; WL: John MacLeod Papers, pp.2–3.

75 HBCA: A.5/5, fo.62d–63d; see J. P. Pritchett and F .J. Wilson, 'A Winter at Hudson Bay, 1811–12', *CHR* (1943), pp.5–8.

76 OA: D31/23/1, James Sutherland to George and John Sutherland, St Margaret's Hope, 29 June 1814.

77 HBCA: A.6/18, fos.175–6.

78 E. E. Rich (ed.), *Journal of Occurrences in the Athabasca Department, by George Simpson, 1820 and 1821, and Report* (Toronto, 1938), p.399; Burley, *Servants*, p.194.

79 HBCA: A.32/23–58.

80 HBCA: A.5/5, fos.115, 129.

81 HBCA: A.5/5, fo.27; A.6/18, fo.21.

82 HBCA: A.6/18, fos.21–2 and (folio illegible), London Committee to William Auld and Thomas Thomas, 31 May 1811.

83 HBCA: A.5/5, fo.43.

84 HBCA: A.1/51, fo.20d.

85 HBCA: A.5/5, fos.31–31d.

86 HBCA: A.1/50, fos.28, 109; A.6/18, fo.228.

87 HBCA: A.5/6, fo.88; A.6/19, fos.31–31d, 58–9; C.1/298.

88 HBCA: A.30/15, fo.33d–34; A.30/16, fo.12.

89 HBCA: A.1/51, fo.67; A.1/48, fo.51d; A.5/5, fo.117; A.5/6, fo.77.

90 NAS: GD136/468/321, Sinclair of Freswick Muniments, William Sinclair at Pultney to William Sinclair of Freswick, 1812; HBCA: A.5/5, fo.117; A.5/6, fo.116d.

91 HBCA: A.6/18, fos.175–6.

92 Pritchett and Wilson, 'A Winter at Hudson Bay, 1811–12', pp.5–11.

93 HBCA: A.10/1, fo.89d; A.5/5, fo.25.

94 HBCA: A.6/17, fos.222–22d; A.5/5, fos.52d–53; Burley, *Servants*, p.85.

95 This included those who had not yet arrived in Hudson's Bay and those due to return home. HBCA: A.6/19, fo.99d; A.10/1, fos.89d, 123, 140; A.5/5, fo.116.

96 HBCA: A.5/5, fos.68, 100.

97 HBCA: A.30/16; A.32/19, 23, 29, 41, 42, 47.

98 HBCA: A.6/19, fo.39; A.5/5, fo.132d.

99 HBCA: A.5/5, fo.185; A.5/6, fo.87d; A.6/19, fo.10, 48d.

100 HBCA: A.5/5, fo.146.

101 HBCA: A.5/5, fo.62d; B.3/a/119b, fo.13.

102 HBCA: A.5/6, fo,154.

103 HBCA: D.1/11, fos.24d–25; A.5/6, fos.87d, 109d, 112d, 126d, 128, 143d, 145d, 154d.

104 HBCA: A.5/6, fo.131.

105 HBCA: A.5/6, fos.155; 158d, 160–62; A.32/40–44.

CHAPTER 3

1 W. R. Scott, 'The Trade of Orkney at the End of the Eighteenth Century', *SHR*, vol. 10, no.4 (1912–13), p.361; Cuthbert (ed.), *Low's History*, p.66.
2 Cuthbert (ed.), *Low's History*, p.37; *OSA*, vol. XX, St Andrews and Deerness, pp.259, 260, 268, 269; vol. XIV, Firth and Stenness, pp.130–2; vol. V, Holme and Paplay, p.410; vol. XVI, Hoy and Gramesay, p.547; vol. VII, Kirkwall and St Ola, pp.552, 540, 564, 569; vol. XIX, Orphir, pp.407, 419; vol. XV, South Ronaldsay and Burray, pp.301–2; vol. XVI, Sandwick and Stromness, pp.421–2, 466; vol. XVII, Walls and Flotta, pp.316–17; vol. XX, Evie and Rendall, pp.252–3.
3 Chappell, *Narrative*, pp.15–16.
4 Cuthbert (ed.), *Low's History*, p.78; *OSA*, vol. VII, Kirkwall and St Ola, p.559; vol. XIV, Birsay and Harray, pp.320, 328; vol. XIV, Firth and Stenness, p.129; Patrick Neill, *A Tour through some of the Islands of Orkney and Shetland, with a View Chiefly to Objects of Natural History, but Including also Occasional Remarks on the State of the Inhabitants, their Husbandry, and Fisheries* (Edinburgh, 1806), pp.13, 61.
5 *OSA*, vol. XV, South Ronaldsay and Burray, p.301.
6 Neill, *A Tour*, pp.61–4; OSA., vol. XV, South Ronaldsay and Burray, p.305; vol. XIV, Birsay and Harray, p.315; vol. XVI, Sandwick and Stromness, p.435; vol. VII, Kirkwall and St Ola, pp.549, 568; vol. V, Holme and Paplay, p.411; Cuthbert (ed.), *Low's History*, pp.32, 78–9.
7 Neill, *A Tour*, p.11.
8 Malcolm Gray, *The Fishing Industries of Scotland 1790–1914: A Study in Regional Adaptation* (Oxford, 1978), pp.124–35; Neill, *A Tour*, pp.8, 11, 61, 65.
9 Neill, *A Tour*, pp.13, 32.
10 Neill, *A Tour*, p.59; Cuthbert (ed.), *Low's History*, p.87; OSA., vol. VII, Cross, Burness, North Ronaldsay and Ladykirk, pp.454–5; vol. XVI, Sandwick and Stromness, p.435; vol. VII, Kirkwall and St Ola, p.539.
11 Glover (ed.), *David Thompson's Narrative*, p.5.
12 *OSA*.,vol. XIX, Orphir, p.407; vol. XVI, Sandwick and Stromness, p.443; vol. XIV, Birsay and Harray, p.320.
13 *OSA*., vol. VII, Kirkwall and St Ola, p.550; Cuthbert (ed.), *Low's History*, pp.47, 86.
14 Cuthbert (ed.), *Low's History*, pp.79, 82; *OSA*., vol. VII, Kirkwall and St Ola, p.536.
15 Neill, *A Tour*, p.19; Cuthbert (ed.), *Low's History*, pp.32, 85–6.
16 *OSA*, vol. VII, Kirkwall and St Ola, pp.550–1; vol. XIV, Birsay and Harray, p.319.
17 *OSA*, vol. VII, Kirkwall and St Ola, p. 551; vol. XIV, Birsay and Harray, p.319; vol. XX, St Andrews and Deerness, p.265; vol. XV, South Ronaldsay and Burray, pp.311–12; Cuthbert (ed.), *Low's History*, pp.47, 55.
18 Ibid., p.86; *OSA*, vol. XV, South Ronaldsay and Burray, pp.311–12; vol. XVI, Sandwick and Stromness, pp.445, 446, 465;vol. VII, Kirkwall and St Ola, p.550.
19 HBCA: A.10/1, fos.87–94; Devine, *Scotland's Empire*, pp.221, 228, 252.
20 HBCA: A.5/3, fos.55, 57d; A.1/48, fo.120d.
21 HBCA: A.32; A.6/13, fo.41; A.5/4, fo.129d.
22 HBCA: A.5/4, fos.113–113d, 129d–130, 137.
23 HBCA: A.1/48, fo.120d; A.5/4, fos.137–137d, 143d–144; A.5/6, fo.86; A.6/15, fo.114.
24 Nicks, 'Orkneymen', p.115.
25 HBCA: A.5/2, fo.137d; A.32/4, fo.14; A.32/5, fo.32.
26 OA: D31/23/1, James Sutherland to John Sutherland, St Margaret's Hope, 24 August 1817.

27 *OSA*, vol. XVI, Sandwick and Stromness, p.445; Brown, *Strangers*, p.28; Burley, *Servants*, p.5.

28 HBCA: A.30/10; A.30/11; A.30/15; A.30/16.

29 HBCA: A.30/15, fos.32d–33, 42d–43; A.30/16, fos.3d–4, 9d–10, 15d–16, 20d–21, 27d–28, 31d–32, 51d–52, 60d–61; A.30/17, fos.1–5; HBC Biographies, George Flett, John Isbister, Joseph Spence; Payne, *'The Most Respectable Place'*, pp.28–9.

30 HBCA: A.5/4, fo.113; A.6/14, fo.39d; A.5/5, fo.56d–57; A.30/2, fos.32d–33; Brown, *Strangers*, p.28.

31 HBCA: A.32/1, fo.90, 156; A.32/2, fos.131, 134, 140,155, 164; A.32/4, fos.36, 37, 39, 40, 148; A.30/2, fo.52d–53d; A.30/4, fo.14d. See also HBCA: A.32/2, fos.40, 92, 93; A.32/5, fo.14.

32 HBCA: A.32/2, fo.143; A.32/4, fo.30; A.32/5, fo.49; A.32/11, fo.44; HBC Biography, John Davey; A.32/5, fo.49; A.32/11, fo.44.

33 HBCA: A.30/2, fos.72d–73; A.30/4, fos.15d–16, 42d–43,68d–69.

34 Jerome Donald Fellmann, Arthur Getis and Judith Getis (eds), *Human Geography: Landscapes of Human Activities* (London, 1997), pp.138–40; Van Kirk, *Many Tender Ties*, pp.3, 65, 292.

35 Sir John Franklin, *Narrative of a Journey to the Shores of the Polar Sea, in the Years 1819, 1820, 1821 and 1822* (London 1823/4), p.289.

36 HBCA: A.5/4, fos.113, 129d.

37 HBCA: A.30/16, fos.6d–7, 12d–13, 57d–58.

38 Burley, *Servants*, p.167; HBCA: B.121/a/4, fo.24.

39 HBCA: HBC Biography, Magnus Spence Sr.; A.32/2, fo.14, 18; A.32/4, fo.147; HBC Biography, James Whitway; A.32/12, fo.97. See also, HBCA: A.32/5, fo.174; A.32/10, fo.25; A.32/13, fo.79; A.30/16, fos.10, 12, 29; A.16/14, fo.19d–20; A.16/15, fo.28d–20.

40 Quoted in Brown, *Strangers*, p.29; HBCA: B.239/a/95, fo.30.

41 HBCA: A.32/5, fo.102; A.32/6, fo.49; B.121/a/4, fos.23d, 30; HBC Biography, James Gaddy Snr; Glover (ed.), *David Thompson's Narrative*, p.45.

42 *David Thompson's Narrative*, p.38; HBCA: B.121/a/4, fos.17, 20; A.32/1, fo.95; A.32/5, fo.97; A.32/8, fo.63; A.30/2, fo.11d; A.30/4, fos.14, 72; A.30/5, fo.80.

43 HBCA: A.5/2, fo.168; A.30/4, fos.23, 78; A.5/3, fo.136; A.6/15, fo.106;A.6/18, fo.184; A.30/16, fo.34.

44 HBCA: A.6/16, fo.37; A.5/4, fo.35d; A.6/18, fo.25; A.16/13, fo.97; A.30/10, fo.24; A.30/11, fos.34, 41; A.30/15, fos.18d–19, 51d; HBC Biographies, William Sinclair 1st; John Ballenden; Alexander Kennedy; James Sutherland 3rd; Brown, *Strangers*, p.30.

45 Brown, *Strangers*, p.29; Van Kirk, 'Fur Trade Social History', p.164.

46 HBCA: A.30/1, fo.80d; A.30/10, fos.25d–26; A.30/11, fos.25d–26; A.32/2, fos.154, 166; A.32/4, fo.146; A.32/6, fo.46; B.121/a/4, fos.2,12, 20; HBC Biography, James Tait (Tate).

47 HBCA: A.30/10, fos.32d–33; A.30/11, fos.36d–37; HBC Biography, James Kirkness.

48 HBCA: A.6/13, fo.1.

49 HBCA: A.6/14, fo.96d.

50 HBCA: A.6/16, fos.151d–152.

51 HBCA: A.6/17, fo.68d.

52 HBCA: A.5/3, fo.56d ; A.6/16, fos.25d, 42d; A.30/1–16; Burley, *Servants*, p.25; Stephen, *Masters and Servants*, pp.261–2.

53 HBCA: A.6/15, fo.129d.

54 HBCA: B.121/a/4, fo.12.

55 Brown, *Strangers*, p.31.

56 HBCA: A.5/4, fo.16d; A.1/52, fo.5d.

57 OA: D31/23/1, James Sutherland to John Sutherland, St Margaret's Hope, 24 August 1817.

58 OA: D31/23/1, James Sutherland to John Sutherland, St Margaret's Hope, 26 August 1825.

59 Brown, *Strangers*, p.48; A.6/15, fo.98d.

60 HBCA: A.5/4, fo.35d; HBC Biography, Alexander Kennedy.

61 HBCA: A.1/49, fo.70; A.5/5, fo.175d; A.1/48, fos.119–122d; A.5/6, fo.71d.

62 HBCA: A.5/3, fo.106d.

63 HBCA: A.30/11, fos.24d–25; A.1/49, fo.70; A.5/4, fo.171; A.6/17, fo.122;A.5/6, fo.155d.

64 HBCA: A.30/10, fos.32d–33; A.30/11, fos.34, 36d–37; A.30/16.; HBC Biography, James Kirkness, William Sinclair.

65 HBCA: A.30/4, fos.13–13b; B.121/a/7, fo.38.

66 HBCA: A.32/1, fo.57; A.5/2, fo.166d.

67 HBCA: A.30/10, fo.27; A.32/12, fo.26.

68 HBCA: A.30/4, fos.14d–15, 44d–45; A.30/10, fos.37d–38; A.32/2, fo.157; B.121/a/7, fo.11d.

69 HBCA: A.32/6, fo.50; A.30/10, fos.35d–36, 37d–38; HBC Biography, James Sandison.

70 HBCA: A.32/1, fo.37; A.30/1, fo.10; HBC Biography, Andrew Graham.

71 HBCA: A.11/116, fo.139; A.5/3, fo.87–8; NA: Prob/11/1595; HBCA: HBC Biography, Andrew Graham.

72 HBCA: HBC Biography, Andrew Graham; A.32/3, fo.111; A.30/10, fos.23d–24; A.5/2, fos.115–17, 137–8.

73 HBCA: B.22/z/1, fos.1–7.

74 HBCA: A.32/4, fo.84; A.30/10, fo.14; A.10/1, fo.111; A.16/7, fos.20, 32, 106.

75 Ibid.

76 HBCA: A.5/5, fo.45.

77 Douglas J. Hamilton, *Scotland, the Caribbean and the Atlantic World 1750–1820* (Manchester, 2005), pp.55–78; Devine, *Scotland's Empire*, p.238. For full discussion of networks see Steve Murdoch, *Network North: Scottish Kin, Commercial and Covert Association in Northern Europe, 1603–1746* (Leiden, 2006), pp.1–48, 228–48; Andrew Mackillop and Steve Murdoch, 'Introduction' in Mackillop and Murdoch (eds), *Military Governors and Imperial Frontiers c. 1600–1800: A Study of Scotland and Empires* (Leiden, 2005); David Armitage and Michael J.Braddick, 'Three Concepts of Atlantic History', in Armitage and Braddick (eds), *The British Atlantic World, 1500–1800* (Basingstoke, 2002), pp.11–27; N. Glaisyer, 'Networking: Trade and Exchange in the Eighteenth-Century British Empire', *HJ*, 47 (2004), pp.451–75; T. M. Devine, *The Tobacco Lords, A Study of the Tobacco Merchants of Glasgow and their Trading Activities c.1740–90* (Edinburgh, 1975), p.83; Devine, *Scotland's Empire*, pp.236–9, 255; Harper, *Adventurers and Exiles*, pp.284–7; Allan I. Macinnes, Marjory-Ann D. Harper, Linda G. Fryer (eds). *Scotland and the Americas, c. 1650– c. 1939: A Documentary Source Book* (Edinburgh, 2002); Andrew Mackillop, 'Europeans, Britons, and Scots: Scottish Sojourning Networks and Identities in Asia, c.1700–1815', in Angela McCarthy (ed.) *A Global Clan: Scottish Emigrant Networks* (London, 2006), pp.19–47. General works: D. Hancock, 'Combining Success and Failure: Scottish Networks in the Atlantic Wine Trade', in David Dickson, Jan Parmentier and Jane Ohlmeyer (eds), *Irish and Scottish Mercantile Networks in Europe and Overseas in the Seventeenth and Eighteenth Centuries* (Ghent, 2007); D. Hancock, *Citizens of the World: London Merchants and the Integration of the British Atlantic Community, 1735–1785* (Cambridge, 1995).

78 OA: D31/23/1, James Sutherland to John Sutherland, St Margaret's Hope, 24 August 1817.

79 Nicks, 'Orkneymen', p.115.
80 Brown, *Strangers*, pp.36–49; Bumsted, *Fur Trade Wars*, p.24; Heather Devine, 'Ambition versus Loyalty: Miles Macdonnell and the Decline of the North West Company' in Jo-Anne Fiske, Susan Sleeper-Smith, and William Wicken (eds), *New Faces of the Fur trade: Selected Papers of the Seventh North American Fur Trade Conference, Halifax, Nova Scotia, 1995* (East Lansing, 1998), p.271.
81 Devine, *Scotland's Empire*, p.238.
82 HBCA: A.30/4; A.30/10; A.30/11; A.30/15; A.30/16; B.198/a/49, fo.8.
83 HBCA: A.6/15, fo.131; A.6/16, fo.69d.
84 HBCA: A.5/3, fo.90; A.6/17, fos.16–16d, 47d.
85 Stephen, *Masters and Servants*, pp.67, 261.
86 HBCA: A.5/5, fos.44d–45.
87 HBCA: A.6/18, fo.216.
88 Devine, *Scotland's Empire*, p.239.
89 HBCA: A.11/117, fo.52.
90 Devine, *Scotland's Empire*, pp.232, 252.
91 HBCA: A.32/1–60; Jennifer S. H. Brown, 'A Parcel of Upstart Scotchmen', *The Beaver* (February, 1988), p.5.
92 J. B. Tyrell (ed.), *David Thompson's Narrative of his Explorations in Western America 1784–1812* (Toronto, 1916), p.320.
93 HBCA: B.121/a/4, fo.31d.
94 HBCA: A.32/4, fo.52; A.32/5, fo.15; A.30/4, fo.14d, 46, 74; A.30/6, fo.34; HBC Biography, Edward Wishart; Quoted in Brown, *Strangers*, p.29.
95 HBCA: A.16/111, fos.16d–56.
96 HBCA: A.6/16, fos.37, 98.
97 HBCA: A.30/15, fos.11d–12, 16; A.16/7, fos.61–61d; A.16/8, fo.17; HBC Biography, George Budge.
98 HBCA: A.6/19. fos.49–49d.
99 HBCA; A.5/6, fos.74d, 144d, 147d.
100 HBCA: A.6/18, fos.212–15; A.30/16, fos.44, 49, 53, 58; A.6/19, fos.49–49d.
101 HBCA: A.6/18, fos.93, 140.
102 Brown, *Strangers*, p.30; Burley, *Servants*, p.37; HBCA: A.6/18, fos.149–220, 244; A.30/16, fos.1–65.
103 HBCA: HBC Biography, John Robertson; A.32/13, fo.93.
104 HBCA: A.6/19, fos.14, 49–49d.
105 HBCA: A.11/118, fo.24; quoted in Brown, *Strangers*, p.30.
106 HBCA: A.30/16, fos.48d–49.
107 HBCA: A.30/16, fos.1–65.
108 HBCA: A.30/15, fos.11d–12; A.30/16, fo.61; A.30/17, fo.1–2d.
109 HBCA: A.30/11, fos.40d–41; A.30/15, fos.6, 51d–52; A.30/16, fos.35d–36, 61d–62; A.30/17, fo.1; A.32/14, fo.34; A.16/16, fo.65; HBC Biography, Donald Sutherland; HBC Biography, Peter Spence. See also HBCA: HBC Biography, George Flett.A.30/11, fos.35d–36; A.30/16, fos.8d–9.
110 HBCA: A.30/16.
111 HBCA: A.30/16, fo.26; Rich (ed.), *Journal of Occurrences*, pp.399–400.
112 HBCA: A.30/4; A.30/10; A.30/12; A.30/15; A.30/16.
113 OA: D31/23/1, James Sutherland to John Sutherland, St Margaret's Hope, 24 August 1817.

114 HBCA: A.5/5, fo.39; A.5/6, fo.87d, *OSA*, vol. XIX, Orphir, p.406.
115 HBCA: A.5/4, fos.129d–130, 136d–137.
116 HBCA: A.6/13, fo.80; A.16/7, fo.27; A.16/16, fo.64; A.5/3, fo.68; A.16/6, fo.125.
117 HBCA: A.30/4; A.30/10; A.30/11; A.30/15; A.6/14, fo.39d; A.6/16, fo.25d.
118 HBCA: B.198/b/4, fo.17.
119 HBCA: A.5/4, fo.113, 129d–130; *OSA*, vol. XVI, Sandwick and Stromness, pp.443; A.32/1; A.30/2, fo.42, A.30/4, fos.3d–4; A.32/5; A.32/10.
120 HBCA: A.16/6, fo.143; A.6/17, fo.68d; A.30/10, fos.3d, 8d, 21.
121 HBCA: A.5/3, fo.72d; A.11/117, fo.120.
122 HBCA: A.6/17, fos.16–16d; A.30/10, fos.5, 12; A.6/16, fos.157d –158.
123 HBCA: A.5/3, fo.72d; A.6/16, fos.157d–158.
124 HBCA: A.6/16, fos.70d, 79,157d –158.
125 HBCA: A.6/16, fos.35d, 42d, 49d–50.
126 HBCA: A.30/2, fos.41d–42; A.11/45, fo.146d.

CHAPTER 4

1 NAS: RH15/14/41, Thomas Bannatyne, Charlton Island, to Anna Bannatyne, 1684.
2 Glyndwr Williams (ed.), *Andrew Graham's Observations on Hudson's Bay, 1767-1791* (London, 1969), p.299.
3 HBCA: B.239/a/120, fo.6d; D.1/11, fos.24d–25.
4 HBCA: D.1/11, p.300.
5 HBCA: B.40/a/1, fo.10; B.59/b/8, fo.15; B.59/a/94, fos.21d–22. See also Edward Umfreville, *The Present State of Hudson's Bay Containing a Full Description of that Settlement, and the Adjacent country, and Likewise of the Fur Trade, with Hints for its Improvement. . .* (London, 1790), p.19.
6 Tyrell (ed.), *David Thompson's Narrative*, p.35.
7 HBCA: A.30/16, fos.54d–55; B.3/a/114, fo.10d.
8 HBCA: B.3/a/120, fos.17–22; A.32/3, fo.234; A.32/14, fo.50, A.32/19, fo.53d.
9 HBCA: B.59/b/19, fos.9–9d.
10 HBCA: B.59/a/94, fo.23d.
11 HBCA: B.3/a/118, fos.14d–15; B.135/a/113a, fo.26.
12 HBCA: B.3/z/2, fo.303; B.42/z/1, fo.4; B.176/a/1, fo.2d; B.169/a/1, fo.3d; B.177/a/6, fo.5.
13 HBCA: B.59/b/28, fo.5d; B.9/a/3, fo.1; B.59/b/30, fo.8.
14 HBCA: B.177/a/1, fos.7d–10d.
15 HBCA: B.22/a/10 fo.2.
16 HBCA: B.169/a/1, fos.2d–3d.
17 HBCA: B.159/a/3, fo.1d; B.40/a/1, fos.15d–19; B.24/a/5, fos.1–4.
18 HBCA: B.40/a/1, fo.5; B.177/a/1, fo.7d; See also B.42/c/1, fo.1.
19 HBCA: B.198/b/4, fo.15.
20 HBCA: A.30/2, fo.33; B.59/b/32, fo.22d.
21 HBCA: B.176/a/1, fos.2d–3d.
22 HBCA: B.59/b/30, fo.8; B.164/a/1, fos.4–5; B.123/a/8, fo.14d.
23 HBCA: B.89/a/1, fo.5.
24 HBCA: B.164/a/1, fos.4–5. See also B.59/b/30, fos.8–9; B.3/z/2, fo.303.
25 HBCA: B.3/z/2, fo.3; B.164/a/2, fos.3–7.
26 HBCA: B.40/a/1, fos.6d–15.

27 HBCA: B.141/a/1, fos.4–4d; B.164/a/1, fos.4–5d; B.3/a/115, fo.12d; Burley, *Servants*, p.164.

28 HBCA: B.141/a/1, fos.4–4d; B.164/a/1, fos.4–5d; B.3/a/115, fo.9.

29 HBCA: B.3/a/120, fos.21d–39.

30 HBCA: B.3/a/120, fos.25, 29d, 30d.

31 HBCA: A.6/15, fo.95; B.3/a/120, fos.22d–24; B.164/a/1, fo.5d.

32 HBCA: A.5/6, fo.17d; B.177/a/5, fos.7d–9; Van Kirk, *Many Tender Ties*, pp.53–73.

33 HBCA: B.59/b/30, fo.5; B.164/a/2, fo.7.

34 HBCA: B.3/a/120, fos.5d–13, 35d.

35 HBCA: C.1/205, fo.1. See also HBCA: B.59/b/12, fo.16.

36 HBCA: B.198/b/3, fos.2d–3; B.59/b/11, fo.3d; B.239/ee/1, fos.125–145d.

37 HBCA: B.135/a/113a, fo.7d; B.372/a/3, fos.22d–23; B.239/a/89, fos.25–25d.

38 HBCA: B.135/a/113a, fo.7d; B.49/f/2, fo.4.

39 HBCA: B.59/b/10, fo.4; B.59/b/32, fo.20d.

40 HBCA: A.6/14, fos.102d–103; A.6/15, fo.108d.

41 HBCA: A.6/14, fos.133, 134, 144.

42 HBCA: A.6/15, fos.74, 95d–96; A.11/45, fo.171.

43 Cynthia Toman, 'George Spence: Surgeon and Servant of the HBC, 1738–41', *CBMH/ BCHM*, Vol.18, 2001, p.31; HBCA: A.6/16, fo.115; B.42/z/1, fo.4.

44 HBCA: B.59/b/21, fo.1d; B.239/a/105, fo.36d; A.11/118, fo.23d.

45 HBCA: B.3/a/120, fos.31; 29d; 39; A.32/18, fos.66, 130.

46 HBCA: B.59/b/32, fos. 18d–22.

47 HBCA: B.59/a/94, fo.23d; Burley, *Servants*, p.215.

48 HBCA: A.11/118, fo.23d.

49 Umfreville, *The Present State*, p.35.

50 HBCA: B.121/a/7, fo.5; B.121/a/4, fo.27d; B.3/a/120, fos.15d, 22–33d; A.10/1, fo.111C; see also B.135/a/66, fo.24.

51 HBCA: B.59/z/1, fos.94, 185–186; B.59/a/92, fos.18d–36.

52 Guy Williams, *The Age of Agony: The Art of Healing c.1700–1800* (London, 1975), p.136; Elliott Coues (ed.), *New Light on the Early History of the Greater Northwest: the Manuscript Journals of Alexander Henry, Fur Trader of the Northwest Company, and of David Thompson, Official Geographer and Explorer of the same Company 1799–1814. . .* 3 vols. (New York, 1897), vol.2, pp.835–6, 868–9, 888; Barry M. Gough, *The Journal of Alexander Henry the Younger, 1799–1814*, vol.2 (Toronto, 1988–1992), pp.679–718.

53 E. E. Rich and A. M. Johnson (eds.), *Cumberland House Journals and Inland Journals, 1775–1782*. First Series, 1775–79 (London, 1952), pp.143–4, 176, 196–8.

54 HBCA: B.198/b/3, fo.5d; B.135/a/105, fo.6.

55 HBCA: B.42/z/1, fo.1; B.3/z/2, fo.19; Williams, *The Age of Agony*, pp.127–135.

56 HBCA: B.59/b/19, fo.18.

57 *OSA*, vol. 20, St Andrews and Deerness, p.265; Payne, 'The Most Respectable Place', p.94.

58 See HBCA: A.5/4, fos.32d, 34; A.16/15, fos.16d–17; A.30/16, fos.42, 46; A.32/2, fo.9; A.32/7, fo.36; A.32/18, fo.77; B.3/a/24, fos.24–25; B.59/b/13, fo.7d; B.59/b/28, fo.23; B.59/a/82, fos. 9d, 20; B.121/a/7, fo.5d; B.141/a/3, fo.4; B.198/b/3, fos.1d, 9d; D.1/11, fo.8. For non-Orcadian employees who drowned see HBCA: A.16/8, fos.2, 167; A.16/15, fo.80; A.16/16, fos.93, 96; A.30/15, fos.5d–7; B.59/a/94, fo.37d; B.135/a/105, fo.28d.

59 HBCA: A.11/118, fos.22–3.

60 HBCA: A.6/14, fo.30; B.198/b/3; fo.1d, A.32/2, fos.9, 112, 142, 181.

61 HBCA: B.59/b/28, fo.23; B.59/b/13, fo.7d.

62 HBCA: B.141/a/3, fo.4, A.32/7, fo.36.

63 HBCA: B.121/a/7, fo.5d.

64 HBCA: A.30/16, fos.42, 46; B.135/a/90, fo.21.

65 HBCA: A.6/15, fos.77–8; B.40/a/1, fos.1–2.

66 HBCA: B.59/b/16, fo.18d; B.135/a/80, fos.3–4; A.32/4, fo.177.

67 HBCA: A.11/45, fo.172; A.32/3, fo.228; see also B.135/a/66, fo.9d; A.30/16, fos.52d–53, A.1/48, fo.67.

68 HBCA: A.30/2, fo.41.

69 HBCA: A.30/16, fos.52d–53.

70 HBCA: B.59/b/19, fo.18; B.135/a/82, fo.41.

71 Burley, *Servants*, p.131.

72 William B. Ewart, 'Causes of Mortality in a Subarctic settlement (York Factory, Man.), 1714–1946', *CMAJ*, vol. 129, No.6 (1983), p.572.

73 HBCA: B.3/a/120, fos.15d, 16, 21, 24d.

74 HBCA: A.6/14, fo.98d; Van Kirk, *Many Tender Ties*, p.260.

75 HBCA: B.198/b/3, fo.8d.

76 HBCA: A.30/15, fos.1d, 2, 2d, 3; A.30/16, fos.13, 57.

77 HBCA: A.30/2, fo.28; A.1/48, fo.12.

78 HBCA: A.6/15, fo.129d; B.3/a/115, fos.8–8d.

79 HBCA: B.22/a/116, fo.2.

80 HBCA: A.6/13, fo.74d; A.6/16, fo.37; B.164/a/1, fo.5; B.135/a/80, fos.9–9d; B.135/a/97, fo.10; A.30/15, fos.17, 29, 30d, 31, 32, 23d, 24, 24d.

81 HBCA: B.142/a/6, fo.11d; B.121/a/4, fo.63; B.59/b/27, fo.39; B.198/b/5, fo.18d; Williams (ed.), *Andrew Graham's Observations*, p.307.

82 HBCA: B.3/a/119b, fo.3.

83 Burley, *Servants*, p.171.

84 HBCA: B.3/a/115, fo.7.

85 HBCA: A.11/45, fo.144.

86 HBCA: A.30/15, fos.27d–27; A.30/16, fos.4d–5,63.

87 HBCA: A.6/19, fo.50.

88 HBCA: B.135/a/113a, fo.23; A.30/16, fo.56.

89 HBCA: A.30/11, fo.44.

90 HBCA: B.3/a/117a, fo.1.

91 HBCA: B.198/b/3, fos.2d–3; A.30/4, fo.48d; B.59/a/94, fo.22; A.5/6, fos.123d, 129d.

92 HBCA: A.6/13, fo.149; A.6/15, fo.130d; A.6/16, fos.37d, 50d; A.5/5, fo.51d.

93 HBCA: A.11/117, fo.22.

94 Van Kirk, *Many Tender Ties*, p.17.

95 HBCA: B.59/a/94, fos.4d–5; B.59/b/8, fos.12d–13.

96 Umfreville, *The Present State*, pp.28–9.

97 HBCA: B.3/z/2, fo.19; B.42/z/1, fo.1; A.6/14, fo.27d; A.1/51, fo.28.

98 HBCA: B.121/a/7, fo.28d.

99 A. M. Johnson (ed.), *Saskatchewan Journals and Correspondence Edmonton House 1795–1800 Chesterfield House 1800–1802* (London, 1967), pp.24–5.

100 HBCA: B.177/a/2, fo.3d.

101 Johnson (ed.), *Saskatchewan Journals*, pp.24–5, 56–7.

102 HBCA: B.24/a/5, fo.7; Johnson (ed.), *Saskatchewan Journals*, pp.128–9.

103 HBCA: A.11/117, fo.179; B.24/a/5, fos.3d–9.

104 HBCA: B.40/a/1, fos. 4d–6; A.32/4, fo.193; A.32/6, fo.67; A.32/12, fo.93.
105 HBCA: A.16/111, fos.55, 71d; A.16/112, fo.43; A.16/113, fo.52.
106 HBCA: A.5/3, fo.28.
107 HBCA: B.121/a/7, fo.28d.
108 HBCA: A.16/112, fo.3 A.16/111, fo.25d.
109 HBCA: A.6/14, fos.133, 134, 144; A.6/13, fo.149.
110 HBCA: A.6/16, fos.129d,158d–159.
111 HBCA: A.11/118, fos.22–23; quoted in Brown, *Strangers*, p.17.
112 Douglas Mackay, *The Honourable Company: A History of the Hudson's Bay Company* (Toronto, 1936), p.72.
113 HBCA: A.5/6, fos.86–86d; A.6/19, fo.24.
114 HBCA: A.5/6, fos.86–86d.
115 HBCA: A.6/19, fo.29d.
116 HBCA: A.6/13, fo.71d.
117 HBCA: A.6/14, fo.96d; A.1/47, fo.36; A.1/48, fo.40.
118 HBCA: A.5/3, fos.127, 262.
119 HBCA: A.5/4, fo.4; A.5/6, fo.92.
120 HBCA: A.1/48, fos.50d, 67, 83d, 79d; A.5/4, fos.100, 121; A.1/52, fo.69; B.59/b/19, fo.18, A.32/4, A.30/10, fo.16d.
121 HBCA: A.1/51, fo.63, A.32/1; A.1/45, fo.54; A.1/49, fo.132d. See also A.36/1a, fo.22d.
122 HBCA: A.1/47, fo.72d.
123 HBCA: A.36/1b, fo.19d; A.5/5, fo.88; A.36/1a, fo.22–22d; A.1/51, fo.36; A.1/52, fos.4, 11d.
124 HBCA, A.5/6, fo.70d.
125 HBCA, A.5/3, fo.262; also see A.1/52, fo.27.
126 HBCA: B.121/a/7, fos. 25d–36.
127 HBCA, A.5/3, fo.172d; A.32/13, fo.12; A.32/18, fo.121; A.1/52, fos.6, 13–13d, 27.
128 HBCA, A.5/4, fo.15.
129 HBCA, A.1/47, fo.112; A.5/4, fos.15, 32d, 46; A.32/1, fo.58; A.1/48, fo.48; A.1/49, fo.7.
130 HBCA, A.16/13, fos.97d–129; A.5/5, fo.27; A.36/1a, fo.22d; A.5/6, fo.111, fo.126d, A.1/52, fo.73.
131 HBCA, A.16/15, fos.1–80; A.5/5, fo.86.
132 Umfreville, *The Present State*, p.22.
133 HBCA, A.5/6, fo.70d.
134 W. S. Wallace (ed.), *Documents Relating to the North West Company* (Toronto, 1934), p.256.
135 Stephen, *Masters and Servants*, pp.254–6; HBCA: A.1/51, fo.46, 47d.
136 HBCA, A.11/117, fo.62; A.6/13, fo.98d.
137 HBCA, D.1/11, fos.24d–25.
138 HBCA, A.30/16, fo.52; A.30/15, fos.5d–6.
139 HBCA, B.198/b/3, fo.9d.
140 Harper, *Adventurers and Exiles*, pp.298–9.

CHAPTER 5

1 Ross Cox, *Adventures on the Columbia River, Including the Narrative of a Residence of Six Years on the Western Side of the Rocky Mountains, among Various Tribes of Indians Hitherto Unknown: Together with a Journey across the American Continent*, 2 vols. (London, 1831), pp.228–9.

2 For instance Bumsted, *Fur Trade Wars*, p.11

3 H. H. Langton (ed.), *Travels in the Interior Inhabited Parts of North America in the Years 1791 and 1792* by Patrick Campbell (Toronto, 1937), p.123.

4 HBCA: B.121/a/3, fo.18d; R. McKenzie, 'Reminiscences', in Louis F. R. Masson (ed.), *Les Bourgeois de la Compagnie du Nord-Ouest: Récits de Voyages, Lettres, et Rapports Inédits Relatifs au Nord-Ouest Canadien* (1st ed. 1889–90) vol.1 (New York, 1960), pp.19–20.

5 HBCA: B.135/a/82, fo.39d.

6 HBCA: A.6/16, fos.83d–84; A.32/4, fo.138; B.7/a/1, fo.2.

7 HBCA: B.177/a/2, fo.12d.

8 D. Cameron, 'The Nipigon Country, 1804' in Masson (ed.), *Les Bourgeois de la Compagnie du Nord-Ouest*, vol.2, p.245; Innis, *The Fur Trade in Canada*, pp.262–3; Arthur J. Ray, *Indians in the Fur Trade: Their Role as Hunters, Trappers and Middlemen in the Lands Southwest of Hudson Bay 1660–1870* (Toronto, 1974), pp.117–19; V. Hopwood (ed.), *David Thompson: Travels in Western North America, 1784–1812* (Toronto, 1971), pp.158–61; HBCA: B.49/c/1, fos.1–2.

9 Hopwood, *David Thompson*, p.161.

10 Cameron, 'The Nipigon Country, 1804', p.245; HBCA: B.89/a/2, fo.35; Bumsted, *Lord Selkirk*, pp.183, 198.

11 Innis, *The Fur Trade in Canada*, p.262; Cameron, 'The Nipigon Country, 1804', p.245; John Lambert, *Travels through Canada, and the United States of North America, in the years 1806, 1807, & 1808*, 2 vols. (London 1813), p.235.

12 HBCA: A.10/1, fos.34–69.

13 HBCA: A.10/1, fos.46, 70–71d.

14 HBCA: A.6/16, fo.70.

15 Coues (ed.), *New Light on the Early History of the Greater Northwest*, vol.1, p.239.

16 Bumsted, *Fur Trade Wars*, p.33.

17 Louis F. R. Masson, 'North-West Agreement, 1804' in Masson (ed.), *Les Bourgeois de la Compagnie du Nord-Ouest*, vol.2, pp.483–4.

18 HBCA: B.59/b/24, fos.11, 19; See also HBCA: B.3/b/41, fo.25d.

19 HBCA: B.41/a/1, fos.18–18d.

20 HBCA: B.176/a/1, fos.7–8. See HBCA: B.59/b/24, fo.33; B.89/a/1, fo.6.

21 HBCA: B.59/b/24, fos.19–20; B.164/a/2, fo.3d.

22 HBCA: B.89/a/1, fos.7–11; A.32/17, fo.117; B.244/a/1, fos.7d–8; Thomas Douglas, fifth earl of Selkirk, *A Sketch of the British Fur Trade in North America; with Observations Relative to the North-West Company of Montreal* (London, 1816), pp.68–9.

23 Ibid.; Glyndwr Williams (ed.), *Hudson's Bay Miscellany, 1670–1870* (Winnipeg, 1973), p.98.

24 HBCA: B.59/b/24, fo.34.

25 HBCA: B.59/b/24, fos.36, 51; A.32/13, fo.20 A.32/13, fo.138; Selkirk, *A Sketch of the British Fur Trade in North America*, pp.70–1.

26 HBCA: B.57/a/2, fos.1d–2d; Glyndwr Williams, 'James Tate's Journal 1809–1812' in Williams (ed.), *Hudson's Bay Miscellany, 1670–1870* (Winnipeg, 1973), p.108.

27 Williams, 'James Tate's Journal', p.100.

28 George Keith, 'Letters' in Masson (ed.), *Les Bourgeois de la Compagnie du Nord-Ouest*, vol.2, pp.94–5.

29 HBCA: F.3/2, fo.113.

30 HBCA: B.89/a/2, fos.1–4.

31 HBCA: B.89/a/2, fos.4–35; Arthur S. Morton (ed.), *The Journal of Duncan M'Gillivray of the North West Company at Fort George on the Saskatchewan, 1794–5* (Toronto, 1929), Appendix, p.2–3; Coues (ed.), *New Light on the Early History of the Greater Northwest.* vol.1, p.190.

32 HBCA: B.89/a/2, fo.34d; F.3/2, fo.108.

33 HBCA: B.89/a/2, fos.5, 27–8; F.3/2, fo.113; Wallace (ed.), *Documents*, p.426.

34 Van Kirk, *Many Tender Ties*, p.89–90.

35 Ibid.; HBCA: B.89/a/2, fos.5–33; B.89/c/1, fo.2.

36 Quoted in Van Kirk, *Many Tender Ties*, p.90.

37 HBCA: B.89/a/2, fos.33–36d.

38 HBCA: F.3/2, fo.108; B.89/a/2, fos.35–36d.

39 HBCA: A.6/15, fo.98; A.6/16, fo.82; A.6/17, fos.17d, 47d, 66d.

40 HBCA: A.6/17, A.6/16, fo.82; A.6/17, fo.98.

41 HBCA: B.89/a/1, fo.9; F.3/2, fos.108–114; B.59/b/24, fos.36–51.

42 HBCA: A.6/18, fo.107.

43 Bumsted, 'The Affair at Stornoway', p.53; Woodcock, *The Hudson's Bay Company*, p.100; Williams, 'The Hudson's Bay Company', p.44; Innis, *The Fur Trade in Canada*, p.162.

44 HBCA: A.6/18, fos.175–6.

45 Burley, *Servants*, pp.43–4.

46 HBCA: F.3/2, fos.108–114.

47 HBCA: A.10/1, fo.99.

48 Thomas Douglas, fifth earl of Selkirk, 'Observations on The Present State of The Highlands, with a View of The Causes and Probable Consequences of Emigration' in J. M. Bumsted (ed.), *The Collected Writings of Lord Selkirk 1799–1809* (Winnipeg, 1984), pp.102–20. J. M. Bumsted, 'Settlement by Chance: Lord Selkirk and Prince Edward Island' in *CHR* 59 (Toronto, 1978), p.170.

49 Bumsted, 'Settlement by Chance', p.175.

50 HoC, *Papers Relating to the Red River Settlement* (London, 1819), p.3; Bumsted, 'The Affair at Stornoway', p.53; Mitchell, 'The Scot in the Fur Trade', p.38.

51 Bumsted, 'The Affair at Stornoway', p.54 ; Pritchett and Wilson, 'A Winter at Hudson Bay', p.1; HBCA: A.5/5, fo.51.

52 Wallace (ed.), *Documents*, p.464; Heather Devine, 'Ambition versus Loyalty: Miles Macdonnell and the decline of the North West Company' in Jo-Anne Fiske, Susan Sleeper-Smith, and William Wicken (eds.), *New Faces of the Fur Trade: Selected Papers of the Seventh North American Fur Trade Conference, Halifax, Nova Scotia, 1995* (East Lansing, 1998), pp.248–52.

53 Pritchett and Wilson, 'A Winter at Hudson Bay', p.1; WL: John MacLeod Papers (Transcript of original letters supplied by the Public Archives of Canada), pp.1–2.

54 Bumsted, *Fur Trade Wars*, p.71.

55 Bumsted, *Fur Trade Wars*, pp.76–7; Campbell, *The North West Company*, p.189.

56 Bumsted, *Fur Trade Wars*, pp.76–7.

57 Bumsted, *Fur Trade Wars*, p.93; HBCA: F.1/1, pp.65–7.

58 Ibid; Wallace (ed.), *Documents*, p.285; Bumsted, *Fur Trade* Wars, p.105.

59 HBCA: E.3/8, '30th August 1814' –'1st September 1814'; A.6/18, fo.145; Bumsted, *Fur Trade Wars*, pp.95, 136.

60 HBCA: E.3/8,'6th September 1814'; A.6/19, fos.20–20d.

61 WL: John MacLeod Papers, p.3.

62 HBCA: E.3/8, entry '28th July 1814'.

63 Bumsted, *Fur Trade Wars*, p.115.

64 HoC, *Papers Relating to the Red River Settlement*, p.4.

65 Horn, 'British Diaspora', p.33.

66 HoC, *Papers Relating to the Red River Settlement*, pp.1–3.

67 HoC, *Papers Relating to the Red River Settlement*, pp.4–5.

68 Bumsted, *Fur Trade Wars*, p.111–16.

69 Ibid.

70 Cox, *Adventures on the Columbia River*, pp.239–40.

71 HBCA: B.176/a/1, fo.7d–9.

72 HBCA: A.10/1, fos.144, 152 (a–g).

73 Bumsted, *Fur Trade Wars*, pp.125–6.

74 Bumsted, *Fur Trade Wars*, p.127.

75 Bumsted, *Fur Trade Wars*, pp.139–141; Campbell, *The North West Company*, p.242; Cox, *Adventures on the Columbia River*, p.238; E. E. Rich, *The Fur Trade and the Northwest to 1857* (London, 1968), p.231.

76 HoC, *Papers Relating to the Red River Settlement*, p.42.

77 HBCA: A.10/1, fos.181–4.

78 HBCA: A.6/18, fos.342–4.

79 Bumsted, *Fur Trade Wars*, pp.138, 154.

80 HoC, *Papers Relating to the Red River Settlement*, p.56; Cox, *Adventures on the Columbia River*, pp.236–9; Bumsted, *Fur Trade Wars*, pp.148–9.

81 Bumsted, *Fur Trade Wars*, p.149.

82 HBCA: B.177/a/9, fo.2d–4.

83 HoC, *Papers Relating to the Red River Settlement*, p.53.

84 Bumsted, *Fur Trade Wars*, pp.157–9; Cox, *Adventures on the Columbia River*, p.237; George Keith, 'Letters' in Masson (ed.), *Les Bourgeois de la Compagnie du Nord-Ouest*, vol.2, p.130.

85 HBCA: A.6/19, fos.18d–20d.

86 HBCA: A.6/19, fos.21–2.

87 HBCA: B.39/z/1, fos.56–56d.

88 HBCA: B.39/z/1, fos.7–7d.

89 Cox, *Adventures on the Columbia River*, p.228.

90 HBCA: A.6/19, fos.51d–54d.

91 Bumsted, *Fur Trade Wars*, p.182; HoC, *Papers Relating to the Red River Settlement*, p.71.

92 HoC, *Papers Relating to the Red River Settlement*, pp.70, 92; HBCA: A.5/5, fos.152d–153d.

93 HoC, *Papers Relating to the Red River Settlement*, p.92; Bumsted, *Fur Trade Wars*, pp.201–2.

94 Nicholas Garry, 'The Diary of Nicholas Garry, Deputy-Governor of the Hudson's Bay Company, from 1822–35: a Detailed Narrative of his Travels in the Northwest Territories of British North America in 1821', *Transactions of the Royal Society of Canada, 1900*, p.569.

95 Cox, *Adventures on the Columbia River*, p.228.

96 Rich, *The Fur Trade and the Northwest to 1857*, p.230–1; Bumsted, *Fur Trade Wars*, p.124.

97 W. F. Wentzel, 'Letters to Roderick McKenzie, 1807–1824', in Masson (ed.), *Les Bourgeois de la Compagnie du Nord-Ouest*, vol.1, pp.125–7.

98 G. P. Glazerbrook (ed.), *The Hargrave Correspondence, 1821–43* (Toronto, 1938), p.1; Rich, *The Fur Trade and the Northwest to 1857*, p.239; E. E. Rich (ed.), *Colin Robertson's Correspondence Book, September 1817 to September 1822* (Toronto 1939), p.xx; Bumsted, *Fur Trade Wars*, p.227.

99 Allan I. Macinnes, *Clanship, Commerce and the House of Stuart, 1603–1788* (East Linton, 1996), pp.37–9, 56.

100 R. B. Ferguson, 'Explaining War', in J. Haas (ed.), *The Anthropology of War* (Cambridge, 1990), p.34.

101 Macinnes, *Clanship, Commerce and the House of Stuart*, pp.5–6, 37–46; Robert A. Dodgshon, *From Chiefs to Landlord: Social and Economic Change in the Western Highlands and Islands, c.1493–1820* (Edinburgh, 1998), pp.8, 38–9, 87–8; K. M. Brown, *Bloodfeud in Scotland, 1573–1625: Violence, Justice and Politics in Early Modern Society* (Edinburgh, 1986), pp.4, 277; Alison Cathcart, 'The Western Gaidhealtachd', in Bob Harris and Alan R. McDonald (eds), *Scotland: The Making and Unmaking of the Nation c.1100–1707*, vol.2 (Dundee, 2007), p.92.

102 Dodgshon, *From Chiefs to Landlords*, pp.8, 15, 87.

103 Bumsted, *Fur Trade Wars*, pp.145.

104 Bumsted, *Fur Trade Wars*, pp.146–8.

105 Bumsted, *Fur Trade Wars*, p.159; Williams (ed.), 'James Tate's Journal 1809–1812', p.223.

106 Cox, *Adventures on the Columbia River*, p.228.

107 S. H. Wilcocke, 'Death of Benjamin Frobisher', in Masson (ed.), *Les Bourgeois de la Compagnie du Nord-Ouest*, vol.2, p.179–226; Bumsted, *Fur Trade Wars*, pp.223–4.

108 HBCA: B.177/a/1, fos.16, 16d; B.177/a/2, fo.6d; B.177/a/3, fo.6; B.177/a/4, fo.6; B.22/a/10, fo.2; Morton (ed.), *The Journal of Duncan M'Gillivray*, Appendix, p.3.

109 Rich (ed.), *Colin Robertson's Correspondence Book, September 1817–1822*, p.85.

110 HBCA: B.3/a/115, fo.7d.

111 HBCA: B.3/a/119b, fos.7–7d.

112 Wilcocke, 'Death of Benjamin Frobisher', p.203.

CHAPTER 6

1 Robert Louis Stevenson, *From Scotland to Silverado*, edited by James D. Hart (Cambridge, 1966), p.210.

2 HBCA: B.22/a/16, fo.6.

3 HBCA: B.177/a/1, fo.16.

4 Neill, *A Tour*, pp.1–2; *OSA*, vol. XVI, Sandwick and Stromness, p.464.

5 HBCA: B.177/a/1, fos.16–16d.

6 HBCA: A.16/111, fos.8–31d. See also HBCA: A.16/111, fos.11,16d; A.16/112, fos.15d, 70; A.16/113, fo.4.

7 Brown, 'A Parcel of Upstart Scotchmen', p.6.

8 HBCA: A.16/111, fos.16d, 21d.

9 Tyrell (ed.), *David Thompson's Narrative*, p.74.

10 Henry Youle Hind, *Narrative of the Canadian Red River Exploring Expedition of 1857 and of the Assinniboine and Saskatchewan Exploring Expedition of 1858* (London, 1860), p.206.

11 Umfreville, *The Present State*, p.109; HBCA: A.6/20, fo.72d.

12 HBCA: A.6/18, fos.252–3; A.11/118, fo.23.

13 Stevenson, *From Scotland to Silverado*, p.210.

14 Cuthbert (ed.), *Low's History*, p.45.

15 *OSA*, vol. XIV, Birsay and Harray, p.331; vol. VII, Kirkwall and St Ola, p.554; Cuthbert (ed.), *Low's History*, p.45.

16 *OSA*, vol. XIV, Birsay and Harray, p.321; vol. XVI, Sandwick and Stromness, p.409; Cuthbert (ed.), *Low's History*, pp.45–6.

17 *OSA*, vol. VII, Kirkwall and St Ola, pp.560–1; vol, XVI, Sandwick and Stromness, pp.460–1; Cuthbert (ed.), *Low's History*, pp.50–3.

18 OA: D31/23/1, James Sutherland to George and John Sutherland, St Margaret's Hope, 29 June 1814.

19 HBCA: A.5/5, fo.110d; A.5/ 6, fo.127d.

20 HBCA: A.11/117, fos.118, 159.

21 HBCA: A.6/18 (folio illegible) London Committee to William Auld and Thomas Thomas, 31 May 31 1811.

22 HBCA: A.11/118, fo.24d.

23 Ibid.

24 HBCA: A.6/19, fo.70; NA: BH1/1782.

25 HBCA: A.30/16, fos.12d–13, 23.

26 *OSA*, vol. XVI, Sandwick and Stromness, p.445.

27 Brown, *Strangers*, pp.12–13, 52–66; Van Kirk, *Many Tender Ties*, pp.4, 14–15, 25–9, 38, 41, 45; Stephen, *Masters and Servants*, pp.286–9.

28 Brown, *Strangers*, pp.78–9; Van Kirk, *Many Tender Ties*, pp.38, 45.

29 Van Kirk, *Many Tender Ties*, pp.xi; 4, 9, 27.

30 William Newton, *Twenty Years on the Saskatchewan* (London, 1897), pp.39–40.

31 Van Kirk, *Many Tender Ties*, p.93; Brown, *Strangers*, p.51.

32 HBCA: A.16/112, fo.19d–20;A.16/113, fos.4–11d.

33 HBCA: A.16/112, fo.13d; Van Kirk, *Many Tender Ties*, p.99.

34 Van Kirk, *Many Tender Ties*, pp.5, 99; HBCA: A.16/111, fos.39d–46; A.16/112, fos.12d–13, 43, 76–76d; A.16/113, fo.4d.

35 HBCA: B.3/a/118, fo.4; Brown, *Strangers*, p.76.

36 HBCA: A.6/19, fo.71.

37 Brown, *Strangers*, pp.83–7; Franklin, *Narrative Of A Journey*, p.134.

38 Devine, *Scotland's Empire*, p.242; Hamilton, *Scotland, the Caribbean and the Atlantic World*, pp.46–8.

39 HBCA: A.6/13, fo.112d; A.6/15, fo.63d; A.6/17, fo.66d; Herbert D. G. Maschner and Katherine L. Reedy-Maschner, 'Marauding Middlemen: Western Expansion and Violent Conflict in the Sub-arctic', *Ethnohistory* 46.4 (1999), p.732; Brown, *Strangers*, pp.xi–xii,13; Van Kirk, *Many Tender Ties*, pp.9, 14, 86.

40 Brown, *Strangers*, pp.xvi, 52.

41 Van Kirk, *Many Tender Ties*, p.5; Brown, *Strangers*, p.52; Franklin, *Narrative Of A Journey*, pp.131–2.

42 OA: D31/23/1, James Sutherland to George and John Sutherland, St Margaret's Hope, 29 June 1814; HBCA: A.36/8, fos.97–103.

43 HBCA: A.6/15, fo.177; A.5/6, fo.75d; HBC Biographies, Joseph Spence. See also HBC Biographies for Andrew Stewart and William Auld.

44 OA: D31/23/1, James Sutherland to George and John Sutherland, St Margaret's Hope, 29 June 1814.

45 Van Kirk, *Many Tender Ties*, p.87.

46 HBCA: A.5/4, fos.80, 88d.

47 Van Kirk, *Many Tender Ties*, p.87.

48 HBCA: A.5/4, fos.49d–50; A.6/16, fo.160; Van Kirk, *Many Tender Ties*, pp.96, 99.

49 HBCA: A.5/4, fos.80, 88d; A.6/19, fo.98d.

50 HBCA: A.6/17, fos.119–20d; B.198/c/1, fo.3; B.59/z/2, fos.1–2; Brown, *Strangers*, p.77.

51 HBCA: A.11/118, fo.3d; Van Kirk, *Many Tender Ties*, p.133.

52 Franklin, *Narrative Of A Journey*, p.133; Van Kirk, *Many Tender Ties*, p.17, 97–9; Brown, *Strangers*, p.72.

53 Van Kirk, *Many Tender Ties*, p.95.

54 Newton, *Twenty Years on the Saskatchewan*, pp.39–40.

55 Newton, *Twenty Years on the Saskatchewan*, p.134.

56 NAS: SC70/1/34, fos.394–8; HBCA: A.16/15, fos.29d–30; A.36/6, fos.135–47; Van Kirk, *Many Tender Ties*, pp.8, 39, 95, 108–9, 122; Brown, *Strangers*, pp.70–9.

57 HBCA: A.6/15, fo.73d; A.6/16, fo.160.

58 HBCA: A.6/16, fos.29d–30; Van Kirk, *Many Tender Ties*, pp.49, 106–7; Brown, *Strangers*, pp.67–9.

59 HBCA: A.6/19, fo.45.

60 HBCA: A.6/19, fo.96d.

61 HBCA: A.6/19, fo.48.

62 HBCA: A.6/19, fo.70d; NA: BH1/1782; HBCA: E.6/13, fos.3d, 4, 6d, 7.

63 HBCA: A.6/19, fo.98d; Brown, *Strangers*, pp.200–1; Van Kirk, 'Fur Trade Social History', p.170.

64 NA: BH1/1783, fos.191–194d; Van Kirk, *Many Tender Ties*, p.145.

65 Nicks, 'Orkneymen', p.122; Burley, *Servants*, p.71; HBCA: A.5/3, fo.95d; A.5/5, fo.26; A.11/117, fos.21d–22, 61d; see also HBCA, Series A.16; *OSA*, vol. XV, Evie and Rendall, p.254.

66 Gough, *The Journal of Alexander Henry*, pp.299–300.

67 HBCA: A.5/3, fos.34, 172d; A.1/48, fo.60; A.5/4, fo.94; A.1/49 fo.15; A.32/2, fo.141; A.32/3, fo.116; A.32/5, fo.180; A.32/13, fos.47, 123. See also HBCA: A.5/4, fo.72.

68 HBCA: A.6/15, fo.99; A.30/4, fo.12; A.32/5, fo.208;A.30/11, fos.37–37d.

69 Brown, *Strangers*, pp.11–12.

70 HBCA: A.5/3, fo.173.

71 Ibid.

72 HBCA: A.5/4, fo.94.

73 HBCA: A.5/3, fo.18.

74 HBCA: A.5/4, fo.175.

75 HBCA: A.5/4, fo.77.

76 HBCA: A.5/6, fo.76; A.5/5, fo.2.

77 HBCA: B.3/a/118, fo.3.

78 OA: D31/23/1, James Sutherland to John Sutherland, St Margaret's Hope, 24 August 1817, p.1.

79 HBCA: A.6/19, fo.71; A.5/6, fo.116d.

80 HBCA: A.5/6, fo.101d; A.5/3, fo.173; see also A.5/5, fo.169.

81 HBCA: A.10/2, fos.64d–65.

82 HBCA: A.5/5, fo.169.

83 HBCA: A.5/6, fo.131.

84 OA: D31/23/1, James Sutherland to John Sutherland, St Margaret's Hope, 26 August 1825, p.1.

85 HBCA: A.5/4, fo.46.

CHAPTER 7

1 Chappell, *Narrative*, p.13; *OSA*, vol. XVI, Sandwick and Stromness, pp.464–5.

2 HBCA: A.5/4, fo.66d; A.5/6, fos.70, 134, 139d; A.6/16, fo.36; C.1/297, fo.8.

3 *Orkney and Zetland Chronicle*, No.3, 28 February 1825, p.28.

4 HBCA: A.25/3, fos.5–7.

5 *OSA*, vol. XVI, Sandwick and Stromness, p.445.

6 HBCA: A.5/4, fos.18, 80d–83; A.5/5, fo.77d; A.5/6, fo.127d.

7 HBCA: A.11/117, fos.21d–22, fo.61d.

8 HBCA: B.59/a/86, fos.31–31d; A.10/2, fos.47d–82.

9 HBCA: A.6/16, fo.137; Van Kirk, *Many Tender Ties*, p.39; .OA: D31/23/1, James Sutherland to John Sutherland, St Margaret's Hope, 26 August 1825, p.1.

10 HBCA: B.143/a/4, fo.1; B.142/a/5, fo.22; B.198/b/5, fos.18–22.

11 HBCA: A.67/9, fo.1.

12 HBCA: B.143/a/4, fo.1; B.142/a/5, fo.22; B.198/b/5, fos.18–22.

13 Burley, *Servants*, p.73; HBCA: A.11/117, fos.21d–22.

14 HBCA: A.5/2, fos.137,176d; A.6/14, fo.125.

15 Burley, *Servants*, p.144.

16 HBCA: A.5/2, fo.137.

17 HBCA: A.5/2, fo.137.

18 HBCA: A.5/2, fos. 137–8, 151–7; A.5/3 fos.178d–179.

19 HBCA: A.6/13, fos.96, 126d; A.5/6, fo.86.

20 HBCA: A.5/4, fo.71–71d; A.6/13, fo.126d.

21 HBCA: A.6/13, fos.122d–134.

22 HBCA: A.6/13, fo.133d; A.6/14, fo.45.

23 HBCA: A.5/2, fos.137, 176d; A.5/3, fos.54d–55d; A.5/5, fo.103d; A.6/14, fo.125; A.11/45, fo.171.

24 HBCA: A.5/5, fo.160; A.5/6, fo.32; A.10/2, fo.52.

25 HBCA: A.5/6, fo.113d.

26 HBCA: A.1/51, fo.90; A.5/3, fo.132d; A.5/5, fo.165d; A.30/16, fo.163; B.198/b/5, fos.18d–22; Burley, *Servants*, p.42.

27 HBCA: A.5/4, fo.29d; A.32/5, fo.35; A.32/8, fo.13; A.16/111, fos.30–7; A.16/112, fos.18d–19.

28 HBCA: A.1/48, fos.35d–36; A.5/5, fos.16d, 102; A.6/16, fo.225; A.30/10, fo.31.

29 HBCA: A.5/3, fo.146d.

30 HBCA: B.3/a/115, fos.8–8d.

31 HBCA: A.1/51, fo.108d; A.10/1, fos.327–33; A.10/2, fo.110.

32 HBCA: A.10/2, fos.49, 64d, 65, 75d.

33 HBCA: A.10/2, fo.47.

34 HBCA: A.5/3, fo.39d; A.11/117, fo.61d.

35 HBCA; A.6/14, fo.125.

36 HBCA: A.5/5, fo.93, 132; A.5/6, fos.32–32d.

37 HBCA: A.5/6, fos.70, 79d, 85d.

38 HBCA: A.5/6, fos.86d–97d.

39 HBCA: A.5/6, fos.99, 128d.

40 HBCA: A.1/52, fo.4; A.5/3, fo.102.

41 HBCA: A.1/51, fo.125; A.1/52, fos.12, 49d; A.5/2, fo.159; A.5/6, fos.16d–17, 46, 84d, 100, 107, 110, 134d.

42 HBCA: A.5/6, fos.110, 153d; A.6/19, fo.96.

43 HBCA: A.5/3, fo.147d.

44 HBCA: B.39/c/1, fo.1.
45 HBCA: A.5/6, fos.85–6.
46 Ibid.
47 HBCA: A.5/4, fos.67, 70–2.
48 HBCA: A.11/117, fo.120; A.5/4, fo.71d.
49 HBCA: A.11/117, fo.67.
50 HBCA: A.1/52, fo.4; A.5/4, fos.113d, 130, 137d; A.5/5, fos.59d, 91.
51 HBCA: A.5/6, fo.100.
52 HBCA: A.5/6, fo.119d.
53 HBCA: A.11/116, fo.112d.
54 HBCA: A.5/3, fo.95d; A.5/5, fo.26.
55 HBCA: A.1/50, fo.95. See also, HBCA: A.5/6, fos.32, 83.
56 HBCA: A.5/4, fo.41d; A.1/52, fo.15; A.5/5, fo.174d; A.5/6, fo.84d.
57 HBCA: A.1/48, fos.60, 121; A.5/3, fo.172d; A.5/5, fos.36d, 65; A.6/17, fo.28d; A.16/7, fo.19.
58 HBCA: A.5/3, fo.179d.
59 HBCA: A.10/2, fo.110.
60 Ibid.
61 HBCA: A.5/6, fo.32–32d.
62 HBCA: A.16/12, fo.29; A.16/15, fos.7d–174; *OSA*, vol. XIV, Firth and Stenness, p.134.
63 HBCA: A.16/15, fos.7d–174.
64 HBCA: A.5/6, fo.113d.
65 HBCA: A.16/7; A.16/8; A.16/12; A.16/13; A.16/14; A.16/15; A.16/16; Gary B. Magee and
    Andrew S. Thomson, 'The Global and Local: Explaining Migrant Remittance Flows in
    the English-speaking World, 1880–1914', *JEH*, vol. 66, no.1 (March 2006), p.177.
66 HBCA: A.16/7, fo.25; A.16/12, fo.33; A.16/16, fos.112, 150.
67 HBCA: A.16/15, fo.23; A.16/7, fos.1–9.
68 Judith Hudson Beattie and Helen M Buss (eds.), *Undelivered Letters to Hudson's Bay
    Company Men on the Northwest Coast of America, 1830–1857* (Vancouver, 2003), pp.19–21;
    Magee and Thomson, 'The Global and Local', p.177.
69 HBCA: A.16/7, fo.33; A.16/15, fo.33.
70 HBCA: A.16/15, fo.38; OA: D31/23/1, James Sutherland to John Sutherland, St Margaret's
    Hope, 24 August 1817, p.2.
71 *NSA*, vol. p.26.
72 HBCA: B.239/c/1, fo.18; A.1/51, fo.104d.
73 Ann M. Carlos, 'The Birth and Death of Predatory Competition in the North American
    Fur Trade: 1810–1821', *Explorations in Economic History*, 19 (April 1982), p.788.
74 HBCA: A.16/15, fos.34d–35, 40, 46d–47, 61d–62.
75 HBCA: A.5/3, fos.147d, 149d; A.5/4, fo.19d.
76 HBCA: A.16/12, fo.25; A.16/15, fos.63d–64, 87d–89.
77 HBCA: A.16/15, fo.59.
78 HBCA: A.16/15, fo.92.
79 HBCA: A.6/17, fo.66.
80 HBCA: A.11/117, fos.105–7.
81 HBCA: A.5/3, fos.53d, 87–88d.
82 Ibid.
83 HBCA: A.6/17, fo.66; A.5/4, fos.113d–130.
84 HBCA: A.5/4, fo.24d–26d; A.16/15, fos.15, 36, 42; A.16/7.

85 HBCA: A.32/4, fos.52, 146; A.32/5, fo.15; A.5/4, fos.24d–26d; A.30/4, fos.14d, 46, 74; A.5/3, fos.87d–88; A.32/2, fos.154, 166; A.32/6, fo.46; A.16/6, fos.133, 142.

86 HBCA: A.5/3, fos.87–88d; A.5/4, fos.23–26d; A.30/2, A.30/4;A.32/1, fos.12, 19, 37, 57, 60, 84, 105, 157; A.32/2, fos.19, 43, 55, 114, 123, 139, 154, 166; A.32/4, fos.50, 171.

87 HBCA: A.5/4, fo.22, 26d; B.239/c/1, fos.7–32.

88 HBCA: A.5/2, fos.156–8.

89 HBCA: A.5/3, fo.164.

90 HBCA: A.5/4, fo.27d; B.239/c/1, fo.24.

91 *OSA*, vol. XIX, Orphir, p.407.

92 *OSA*, vol. XIV, Firth and Stenness, pp.133–4.

93 Ibid.

94 Ibid.

95 *OSA*, vol. XIX, Orphir, p.407.

96 Ibid.

97 NAS: RS46/6.89 (407); RS46/10.184 (730); RS46/11.29 (755); RS46/12.277 (904); RS46/13.194 (950); RS46/14.137 (1026); RS46/17.146 (1254); RS46/18.10 (1307); RS46/18.96 (1338); RS46/14.110 (1011); RS46/14.213 (1048); RS46/15.26 (1081); RS46/15.175 (1118); RS46/15.115(1105); RS46/17.168 (1261); RS46/17.168 (1262); RS46/18.18 (1309); RS46/19.167 (1452); RS46/20.101 (51); RS46/6.163 (426); RS46/11.186 (805); RS46/11.120 (789); RS46/13.64 (930); RS46/949.74 (941); RS46/4.425 (199); RS46/5.517 (385).

98 Quoted in Brown, *Strangers*, p.27.

99 NAS: RS46/18/10 (1307); RS46/21/140 (126); RS46/20/176 (72); RS46/14/110 (1011); RS46/18/8 (1309); HBCA: A.30/16, fos.33d–34.

100 NAS: RS46/4/425 (199); RS46/11/186 (805); RS46/17/146 (1254); RS46/949/74 (941); HBCA: A.16/6, fo.159; A.16/7, fo.7; A.30/4 fos.49d–50; A.30/10 fos.42d–43; A.30/11, fos.3d–4, 8d–9, 33d–34; A.32/5, fos.144, 168; A.32/13, fo.20: A.32/18, fo.40.

101 Devine, *The Tobacco Lords*, pp.22–4.

102 NAS: RS46/6/163 (426); RS46/23/41 (252); RS46/25/3 (393); HBCA: A.30/10, fos.44d–45; A.30/11, fos.17d–18.

103 NAS: RS46/13/64 (930); RS46/13/194 (950); RS46/15/175; HBCA: A.30/11, fo.44d–45; A.16/15, fo.83.

104 NAS: RS46/20.101 (51); RS46/15/115 (1105); RS46/26/80 (489); RS46/15/175 (1118); RS46/23/211 (292); RS46/20/218 (81).

105 NAS: RS46/14/213 (1048); RS46/10/184; RS46/20/215; NA: Prob 11/1565, fos.356–356d; HBCA: A.30/11, fo.34; A.32/1 fo.84; HBC Biography, William Sinclair, James Robertson Sr.

106 NA: Prob.11/1595, fos.44d–46.

107 HBCA: A.5/4, fos.27–33d, 137; A.5/5, fo.39; A.5/6, fo.143d.

108 HBCA: A.36/7, fo.127; A.36/11, fos.204–206; A.36/13, fos.2–65; NAS: RS46/19.167 (1452).

109 NA: Prob 11/1565, fos.356–356d; HBCA: A.32/1, fo.84; HBC Biography, James Sr Robertson.

110 NAS: CC8/8/135, fos.240–1.

111 OA: D31/23/1, James Sutherland to John Sutherland, St Margaret's Hope, 26 August 1825, p.1; HBCA: A.36/12, fo.255; A.36/1b, fo.29.

112 Quoted in Brown, *Strangers*, p.138.

113 HBCA: A.36/1b, fos.12–13; A.36/8, fos.83–195; E.6/9; E.6/12.

114 NA: Prob 11/1840, fo.46d.

115 HBCA: A.6/19, fo.45d; A.36/1a, fos.7d, 16d.

116 HBCA: A.36/3, fos.180–4.
117 HBCA: A.36/6, fos.135–47; NAS: SC170/1/34.
118 HBCA: B.24/a/3, fo.2d; A.6/18, fo.351; A.36/1a, fos.18d–19; A.36/12.
119 HBCA: A.5/4, fo.27.
120 HBCA: A.6/18, fo.226.
121 HBCA: A.36/1b, fos.12–13; A.36/8, fos.83–195; A.36/12, fo.255; A.36/1b, fo.29; NA: Prob
     11/1840, fo.46d.
122 *OSA*, vol. XIX, Orphir, pp.406–7.
123 OA: D31/23/2; HBCA: A.11/116, fo.142.
124 OA: D31/23/2, pp.1–7.
125 *The Orcadian*, 16 September 1911, p.3a.
126 NAS: CC8/8/135, fos.240–1; HBCA: HBC Biography, Magnus Twatt.
127 HBCA: A.36/1b, fos.24–5.
128 Ibid.; NA: Prob 11/1944, fos.216d–217d.
129 NAS: CC8/8/135, fos.240–1; *NSA*: vol. XV, South Ronaldsay and Burray, p.195; NA: Prob
     11/1944, fos.216d–217d; NAS: SC11/41/1.
130 Devine, *The Tobacco Lords*, pp.18–33; Hamilton, *Scotland, the Caribbean and the Atlantic
     World*, pp.195–220; Stephen, *Masters and Servants*, p.16.

Bibliography

MANUSCRIPT SOURCES

Hudson's Bay Company archives, Provincial Archives of Manitoba, Winnipeg

SERIES A: HEADQUARTERS RECORDS

A.1/45–52, London Minute Book, 1776–1821
A.5/2–6, London Correspondence Books Outwards – General Series, 1776–1822
A.6/13–20, London Correspondence Books Outwards – HBC Official, 1781–1824
A.10/1–2, London Inward Correspondence – General, 1712–1835
A.11/45–46, London Inward Correspondence – From Posts, Moose
A.11/116–118, London Inward Correspondence – From Posts, York
A.16/7–8, Officers' and Servants' Ledger – Albany, 1802–1819
A.16/12, Officers' and Servants' Ledger – Churchill, 1813–1819
A.16/13, Officers' and Servants' Ledger – Eastmain, 1787–1813
A.16/14–15, Officers' and Servants' Ledger – Edmonton, 1810–1813
A.16/16, Officers' and Servants' Ledger – Moose, 1791–1813
A.16/111–113, Officers' and Servants' Account Book – Servants' Commissions, 1787–1897
A.25/3, Merchandise Exported, 1778–1799
A.25/4, Merchandise Exported, 1800–1812
A.30/2, Names &c of the Company's Servants at Hudson's Bay, 1780–1783
A.30/4, Names &c of the Company's Servants at Hudson's Bay, 1788–1790
A.30/10–11, Names &c of the Company's Servants at Hudson's Bay, 1800–1812
A.30/15–17, Names &c of the Company's Servants at Hudson's Bay, 1815–1821
A.32/1–60, Servants' Contracts, 1776–1926
A.36/1a–15, Officers' and Servants' Wills, 1763–1921
A.66/2, Papers re. Pension and Benefit Schemes, 1711–1863
A.67/1, Miscellaneous Papers, 1719–1870
A.67/9, Servants' Cash and Clothing Tickets, 1812

SERIES B: POST RECORDS

B.3/a/114–120, Albany – Post Journal, 1810–1817
B.3/b/41, Albany – Correspondence Book, 1804–1805
B.3/z/2, Albany – Miscellaneous Records, 1696–1865
B.4/z/1, Fort Alexander – Miscellaneous Accounts, 1817–1865
B.7/a/1, Ash Fall – Post Journal, 1798–1799

B.18/a/1, Big Fall – Post Journal, 1802–1803
B.22/a/10, Brandon House – Post Journal, 1802–1803
B.22/a/16, Brandon House – Post Journal, 1808–1809
B.22/a/18, Brandon House – Post Journal, 1810–1811
B.22/z/1, Brandon House and Upper Red River District – Miscellaneous Records, 1810–1824
B.23/a/1–14, Brunswick House – Post Journal, 1777–1791
B.24/a/1–6, Buckingham House – Post Journal, 1792–1799
B.39/c/1, Fort Chipewyan – Correspondence Inwards, 1823–1826
B.39/z/1, Fort Chipewyan – Miscellaneous, 1815–1870
B.40/a/1, Chipewyan Lake – Post Journal, 1800–1801
B.41/a/1, Chiswick House – Post Journal, 1803–1804
B.42/c/1, Fort Churchill – Correspondence Inwards, 1799–1862
B.42/z/1, Churchill – Miscellaneous (Indents), 1797–1870
B.49/c/1, Cumberland House – Correspondence Inwards, 1801–1856
B.49/f/2, Cumberland House – Servants' List, 1795–1796
B.49/z/1, Cumberland House – Miscellaneous, 1817–1870
B.57/a/2, Eagle Lake – Post Journal, 1809–1810
B.59/a/70, Eastmain – Post Journal, 1793–1794
B.59/a/74, Eastmain – Post Journal, 1797–1798
B.59/a/78, Eastmain – Post Journal, 1800–1801
B.59/a/82–83, Eastmain – Post Journal, 1804–1806
B.59/a/85–87, Eastmain – Post Journal, 1807–1810
B.59/a/94, Eastmain – Post Journal, 1815–1816
B.59/a/103, Eastmain – Post Journal, 1819–1820
B.59/b/8–32, Eastmain – Correspondence Book, 1788–1816
B.59/z/1, Eastmain – Register of Baptisms and Burials, 1806–1826
B.59/z/2, Eastmain – School Register and Indent, 1810–1812
B.78/a/24–26, Gloucester House – Post Journal, 1815–1818
B.81/z/1, Gordon House (Rock Depot) – Miscellaneous Records, 1818–1821
B.89/a/1–2, Isle à la Crosse – Post Journal, 1805–1811
B.89/c/1, Isle à la Crosse – Correspondence Inwards, 1811–1862
B.9/a/3, Lake Athabasca – Post Journal, 1790–1792
B.121/a/3–4, Manchester House – Post Journal, 1788–1790
B.121/a/7, Manchester House – Post Journal, 1791–1792
B.122/a/1, Manitoba Lake – Post Journal, 1815–1816
B.123/a/1, Martin Fall – Post Journal, 1794–1795
B.123/a/8, Martin Fall – Post Journal 1803–1804
B.135/a/62, Moose – Post Journal, 1780–1781
B.135/a/66, Moose – Post Journal, 1782–1783
B.135/a/77, Moose – Post Journal, 1790–1791
B.135/a/80, Moose – Post Journal, 1793–1794
B.135/a/87, Moose – Post Journal, 1799–1800
B.135/a/90, Moose – Post Journal, 1802–1803
B.135/a/97, Moose – Post Journal, 1808–1809

B.135/a/102, Moose – Post Journal, 1811–1812
B.135/a/105, Moose – Post Journal, 1814–1815
B.135/a/111, Moose – Post Journal, 1815–1816
B.135/a/82, Moose Fort – Correspondence, 1794–1795
B.141/a/1, Nelson House (Churchill River) – Post Journal, 1802–1803
B.141/a/3, Nelson House (Churchill River) – Post Journal, 1809–1810
B.141/a/5, Nelson House (Churchill River) – Post Journal, 1811–1812
B.141/a/9–11, Nelson House (Churchill River) – Post Journal, 1815–1819
B.142/a/1–9, Nemiskau – Post Journal, 1794–1809
B.143/a/1–4, Neoskweskau – Post Journal, 1793–1797
B.158/a/1, Pelican Lake – Post Journal, 1818–1819
B.159/a/1–3, Fort Pelly – Post Journal, 1793–1797
B.164/a/1–2, Pine Lake – Post Journal, 1810–1812
B.166/a/1–3, Portage de l'Isle – Post Journal, 1793–1795
B.169/a/1, Portland House – Post Journal, 1796–1797
B.177/a/1–10, Red Lake – Post Journal, 1790–1818
B.176/a/1, Red Deer River (Swan River) – Post Journal, 1812–1813
B.198/a/47–50, Severn – Post Journal, 1795–1799
B.198/a/52–53, Severn – Post Journal, 1799–1808
B.198/b/3–5, Severn – Correspondence Book, 1788–1808
B.198/c/1, Severn – Correspondence Inwards, 1808–1825
B.239/a/89, York Factory – Post Journal, 1788–1789
B.239/a/92, York Factory – Post Journal, 1791–1792
B.239/a/105, York Factory – Post Journal, 1800–1801
B.239/a/120, York Factory – Journal, 1812–1813
B.239/c/1, York Factory – Correspondence Inwards, 1807–1828
B.239/ee/1, York Factory – Indents, 1783–1790
B.244/a/1, Bad Lake – Post Journal, 1805–1806
B.372/a/3, Great Whale River – Post Journal, 1815–1816

SERIES C: SHIP RECORDS

C.1/206, Ship Log – Beaver, 1793
C.1/297–298, Ship Log – Eddystone, 1812–1813
C.1/398, Ship Log – King George (III), 1795
C.1/415–416, Ship Log – King George (III), 1804–1805
C.4/1, Ships' Movements Book, 1719–1929

SERIES D: GOVERNORS' PAPERS

D.1/11, Governor William Williams – Correspondence Book Inwards, 1818–1819

SERIES E: MISCELLANEOUS RECORDS

E.3/8 (also B.235/a/3), Red River Settlement journal kept by Peter, Thomas and Charles Fidler, 1814–1815
E.41/1, The Cameron Family Correspondence: Inward – General, 1787–1803

E.41/2–3, The Cameron Family Correspondence: Inward – Official, 1788–1815
E.6/4, Red River Land Register Book, 1823–1825
E.6/9, Red River Settlement – Land Sales Memoranda, 1830–1831
E.6/12–13, Red River Settlement – References to Plans, 1835–1836
E.7/28, Red River Settlement – Account Book, 1825–1826

SERIES F: RECORDS OF ALLIED AND SUBSIDIARY COMPANIES

F.1/1, Northwest Company Minute Book, 1807–1814
F.3/2, Northwest Company Correspondence, 1791–1827

The National Archives, Kew, London

BH1/1782, Red River Settlement Census, 1827
BH1/1783, Red River Settlement – Register of Marriages and Burials, 1820–1841
BH1/370, Merchandise Exported, 1778–1799
BH1/371, Merchandise Exported, 1800–1812
Wills of the Probate Court

National Archives of Scotland, Edinburgh

GD136, Sinclair of Freswick Muniments
GD176, Mackintosh Papers
RH15, Miscellaneous Papers
Register of Sasines – Orkney, Caithness
Wills and Testaments

Orkney Library & Archive, Kirkwall

D31, Ernest Marwick Papers

Western Isles Library

John MacLeod Papers (Transcript of original letters supplied by the Public Archives of
    Canada).

Contemporary newspapers and magazines

Edinburgh Evening Courant
French Gazette
Old Parish Register
Orkney and Zetland Chronicle
The Saturday Magazine
The Scotsman

PRINTED PRIMARY SOURCES

Amicus, *Eight Letters on the Subject of the Earl of Selkirk's Pamphlet, as they lately appeared under the signature of Amicus in one of the Edinburgh newspapers* (Edinburgh, 1806).

Atcheson, Nathaniel (Henry, John), *On the Origin and Progress of the North-West Company of Canada with a History of the Fur Trade, as Connected with that Concern, and Observations on the Political Importance of the Company's Intercourse with, and Influence Over the Indians or Savage Nations of the Interior, and on the Necessity of Maintaining and Supporting the System from Which that Influence Wrises, and by Which Only it can be Preserved.* (London, 1811).

Bain, J. (ed.), *Travels and Adventures in Canada and the Indian Territories between the Years 1760 and 1776. By Alexander Henry, Fur Trader* (Toronto, 1901).

Beattie, Judith Hudson and Buss, Helen M. (eds), *Undelivered Letters to Hudson's Bay Company Men on the Northwest Coast of America, 1830–1857* (Vancouver, 2003).

Belyea, B. (ed.), *David Thompson: Columbia Journals* (Kingston and Montreal, 1994).

Belyea, B. (ed.), *A Year Inland: The Journal of a Hudson's Bay Company Winterer* (Waterloo, 2000).

Brown, R., *Strictures and Remarks on the Earl of Selkirk's Observations on the Present State of the Highlands of Scotland, with a view of the causes and probable consequences of emigration* (Edinburgh, 1806).

Bumsted, J. M. (ed.), *The Collected Writings of Lord Selkirk*, vol.1, 1799–1809. (Winnipeg, 1984).

Cameron, D., 'The Nipigon Country, 1804' in L.R. Masson (ed.), *Les Bourgeois de la Compagnie du Nord-Ouest*, vol.2 (New York, 1960).

Chappell, Edward, *Narrative of a Voyage to Hudson's Bay in His Majesty's Ship Rosamond containing some Account of the North-Eastern Coast of America and of the Tribes Inhabiting that Remote Region* (London, 1817).

Coues, E. (ed.), *New Light on the Early History of the Greater Northwest: The Manuscript Journals of Alexander Henry, Fur Trader of the Northwest Company, and of David Thompson, Official Geographer and Explorer of the same Company, 1799–1814; Exploration and Adventure among the Indians on the Red, Saskatchewan, Missouri and Columbia Rivers*, 3 vols. (New York, 1897).

Cox, Ross, *Adventures on the Columbia River, Including the Narrative of a Residence of Six Years on the Western Side of the Rocky Mountains, among Various Tribes of Indians Hitherto Unknown: Together with a Journey across the American Continent*, 2 vols. (London, 1831).

Cuthbert, Olaf D. (ed.), *A History of The Orkneys Introduced by A Description of the Islands and Their Inhabitants by George Low* (Orkney, 2001).

Davies, K. G. (ed.), *Letters From Hudson Bay, 1703–40* (London, 1965).

Fauche, Gaspard Adolphe, *Account of the Transactions at Fort William, on Lake Superior, in August 1816 ...* (London, 1817).

Franklin, Sir J., *Narrative of a Journey to the Shores of the Polar Sea, in the Years 1819, 1820, 1821 and 1822: With an Appendix on Various Subjects Relating to Science and Natural History.* (London, 1824).

Franklin, Sir J., *Thirty years in the Arctic Regions, or, The Adventures of Sir John Franklin* (New York, 1859).

Garry, Nicholas, 'The Diary of Nicholas Garry, Deputy-Governor of the Hudson's Bay Company, from 1822–35: a Detailed Narrative of his Travels in the Northwest Territories of British North America in 1821', *TRSC*, 1900, p.569.

Glazerbrook, G. P., 'A Document Concerning the Union of the Hudson's Bay Company and the Northwest Company', *CHR* vol.14, no.2 (1933).

Glazerbrook, G. P., *The Hargrave Correspondence, 1821–43* (Toronto, 1938).

Glover, Richard. (ed.), *A Journey from the Prince of Wales Fort in Hudson's Bay to the Northern Ocean, 1769, 1770, 1771, 1772, by Samuel Hearne* (Toronto, 1958).

Glover, Richard (ed.), *David Thompson's Narrative 1784–1812* (Toronto, 1962).

Gough, Barry M., *The Journal of Alexander Henry the Younger, 1799–1814*, vol.2 (Toronto, 1988–1992).

House of Commons, *Papers Relating to the Red River Settlement: viz. Return to an Address from the Honourable House of Commons to His Royal Highness The Prince Regent, dated 24th June, 1819* (London, 1819).

Halkett, J., *Statement Respecting the Earl of Selkirk's Settlement of Kildonan upon the Red River in North America: its Destruction in the years 1815 and 1816 ; and the Massacre of Governor Semple and His Party; with Observations upon a Recent Publication, Entitled 'A Narrative of Occurrences in the Indian Countries,' &c* (London, 1817).

Hind, Henry Youle, *Narrative of the Canadian Red River Exploring Expedition of 1857 and of the Assinniboine and Saskatchewan Exploring Expedition of 1858* (London, 1860).

Hopwood, V. (ed.), *David Thompson: Travels in Western North America, 1784–1812* (Toronto, 1971).

Irvine, Alexander, *An Inquiry into the Causes and Effects of Emigration from the Highlands and Western Islands of Scotland, with Observations on the Means to be Employed for Preventing It* (Edinburgh, 1802).

Johnson, A. M. (ed.), *Saskatchewan Journals and Correspondence: Edmonton House 1795–1800; Chesterfield House 1800–1802* (London, 1967).

Keith, George, 'Letters' in L. R. Masson (ed.), *Les Bourgeois de la Compagnie du Nord-Ouest*, vol.2 (New York, 1960).

Lamb, W. Kaye (ed.), *Sixteen Years in the Indian Country: The Journal of Daniel Williams Harmon, 1800–1816* (Toronto, 1957).

Lamb, W. Kaye (ed.), *The Letters and Journals of Simon Fraser, 1806–1808* (Toronto, 1960).

Lamb, W. Kaye (ed.), *The Journals and Letters of Alexander MacKenzie* (Cambridge, 1970).

Lambert, John, *Travels through Canada, and the United States of North America, in the Years 1806, 1807, & 1808*, 2 vols (London, 1813).

Langton, H. H. (ed.), *Travels in the Interior Inhabited Parts of North America in the Years 1791 and 1792* by Patrick Campbell (Toronto, 1937).

Long, John, *Voyages and Travels of an Indian Interpreter and Trader* (London, 1791).

McGowan, Ian (ed.), *Samuel Johnson & James Boswell: Journey to the Hebrides. A Journey to the Western Islands of Scotland by Samuel Johnson. The Journal of a Tour to the Hebrides with Samuel Johnson by James Boswell* (Edinburgh, 2001).

Macinnes, Allan I., Harper, Marjory-Ann D., Fryer, Linda G. (eds), *Scotland and the Americas, c. 1650–c. 1939: A Documentary Source Book* (Edinburgh, 2002).

Mackenzie, Alexander, *Voyages from Montreal, on the River St. Laurence, Through the*

Continent of North America to the Frozen and Pacific Oceans in the Years 1789 and 1793 (London, 1801).

Masson, Louis F. R. (ed.), *Les Bourgeois de la Compagnie du Nord-Ouest: Récits de Voyages, Lettres, et Rapports Inédits Relatifs au Nord-Ouest Canadien*, 2 vols. (New York, 1960).

Morton, Arthur S. (ed.), *The Journal of Duncan M'Gillivray of the North West Company at Fort George on the Saskatchewan, 1794–5* (Toronto, 1929).

Neill, Patrick, *A Tour Through Some of the Islands of Orkney and Shetland, with a View Chiefly to Objects of Natural History, but Including also Occasional Remarks on the State of the Inhabitants, Their Husbandry, and Fisheries* (Edinburgh, 1806).

Newton, William, *Twenty Years on the Saskatchewan, N. W. Canada* (London, 1897).

Pritchett, J. P. and Horowitz, M., 'Five "Selkirk" Letters', *CHR* vol.22, no.2 (1941).

Rich, E. E. (ed.), *Journal of Occurrences in the Athabasca Department by George Simpson, 1820 and 1821, and Report.*(Toronto, 1938).

Rich, E. E. (ed.), *Colin Robertson's Correspondence Book, September 1817 to September 1822* (Toronto, 1939).

Rich, E. E. (ed.), *Minutes of the Hudson's Bay Company, 1671–1674* (Toronto, 1942).

Rich, E. E. (ed.), *Minutes of the Hudson's Bay Company, 1679–1684: First Part, 1679–1682* (Toronto, 1945).

Rich, E. E. (ed.), *Minutes of the Hudson's Bay Company, 1679–1684: Second Part, 1682–1684* (Toronto, 1946).

Rich, E. E. (ed.), *Copy Book of Letters Outward & c. Begins 29th May, 1680 Ends 5 July, 1687* (Toronto, 1948).

Rich, E. E. (ed.), *James Isham's Observations on Hudson's Bay 1743 and Notes and Observations on a Book Entitled A Voyage to Hudsons Bay in the Dobbs Gallery, 1849* (Toronto, 1949).

Rich, E. E. (ed.), *Moose Fort Journals, 1783–85* (London, 1954).

Rich, E. E. (ed.), *Hudson's Bay Copy Booke of Letters Commissions Outward, 1688–1696* (London, 1957).

Rich, E. E. and Johnston, A.M. (eds), *Cumberland House Journals and Inland Journals, 1775–1782*, 2 vols. (London, 1952).

Selkirk, Thomas Douglas, fifth earl of, *A Sketch of the British Fur Trade in North America; with Observations Relative to the North-West Company of Montreal* (London, 1816).

Selkirk, Thomas Douglas: *see also* Bumsted, Pritchett, Whit (edited volumes).

Stevenson, Robert Louis, *From Scotland to Silverado*, edited by James D. Hart (Cambridge, 1966).

Tyrell, J. B. (ed.), *A Journey from Prince of Wales's Fort in Hudson's Bay, to the Northern Ocean, in the Years 1769, 1770, 1771 and 1772 by Samuel Hearne* (Toronto, 1911).

Tyrell, J. B. (ed.), *David Thompson's Narrative of his Explorations in Western America 1784–1812* (Toronto, 1916).

Tyrell, J. B. (ed.), *Journals of Samuel Hearne and Philip Turnor* (New York, 1968).

Umfreville, E., *The Present State of Hudson's Bay, Containing a Full Description of that Settlement, and the Adjacent Country, and likewise of the Fur Trade, with Hints for its Improvement, &c. &c.: To Which are Added, Remarks and Observations Made in the Inland Parts, During a Residence of Nearly Four Years, a Specimen of Five Indian*

Languages, and a Journal of a Journey from Montreal to New York (London, 1790).

University of Edinburgh, University of Glasgow (1999), *The Statistical Account of Scotland 1791–99* (http://edina.ac.uk/statacc/).

Wallace, W. S. (ed.), *Notes of a Twenty-five Year's Service in the Hudson's Bay Territories by John Maclean* (Toronto, 1932).

Wallace, W. S. (ed.), *Documents Relating to the North West Company* (Toronto, 1934).

Weld, Isaac, *Travels through the States of North America and the Provinces of Upper and Lower Canada, during the Years 1795, 1796, and 1797* (London, 1799).

Wentzel, W. F., 'Letters to Roderick McKenzie, 1807–1824' in L. R. Masson (ed.), *Les Bourgeois de la Compagnie du Nord-Ouest*, vol.2 (New York, 1960).

White, Patrick C. T. (ed.), *Lord Selkirk's Diary 1803–04: A Journal of His Travels in British North America and the Northeastern United States* (Toronto, 1958).

Wilcocke, Samuel Hull, 'Death of Benjamin Frobisher' in Louis F. R. Masson (ed.), *Les Bourgeois de la Compagnie du Nord-Ouest*, vol.2 (New York, 1960).

Wilcocke, Samuel Hull, McGillivray, Simon and Ellice, Edward, *A Narrative of Occurrences in the Indian Countries of North America: Since The Connection Of The Earl Of Selkirk With The Hudson's Bay Company* (London, 1817).

Williams, Glyndwr (ed.), *Andrew Graham's Observations on Hudson's Bay, 1767–91* (London, 1969).

Williams, Glyndwr (ed.), *Hudson's Bay Miscellany, 1670–1870* (Winnipeg, 1973).

Winterbotham, W., *An Historical Geographical, Commercial, And Philosophical View of the American United States, and of the European Settlements in America and the West-Indies* (London, 1795).

SECONDARY BOOKS AND ARTICLES

Adams, Ian H. and Somerville, Meredyth, *Cargoes of Despair and Hope* (Edinburgh, 1993).

Anderson, R. D., *Education and the Scottish People, 1750–1918* (Oxford, 1995).

Armitage, David and Braddick, Michael J., 'Three Concepts of Atlantic History' in David Armitage and Michael J. Braddick (eds), *The British Atlantic World, 1500–1800* (Basingstoke, 2002).

Bailey, Patrick, *Orkney* (London, 1971).

Barth, Fredrik, 'Enduring and Emerging Issues in the Analysis of Ethnicity' in Hans Vermuelen and Cora Govers (eds), *The Anthropology of Ethnicity: Beyond 'Ethnic Groups and Boundaries'* (Amsterdam, 1994).

Berry, John W., Poortinga, Ype H., Segall, Marshall H., Dasen, Pierre R., *Cross-cultural Psychology: Research and Applications* (Cambridge, 1992).

Bolus, Malvina (ed.), *People and Pelts: Selected Papers of the Second North America Fur Trade Conference* (Winnipeg, 1972).

Brown, Jennifer S. H., *Strangers In Blood: Fur Trade Company Families in Indian Country* (Vancouver, 1980).

Brown, Jennifer S. H., 'Linguistic Solitudes and Changing Social Categories' in Carol M. Judd and Arthur J. Ray (eds), *Old Trails and New Directions: Papers of the Third North American Fur Trade Conference* (Toronto, 1980).

Brown, Jennifer S. H., 'A Parcel of Upstart Scotchmen', *The Beaver* (February, 1988).

Brown, K. M., *Bloodfeud in Scotland, 1573–1625: Violence, Justice and Politics in Early Modern Society* (Edinburgh, 1986).

Bryce, George, *The Remarkable History of the Hudson's Bay Company* (London, 1910).

Bumsted, J. M., 'Settlement by Chance: Lord Selkirk and Prince Edward Island', *CHR* vol.59, no.2 (1978).

Bumsted, J. M., 'The Affair at Stornoway, 1811', *The Beaver* (Spring, 1982).

Bumsted, J. M., *The Scots in Canada* (Ottawa, 1982).

Bumsted, J. M., *The People's Clearance, 1770–1815* (Edinburgh, 1982).

Bumsted, J. M., *Fur Trade Wars: The Founding of Western Canada* (Winnipeg, 1999).

Bumsted, J. M., *Lord Selkirk: A Life* (Michigan, 2009).

Burley, Edith I., *Servants of the Honourable Company: Work, Discipline, and Conflict in the Hudson's Bay Company, 1770–1879* (Toronto, 1997).

Cage, R. A. (ed.), *The Scots Abroad: Labour, Capital, Enterprise. 1750–1914* (London, 1985).

Campbell, M. W., *The North West Company* (Toronto, 1957).

Campey, Lucille H., *The Silver Chief: Lord Selkirk and the Scottish Pioneers of Belfast, Baldoon and Red River* (Toronto, 2003).

Campey, Lucille H., *The Scottish Pioneers of Upper Canada, 1784 –1855. Glengarry and Beyond* (Toronto, 2005).

Carlos, Ann, 'The Causes and Origins of the North American Fur Trade Rivalry: 1804–1810', *JEH* vol.41, no.4 (December, 1981).

Carlos, Ann M., 'The Birth and Death of Predatory Competition in the North American Fur Trade: 1810–1821', *Explorations in Economic History* vol.19 (April, 1982).

Carlos, Ann M., 'Agent Opportunism and the Role of Company Culture: The Hudson's Bay and Royal African Companies Compared', *Business and Economic History*, Second Series, vol.20 (1991).

Carrothers, W. A., *Emigration from the British Isles: with Special Reference to the Development of the Overseas Dominions* (London, 1965).

Cathcart, Alison, 'The Western Gaidhealtachd' in Bob Harris and Alan R MacDonald (eds), *Scotland: The Making and Unmaking of the Nation c.1100–1707*, vol.2 (Dundee, 2007).

Checkland, S. G., *Scottish Banking: A History, 1695–1973* (London, 1975).

Clouston, J. Storer, 'Orkney and the Hudson's Bay Company', *The Beaver* (December, 1936).

Cowan, H. I., 'Selkirk's Work in Canada: An Early Chapter', *CHR* vol.9, no.4 (1928).

Decker, Jody F., 'The York Factory Medical Journals, 1846–52', *CBMH/BCHM* vol.14 (1997).

Devine, Heather, 'Roots in the Mohawk Valley: Sir William Johnson's Legacy in the North West Company' in Jennifer S. H. Brown, W. J. Eccles and Donald P. Heldman (eds), *The Fur Trade Revisited: Selected Papers of the Sixth North American Fur Trade Conference, Mackinac Island* (Michigan, 1991).

Devine, Heather, 'Ambition versus Loyalty: Miles Macdonnell and the Decline of the North West Company' in Jo-Anne Fiske, Susan Sleeper-Smith and William Wicken (eds), *New Faces of the Fur Trade: Selected Papers of the Seventh North American Fur Trade Conference, Halifax, Nova Scotia, 1995* (East Lansing, 1998).

Devine, T. M., *The Tobacco Lords: A Study of the Tobacco Merchants of Glasgow and their Trading Activities, c.1740–1790* (Edinburgh, 1975).

Devine, T. M., 'The Emergence of the New Elite in the Western Highlands and Islands, 1800–1860' in T. M. Devine (ed.), *Improvement and Enlightenment* (Edinburgh, 1989).

Devine, T. M. (ed.), *Improvement and Enlightenment: Proceedings of the Scottish Historical Studies Seminar, University of Strathclyde 1987–88* (Edinburgh, 1989).

Devine, T. M. (ed.), *Scottish Emigration and Scottish Society: Proceedings of the Scottish Historical Studies Seminar, University of Strathclyde, 1990–91* (Edinburgh, 1992).

Devine, T. M., *Clanship to Crofters' War: The Social Transformation of the Scottish Highlands* (Manchester, 1994).

Devine, T. M., *The Transformation of Rural Scotland: Social Change and the Agrarian Economy, 1600–1815* (Edinburgh, 1994).

Devine, T. M., *The Scottish Nation: 1700–2000* (London 1999).

Devine, T. M., *Scotland's Empire 1600–1815* (London, 2003).

Devine, T. M. and Mitchison Rosalind (eds), *People and Society in Scotland, vol.1: 1760–1830* (Edinburgh, 1988).

Dobson, David, *Scottish Emigration to Colonial America, 1607–1785* (London, 1994).

Dodgshon, Robert A., *From Chiefs to Landlord: Social and Economic Change in the Western Highlands and Islands, c.1493–1820* (Edinburgh, 1998).

Ewart, William B., 'Causes of Mortality in a Subarctic Settlement (York Factory, Man.), 1714–1946', *CMAJ* vol.129, no.6 (1983).

Fellman, Jerome Donald, Getis, Arthur and Getis, Judith, *Human Geography: Landscapes of Human Activities* (London, 1997).

Fenton, A., *The Northern Isles: Orkney and Shetland* (Edinburgh, 1978).

Ferguson, R. Brian, 'Explaining War' in J. Haas (ed.), *The Anthropology of War* (Cambridge, 1990).

Finlay, Richard J., 'Caledonia or North Britain? Scottish Identity in the Eighteenth Century' in Dauvit Broun, R. J. Finlay and Michael Lynch (eds), *Image and Identity: the Making and Re-making of Scotland Through the Ages* (Edinburgh, 1998).

Fleming, R. H. 'The Origin of "Sir Alexander Mackenzie and Company"', *CHR* vol.9, no.2 (1928).

Fleming, Rae (ed.), *The Lochaber Emigrants to Glengarry* (Toronto, 1994).

Flinn, Michael (ed.), *Scottish Population History from the Seventeenth Century to the 1930s* (Cambridge, 1977).

Francis, Daniel and Morantz, Toby, *Partners in Furs: A History of the Fur Trade in Eastern James Bay 1600–1870* (Kingston and Montreal 1983).

Fry, Michael, *The Scottish Empire* (Edinburgh, 2001).

Glaisyer, N., 'Networking: Trade and Exchange in the Eighteenth–Century British Empire', *HJ* 47 (2004).

Glover, Richard, 'The Difficulties of the Hudson's Bay Company's Penetration of the West', *CHR* vol.29, no.3 (September, 1948).

Goldring, Philip, 'Lewis and the Hudson's Bay Company in the Nineteenth Century', *SS* 24 (1980).

Goldring, Philip, 'Labour Records of the Hudson's Bay Company, 1821–1870', *Archivaria* 11 (1980/1981).

Gray, John Morgan, *Lord Selkirk of Red River* (London, 1963).

Gray, Malcolm, *The Fishing Industries of Scotland 1790–1914: A Study in Regional Adaptation* (Oxford, 1978).

Haas, J. (ed.), *The Anthropology of War* (Cambridge, 1990).

Hamilton, Douglas J., *Scotland, the Caribbean and the Atlantic World, 1750–1820* (Manchester, 2005).

Hancock, D., *Citizens of the World: London Merchants and the Integration of the British Atlantic Community, 1735–1785* (Cambridge, 1995).

Hancock, D., 'Combining Success and Failure: Scottish Networks in the Atlantic Wine Trade' in David Dickson, Jan Parmentier and Jane Ohlmeyer (eds), *Irish and Scottish Mercantile Networks in Europe and Overseas in the Seventeenth and Eighteenth Centuries* (Ghent, 2007).

Harper, Marjory, 'British Migration and the Peopling of the Empire' in Andrew Porter (ed.), *The Oxford History of the British Empire, Vol.3: The Nineteenth Century* (Oxford, 1999).

Harper, Marjory, *Adventurers and Exiles: The Great Scottish Exodus* (London, 2004).

Harper, Marjory and Vance, Michael E. (eds), *Myth, Migration and the Making of Memory: Scotia and Nova Scotia, c.1700–1990* (Edinburgh, 1999).

Horn, James, 'British Diaspora: Emigration from Britain, 1680–1815' in P. J. Marshall (ed.), *The Oxford History of the British Empire, Vol.2, the Eighteenth Century* (Oxford, 1999).

Huck, Barbara, *Exploring the Fur Trade Routes of North America: Discover the Highways That Opened a Continent* (Winnipeg, 2000).

Innis, H. A. 'The Northwest Company', *CHR* vol.8, no.4 (1927).

Innis, H. A., *The Fur Trade in Canada* (Yale, 1930).

Johnson, Dennis F., *York Boats of the Hudson's Bay Company: Canada's Inland Armada* (Calgary, 2006).

Judd, Carol M., '"Mixt Bands of Many Nations": 1821–1870' in Carol M. Judd and Arthur J. Ray (eds), *Old Trails and New Directions: Papers of the Third North American Fur Trade Conference* (Toronto, 1980).

Karras, Alan L., *Sojourners in the Sun: Scottish Migrants in Jamaica and the Chesapeake, 1740–1800* (New York, 1992).

Linklater, Eric, *Orkney and Shetland: an Historical, Geographical, Social and Scenic Survey* (London, 1980).

MacDonald, Donald, *Lewis – A History of the Island* (Edinburgh, 1978).

MacGregor, J. G., *Peter Fidler: Canada's Forgotten Surveyor 1769–1822* (Toronto, 1966).

Macinnes, Allan I., *Clanship, Commerce and the House of Stuart, 1603–1788* (East Linton, 1996).

MacKay, Douglas, *The Honourable Company: A History of the Hudson's Bay Company* (New York, 1936).

Mackillop, Andrew, *'More Fruitful than the Soil': Army, Empire and the Scottish Highlands, 1715–1815* (East Linton, 2000).

Mackillop, Andrew, 'Europeans, Britons, and Scots: Scottish Sojourning Networks and Identities in Asia, c.1700–1815' in Angela McCarthy (ed.) *A Global Clan: Scottish Migrant Networks and Identities since the Eighteenth Century* (London, 2006).

Magee, Gary B., and Thomson, Andrew S., 'The Global and Local: Explaining Migrant Remittance Flows in the English-speaking World, 1880–1914', *JEH* vol.66, no.1 (March 2006).

Marshall, P. J. (ed.), *The Oxford History of the British Empire, Vol.2: The Eighteenth Century* (Oxford, 1998).

Maschner, Herbert D. G. and Reedy-Maschner, Katherine L., 'Marauding Middlemen: Western Expansion and Violent Conflict in the Sub-arctic', *Ethnohistory* 46.4 (1999).

Mitchell, David E., *Lords and Proprietors: A Reader's Guide to the Hudson's Bay Company Charter* (Toronto, 2004).

Mitchell, E. A., 'The North West Company Agreement of 1795', *CHR* vol.36, no.2 (1955).

Mitchell, E. A., 'The Scot in the Fur Trade' in W. Stanford Reid (ed.), *The Scottish Tradition in Canada* (Toronto, 1976).

Morton, A. S., *A History of the Canadian West to 1870–71: Being a History of Rupert's Land (the Hudson's Bay Company's Territory) and of the North-West Territory (including the Pacific slope)* (Toronto, 1973).

Murdoch, Steve, *Network North: Scottish Kin, Commercial and Covert Association in Northern Europe, 1603–1746* (Leiden, 2006).

Mackillop, Andrew and Murdoch, Steve , 'Introduction' in Andrew Mackillop and Steve Murdoch (eds), *Military Governors and Imperial Frontiers c. 1600–1800: A Study of Scotland and Empires* (Leiden, 2005).

Nicks, John, 'Orkneymen in the Hudson's Bay Company, 1780–1821' in Carol M. Judd and Arthur J. Ray (eds), *Old Trails and New Directions: Papers of the Third North American Fur Trade Conference* (Toronto, 1980).

O'Leary, Michael, Orlikowski, Wanda and Yates, JoAnne, 'Distributed Work over the Centuries: Trust and Control in the Hudson's Bay Company, 1670–1826' in Pamela J. Hinds and Sara Kiesler (eds), *Distributed Work* (Cambridge, 2002).

Osaki, Keiko, 'Migrant Remittances in Thailand: Economic Necessity or Social Norm?', *JPR* vol.20, no.2 (2003).

Parker, James G., 'Scottish Enterprise in India, 1750–1914' in R. A. Cage (ed.), *The Scots Abroad: Labour, Capital, Enterprise, 1750–1914* (London, 1985).

Payne, Michael, *'The Most Respectable Place In the Territory': Everyday Life in Hudson's Bay Company Service York Factory, 1788–1870*, Studies in Archaeology, Architecture and History, National Historic Parks and Sites, Canadian Parks Service, Environment Canada (Ottawa, 1989).

Pritchett, J. P. and Wilson, F. J., 'A Winter at Hudson Bay, 1811–12', *CHR* vol.24, no.1(1943).

Rasporich, A., 'Ethnicity in Canadian Historical Writing, 1970–1990' in J. W. Berry and J. A. Laponce (eds), *Ethnicity and Culture in Canada: The Research Landscape* (Toronto, 1994).

Ray, Arthur J., *Indians in the Fur Trade: Their Role as Hunters, Trappers and Middlemen in the Lands Southwest of Hudson Bay 1660–1870* (Toronto, 1974).

Ray, Arthur J. and J. B. Freeman, *'Give Us Good Measure': An Economic Analysis of Relations Between the Indians and the Hudson's Bay Company Before 1763* (Toronto, 1978).

Reid, Marjorie G., 'The Quebec Fur Traders and Western Policy, 1763–1774' *CHR* vol.6, no.1 (1925).

Reyna, S. P., 'A Mode of Domination Approach to Organised Violence' in S. P. Reyna and R. E. Downs (eds), *Studying War: Anthropological Perspectives* (Amsterdam, 1994).

Rich, E. E., *History of the Hudson's Bay Company, 1670–1870*, 2 vols (London, 1958).

Rich, E. E., *The Fur Trade and the Northwest to 1857* (London, 1968).

Roberts, John L., *Feuds, Forays and Rebellions: History of the Highland Clans, 1475–1625* (Edinburgh, 1999).

Roosens, Eugeen, 'The Primordial Nature of Origins in Migrant Ethnicity' in Hans Vermuelen and Cora Govers (eds), *The Anthropology of Ethnicity: Beyond 'Ethnic Groups and Boundaries'* (Amsterdam, 1994).

Ruggles, Richard I., *A Country So Interesting: The Hudson's Bay Company and Two Centuries of Mapping, 1670–1870* (Montreal, 1992).

Sauberlich, Howerde E., 'A History of Scurvy and Vitamin C' in Lester Packer and Jürgen Fuchs (eds), *Vitamin C in Health and Disease* (New York, 1997).

Saville, Richard, *Bank of Scotland: A History 1695–1995* (Edinburgh, 1996).

Schei, Liv Kjørsvik, *The Islands of Orkney* (Grantown-on-Spey, 2000).

Scott, W. R., 'The Trade of Orkney at the End of the Eighteenth Century', *SHR* vol.10, no.4 (1912–13).

Shaw, Frances J., *The Northern and Western Islands of Scotland: Their Economy and Society in the Seventeenth Century* (Edinburgh, 1980).

Smith, Janet Adam, 'Some Eighteenth Century Ideas of Scotland' in N. T. Phillipson and Rosalind Mitchison (eds), *Scotland in the Age of Improvement: Essays in Scottish History in the Eighteenth Century* (Edinburgh, 1996).

Stanley, G. F. G., 'Documents Relating to the Swiss Immigration to Red River in 1821', *CHR* vol.22, no.1 (1941).

Thomson, William P. L., *The New History of Orkney* (Edinburgh, 2001).

Toman, Cynthia, 'George Spence: Surgeon and Servant of the HBC, 1738–41'. *CBMH/BCHM* vol.18 (2001).

Troup, James A., 'The Canadian Connection' in Donald Omand (ed.), *The Orkney Book* (Edinburgh, 2003).

Van Kirk, Sylvia, *Many Tender Ties: Women in Fur-Trade Society in Western Canada, 1670–1870* (Winnipeg, 1980).

Van Kirk, Sylvia, 'Fur Trade Social History: Some Recent Trends' in Carol M. Judd and Arthur J. Ray (eds), *Old Trails and New Directions: Papers of the Third North American Fur Trade Conference* (Toronto, 1980).

Wenham, Sheena, *A More Enterprising Spirit: The Parish and People of Holm in 18th Century Orkney* (Orkney, 2001).

Williams, Glyndwr., 'Arthur Dobbs and Joseph Robson; New Light on the Relationship Between Two Early Critics of the Hudson's Bay Company', *CHR* vol.40, no.2 (1959).

Williams, Glyndwr, 'The Hudson's Bay Company and the Fur Trade: 1670–1870', *The Beaver* (Autumn, 1983).

Williams, Guy, *The Age of Agony: The Art of Healing c.1700–1800* (London, 1975).

Withrington, Donald J., 'Schooling, Literacy and Society' in T. M. Devine and Rosalind Mitchison (eds), *People and Society in Scotland, vol.1: 1760–1830* (Edinburgh, 1988).

Woodcock, George, *The Hudson's Bay Company: From Trading Post to Emporium - a Tricentennial History of Canada's Pioneering Fur-Traders* (Toronto, 1970).

Youngson, A. J., *Beyond the Highland Line: 'Three Journals of Travel in Eighteenth Century Scotland'* (London, 1974).

Unpublished PhD theses

Stephen, Scott P., '"Masters and Servants", The Hudson's Bay Company and its Personnel, 1668–1782' (University of Manitoba, 2006).

Rigg, S., 'Scots in the Hudson's Bay Company, c.1779–1821' (University of Aberdeen, 2008).

Index

as means of controlling debt and
　private trade 140–2
as means of encouraging recruitment
　89, 149–50, 173
welfare of employees' dependants
　86–9, 134, 148–150, 161, 173
welfare of servants 84–90, 173
Pangman, Bostonais 102, 104
patronage 43, 49–56, 168, 179
Patterson, Thomas 153
Peace of Amiens xix, 22
Perthshire 14, 31, 107
pensions 84, 86–9, 172
petition 21, 52, 86–8, 133–4
Petrie, John 156
Pine Lake (post) 69–70, 94
plantations (Caribbean) 2, 40, 55, 125, 166
Plowman, William 95
poor relief 86–9, 164–6, 172
Porcupine Lake 76
portage 5–6, 12
Portage de l'Isle (post) 48
Portland House (post) 68
posts *see individual post name*
post journals *see journals*
Prince Edward Island 101
prisoners *see imprisonment*
Pritchard, John 114
private trade 141–2
profits 6, 100, 112, 147
promotion 43–4, 46–9, 51, 53–5, 57–60,
　159, 168, 170
protestant 121–2, 131
Pultney 33
punishment 19, 27, 75, 143–4, 147

Quebec xii, xix, 12, 23

Radisson, Pierre 1
Rae, John (Orkney agent and father of
　explorer Dr John Rae) 33, 35, 50,
　85, 138
Rae, John Dr 33
rapids 5, 76, 84
Reay 31

recreation
　books /reading 57, 84, 131, 135
　music and song 117–19, 143
　social occasions 79, 115, 117–18, 169
recruitment xix, xx, 22–3, 25–6, 29–30,
　32–3, 35, 41–2, 49–50, 65, 85–6,
　111, 120, 134, 138, 141–2, 145–50,
　152, 154–5, 157, 159, 167–8, 170
　age of recruits 12, 27, 32
　captains as recruiting agents 12, 16
　criticism of recruits 13, 15, 27, 29,
　　32–5, 68–9, 168
　criticism of recruitment demands in
　　Orkney 20–21
　establishment of recruiting agent in
　　Orkney 16, 19
　ethos 3, 29
　methods 16, 25, 41
　policies 11–12, 16, 24, 27, 29–31, 35
　propaganda 41–2, 140, 160
　re-engagement 14–15, 18, 21–2, 26, 28,
　　34, 41, 44, 46, 51–2, 62–3, 147, 170
　shortage *see* labour shortage
　see also agents, bonuses and bounties,
　　contract, Caithness, Lewis,
　　Inverness, Shetland, Sutherland,
　　Glasgow, Canada
Red Deer River (post) 69, 106
Red Lake (post) 91, 109, 115
　armed robbery 95
　Christmas 115
　contrast in provisions between HBC
　　post and North West Company
　　post 67–8
　hunting and fishing 68, 70
　shortage of medicine 82
Red River boat 6
Red River colony
　abandoned 106–7
　base for crippled servants 89
　destroyed 105–8
　land grants 7, 30, 130, 136, 162–3, 172
　massacre and murder xx, 109–11, 135
　opposition to 9, 101, 104, 113, 171
　organisation of 122

unofficial increase 62–4
war wages 18, 29, 61
see also bonuses and bounties,
    pensions, remittance
Walker, William 15, 51, 56–7
Walls 66, 162
war
    War of 1812 xx, 100–3, 171
    War of the Spanish Succession xix,
        3–4
    Seven Years' War xix
    Revolutionary War with France xix, 6,
        17, 20, 84
    see also fur trade conflict, Napoleonic
        wars
Wass, James 42
Wass, William 42
Watson, James Rev (Minister for South
    Ronaldsay and Burray) 17
Wedderburn, Andrew *see Colvile*
welfare *see* paternalism, pensions
Wentzel, Willard 112,
West Indies *see* Caribbean
West, John Rev (Church of England
    missionary)131
Western Isles xx, 7, 29, 175; *see also*
    Lewis, Stornoway
whaling 39–40, 90

Whitby 39–40
Whitefish Lake 94
Whitway, James 46, 154
Whymester, Thomas 77
Wick 33, 37, 95
widows 86–8, 144, 172
Williams, William 115
wills 129, 161–6
Wilson, William 151–2
Winnipeg 5, 50
Wishart, Edward 57, 155
women
    trafficking 125
    see also country wives; *see under*
        Orcadian employees
writers 41, 43, 47–51, 57, 60, 80, 88

XY Company xix–xx, 93–4, 96, 112,
    115–16

Yorkshire 31
York Factory (post) 2, 6, 12–13, 21–2,
    27, 31, 47–8, 51–2, 67, 71–2, 80–2,
    102, 115–16, 118, 144, 160, 162–5
York boat 6
Yorston, William (Brandon House) 52–4
Yorston, William (Eastmain) 88